THE ALFRED I. duPONT
COLUMBIA UNIVERSITY
SURVEY OF
BROADCAST
JOURNALISM
1971-1972

THE ALFRED I. DUPONT–COLUMBIA UNIVERSITY SURVEY AND AWARDS IN BROADCAST JOURNALISM

THE JURORS

Richard T. Baker
Edward W. Barrett
Dorothy Height

John Houseman
Sig Mickelson
Michael Novak

Elie Abel, chairman

Marvin Barrett, director

Jane Vittengl, administrative aide

Louis G. Cowan, director of special projects,
Columbia University Graduate School of Journalism

JURORS EMERITUS

Arthur Morse, 1968–1969
Sir William Haley, 1968–1969
Michael Arlen, 1968–1970
Marya Mannes, 1968–1970

DUPONT FELLOWS

William Seifert, 1968–1969
Thomas Goldstein, 1968–1969
Michael Hanson, 1969–1970
Helen Epstein, 1970–1971
Michael Meadvin, 1971–1972
Steven Petrou, 1971–1972

THE ALFRED I. duPONT
COLUMBIA UNIVERSITY
SURVEY OF BROADCAST JOURNALISM

1971-1972

THE POLITICS OF BROADCASTING

EDITED BY MARVIN BARRETT

Thomas Y. Crowell Company
New York • Established 1834

Manufactured in the United States of America

ISBN 0-690-64696-8

1   2   3   4   5   6   7   8   9   10

Library of Congress Cataloging in Publication Data

Barrett, Marvin.
   The politics of broadcasting.

   1.   Television in politics--United States.
2. Radio in politics--United States.   I. Titl
HE8689.7.P6B37   384.55'4   73-39
ISBN 0-690-64696-8

Contents

Introduction   1
1   The Year in Broadcast Journalism   5
2   No News Is Good News (I)   39
3   No News Is Good News (II)   67
4   Who Pays?   76
5   The Broadcasting of Politics (I): The Primaries   97
6   The Broadcasting of Politics (II): The Conventions   117
7   The Broadcasting of Politics (III): The Campaign   132
Observations   155
The Alfred I. duPont–Columbia University Awards,
      1971–1972   159

REPORTS AND COMMENTARIES:
  Blurred Image in the Electric Mirror
      by Sig Mickelson   163
  Notes on the Drama of Politics and the Drama of
      Journalism
      by Michael Novak   169
  Radio News—Promise and Performance
      by Steve Knoll   178
  Sports and Television: The Perfect Marriage
      by Dick Schaap   197
  TV Drama in the U.S.A.: The Great Drought of
      1971–1972
      by John Houseman   203

APPENDICES:
  I. Remarks of Clay T. Whitehead to the International
      Radio and Television Society   213
  II. Remarks of Clay T. Whitehead to the National
      Association of Educational Broadcasters   219

III. Message from President Nixon to the House of
     Representatives   226

IV. Remarks of Clay T. Whitehead at the
    Sigma Delta Chi Luncheon   228

Some Information About the Alfred I. duPont–Columbia
    University Awards for 1972–1973   235

Acknowledgments   237

Index   239

Introduction

IN ITS FOURTH YEAR, the Alfred I. duPont–Columbia University Survey of Broadcast Journalism completes a cycle. The first Survey, covering the period from July 1, 1968, to June 30, 1969, contained a careful analysis of broadcasting's part in the painful and historic events of the 1968 presidential campaign. By extending the scope of this year's Survey to include the election of 1972, we have brought broadcast journalism full circle to the next of its quadrennial confrontations with the nation's top politicians.

Beginning with the primaries, the coverage of the presidential race every four years has become the Olympic Games of electronic journalism. The victories won from spring to fall, particularly at the conventions, have traditionally determined the prestige and competitive standing of networks and their news executives, reporters, and anchormen.

The campaign of 1972 was different, and in that difference lies the clue to much of what has changed in broadcast journalism since the DuPont-Columbia Survey began four years ago.

The battle between network and network, particularly at the conventions, seemed inconsequential this time, with little to distinguish one performance from another. The floor men were busy; the anchormen, laconic. In the end it was up to the listener, and the viewer, to gauge the true temper of the gathering. Indeed it may have always been so, but the truth was all at once unavoidable.

Summing it up, the affair seemed a mild distraction from the broader struggle that was going on between politician and broadcaster, a struggle which was already having a dangerous effect on the nation's broadcast journalism and perhaps its politics. In this war between management-stockholder and politician-bureaucrat, the broadcast journalist was the "noncombatant," used and abused, first by one side and then the other, suspected, held hostage, and in some instances, eliminated.

He was by turns weapon and target, depending upon which adversary you chose to believe and the strategic requirements of the moment. As usual in such battles, it was the public who paid, with cash and with the loss of essential services.

The hustings and the polls were only part of the battleground. There were the bureaus of Washington, the chambers of Congress, and the boardrooms of Manhattan as well.

If a broadcaster could damage a politician's reputation, a politician could and did respond with regulatory feints which threatened the broadcaster where he was most vulnerable, in his pretensions and his pocketbook. In this endless jockeying, credibility dwindled and cynicism grew. This was particularly disturbing when one acknowledged that on the one side were broadcasting and broadcast journalism, which have steadily reinforced their hold on the minds of the American people as their primary source of news and information, while on the other side were the men and women who directed the increasingly critical affairs of the republic.

For this and other reasons, we have chosen to call the fourth annual DuPont-Columbia Survey *The Politics of Broadcasting,* with the implied subtitle "The Broadcasting of Politics."

The confrontation between politics and broadcasting described in the following pages did not, of course, begin with the primaries, nor did it end on Election Day. Our task was not a simple matter of how best to tell the story of the 1972 elections, or how to describe the way in which broadcasting was used to win votes. The broadcasters were engaged in a desperate struggle to keep their wealth, their power, and their self-respect—possibly in that order. The politicians, in the interest of their incumbencies, and perhaps their sense of propriety, seemed bent at one time or another upon depriving them of all three.

It was not an edifying spectacle, and, to anyone who cared about the integrity of the nation's press, it had deeply disturbing passages.

Granted the primacy of electronic news among all the media, its practitioners still seemed to have the most precarious of platforms from which to launch their reports and commentaries. And the uncertainty of their footing did not come primarily from bad research or faulty information—although these played a part. It came from the very nature of U.S. broadcasting: a merchandising operation, managed by entrepreneurs, paid for by businessmen, licensed and regulated by politicians in "the public interest, convenience, and necessity." Uncertain budgets and time allotments for news and public affairs, growing in some cases from managerial nerves, or sponsor disapproval or public indifference, could also be blamed on the acts and threats of the adversary in Washington who often seemed more intent upon emasculating than reforming the broadcaster's vast enterprise.

In this Laocoön tangle, there were some signs of freedom and strength. Importuned to bring only glad tidings, U.S. broadcasters, more than ever before, attended to the depressing conditions of the poor, the sick, the handicapped, and the old who made up the nation's real silent majority. Broadcasters, perhaps trying to steer clear of controversy, sometimes found deeper, more universal, and ultimately more upsetting human failures than the political or economic to attend to. If as corrector, investigator, and gadfly, electronic journalism had its least effective season in several years, as observer, seeing life steadily and whole, and adding a few question marks to some of America's smuggest and most strongly held assumptions, it had seldom been more perceptive.

During this period the broadcasting industry had other losses: notable among them the passing of David Sarnoff, its founder and symbolic head; the death of Charles Ireland, the recently appointed president of CBS, its newest, untried leader; and the retirement of Jack Gould of *The New York Times,* the dean of U.S. broadcast editors, which left broadcasters without their wisest counselor. They could ill afford the loss of such a friend or constructive critic.

As usual the Survey is indebted to its network of sixty-five correspondents who report regularly and astutely on the good and bad things they see and hear. This year special thanks is due the National Board of the YWCA and the League of Women Voters, who participated in special monitoring projects concerning minority and political coverage. But again, our primary contributors are the nation's news and public affairs staffs, network and local, whose work is the stuff this Survey is made of, and whose trials and triumphs are ours.

The DuPont-Columbia Awards—the largest number distributed in one year since the program began—are listed on page 159.

The Reports and Commentaries this year are five in number —two dealing with the year's political coverage by Sig Mickelson and Michael Novak; one on the decline of television drama in the United States and its effect upon the news by John Houseman; a report on sports and television by Dick Schaap; and a report on radio news by Steve Knoll.

An important statement from the jurors begins on page 155.

With this year's Survey and Awards we again wish to honor the late Mrs. Jessie Ball duPont, who established the original DuPont Awards Program thirty years ago in memory of her husband, Alfred I. duPont. The past three decades have seen an enormous change in the functions of broadcasting and a staggering growth in its size and importance. Nor does the need, year by year, to observe and encourage the best of broadcasting, the original purpose of Mrs. duPont's grant, grow less. And to us the best of broadcasting has always been and remains the capturing and communicating and commenting on the real world which is broadcast journalism.

MARVIN BARRETT, director

1 • The Year in Broadcast Journalism

CHINA AND RUSSIA, Bangladesh and Vietnam, the Olympics and the moon, the primaries, the conventions, and the campaign. In a period that called for such a massive deployment of broadcast journalists, it may seem ungracious to point out that the industry seemed to be losing ground.

But that was indeed the case. Nor was it a shift that could be blamed solely on the broadcasters. If they had resisted the forces of inertia too little and too late, still everyone else concerned—the regulators, the sponsors, the public—had now apparently joined forces to push them off course.

Nevertheless, for the faithful viewer it was a remarkable, indeed a hallucinatory year. At times he could have been dreaming—or having nightmares.

Among many incredible sights, perhaps the most incredible was President Nixon clinking glasses with the rulers of Red China in Peking's Great Hall of the People, while a local band struck up impeccable renditions of "America the Beautiful" and "Home on the Range." And then as if to prove the fantasy was reality, there he was again, three months later, addressing the Russian (and American) TV audience from a brocade-hung studio in the Kremlin.

As for nightmares, there was the governor of Alabama being gunned down on camera in a Maryland shopping center, or a naked nine-year-old girl, with arms outstretched in terror and supplication, running down a Vietnam road toward the viewer.

In other words, it was the kind of year Americans had come to expect from U.S. broadcast journalism, with most of the day's disasters and achievements spread out before them if they chose to look and listen.

And America was undoubtedly looking and listening. Television viewing in U.S. homes had, by some calculations, shot above the seven-hour-per-day mark for the first time, and radio was claiming 153 million regular listeners.

Whether these millions were devoting much of that time to news and public affairs was another matter. Figures indicated that the network newscasts had been losing viewers during the last year. The total for the three evening newscasts dropped by some 900,000 households.* Explanations ranged from loss of network credibility, and too much unpleasant news, to the prime-time access rule which separated the newscasts from the popular network entertainment programs with locally provided fare, thus discouraging a sizable number of Americans who watched the news only by accident or because they were afraid they might miss a minute or two of their favorite game or adventure show. Whatever the explanation, the fact remained that in a year when both the use of sets and number of sets in use increased substantially, news watching was down.

Network News Audience (in Millions) †

	1968	1969	1970	1971	1972
Total TV households	56.0	57.0	58.5	60.1	62.1
Households using TV at time of network newscasts	30.2	30.8	31.4	33.7	34.3
Households watching network newscasts	25.3	24.3	24.1	25.6	24.7

† Above figures calculated for the month of February. Source: A. C. Nielsen Co.

A survey conducted by the National Opinion Research Center for the National Association of Broadcasters (NAB) in 1970 and finally released in February 1972 showed a general decline in enthusiasm for the media, particularly on the part of blacks who in former years had been radio and TV's most devoted fans. Between 1966 and 1970, according to the report, the percentage of blacks "with a favorable attitude toward TV programs" had dropped from 60 to 41, and the percentage of blacks with a favorable attitude toward radio went down from 57 to 41.

* According to A. C. Nielsen, network newscasts are being watched by fewer people per TV household and watched less frequently.

A survey by Nielsen revealed that about 2.0 viewers per household watched network news in 1968. Four years later that number dropped to 1.7.

Out of twenty network newscasts in 1968, the average viewing home saw 6.1. Out of the same number of newscasts in 1972, the average viewing home saw 5.8.

More ominous was the discovery by the Center that respondents in favor of increased government controls on television had increased from 20 percent in 1966 to 26 percent in 1970. The jump for those labeled "pro broadcasting" was even greater—from 12 percent in 1966 to 28 percent in 1970.

Another study, also underwritten by the NAB, conducted by Andrew Stern of the University of California at Berkeley, indicated the disconcerting fact that even if television remained the nation's prime source of news, it did not mean anyone was necessarily paying attention.

Of 232 respondents who were asked, "What do you recall from tonight's broadcast?" with an average of nineteen items to point to, 51 percent could not recall a single story a few minutes after the newscast was off the air. Among the 49 percent who could summon up at least one item, the last thing they heard, the windup commentary by Eric Sevareid or Harry Reasoner, was least remembered.

Stern, who once worked as a producer for ABC News, concluded:

> Since other studies show that television news is now the prime source of the public's news information, the broadcast industry has an enormous responsibility. It is quite evident that if you want a better-informed public— one that retains a news item better, possibly even one that has time to think about it—scheduling the news away from the dinner hour—and other early evening distractions—would seem to be the best answer. Particularly now might be the time for the networks to ponder such a switch. Since the FCC has reduced the number of prime-time network hours to three, and since we are seeing that the extra half hour which reverted to the local stations is only being filled by generally inferior syndication entertainment programs, how about putting network news on at 10:30?

Another form of attrition was reported by Professor Scott Ward of the Harvard Business School. The new generation of television viewers appeared to be building up an immunity to what they saw. According to Professor Ward, by second grade a great many children have already begun to develop cynicism about television, specifically advertising, and by the sixth grade over two-thirds of the children he tested were responding negatively to what they saw on the screen.

The regular network commitment to news and public affairs, exclusive of special events, was barely holding its own in 1972.

In some instances cuts in budget and staff made during the recession of 1970, and further excused by the loss of over $200 million in annual cigarette advertising in 1971, had not yet been reinstated, although profits had revived. The old-fashioned investigative documentary seemed in for a bad time.

Martin Carr, producer of a long string of outstanding hours culminating in last season's "Migrant" and "This Child Is Rated X" (see *Survey of Broadcast Journalism, 1970–1971*), and this year's "Leaving Home Blues," left network employment in midseason with no plans to return. Carr, who had departed from CBS two years earlier in favor of NBC, because CBS had him "pushing around paper clips" for fourteen months following the congressional flap over his documentary "Hunger in America," found himself, if anything, "too busy" at NBC. This meant, said Carr, that he was given inadequate time to prepare and was understaffed, and that work on his last two documentaries overlapped. Also, he could not figure out how to communicate with the decision makers. When "Leaving Home Blues," which dealt with rural migrations in the United States, was put on the air on a Friday night in August, a time slot roughly the equivalent of Easter Sunday at 11:00 A.M., with little prospect of being repeated, Carr finally decided to give up. "Each year a few like me, who are really serious, who don't like cranking them out, take off."

Peter Davis, producer of "The Selling of the Pentagon," took a leave of absence from CBS seventeen months after his controversial program went on the air. In the period between, he did two segments for "60 Minutes": one on the disappearance of college rebels, the other on the use of new antipersonnel weapons in Vietnam. The second, according to reports, had been subject to drastic cuts. Davis insisted that CBS had been more than considerate in its treatment of him and that the leave was his personal decision.

However, he had some comments to make about those "network executives, not only at CBS, who have latched onto the New Journalism term 'advocacy journalism' to excuse their rejecting anything they consider too tough. It is not advocacy journalism at all, just better, more effective journalism than they are accustomed to. It is unfortunate that the New Journalism coined a phrase that everyone can use as an excuse for avoiding controversy. I know of really first-rate pieces of journalism which have been turned down with that reason, and no other, being given."

Davis left to work on a film on Vietnam; Carr was "free-lancing."

Network television in 1972, which had failed to hang on to the top dramatic talent it developed in its early years (see report on page 203), looked as though it were trying to lose its documentarians through the same treatment—refusing them the opportunity to do their best, cutting off their time and money, keeping them from prime spots on the schedules.

The loss of two talented producers, serious as it may have seemed to those who cared about quality documentaries, was scarcely felt, since the regular weekly network prime time allotted to news and public affairs, which stood at one hour in 1970–1971, hit bottom with zero hours in 1971–1972 and stayed there.

For the new season, NBC news and public affairs did the best, speaking for the 10:00 to 11:00 P.M. slot on Tuesday evenings. "Chronolog," once again called "First Tuesday," was cut to half its former length and outside elements were scheduled for the slot—notably thirteen one-hour segments of Alistair Cooke's "America," produced by the BBC and Time-Life Films. However, an increased number of NBC White Papers were promised throughout the year.

CBS was again without a regular prime-time slot for public affairs. CBS News, which had once been allotted a regular prime-time hour, had no set time slot in the fall schedule for its promised twenty-five "Reports" and "News Specials." For the second year, CBS' first-rate magazine show "60 Minutes" was scheduled outside of prime time at the far end of the Sunday afternoon ghetto. The network pointed out that it had a substantially larger audience, by 1.6 million households, than it had ever had on prime time. This statistic, when it was combined with the unspectacular rating record of most one-shot news and public affairs specials,* might have seemed threatening to the future of regular prime-time network public affairs programming, if there had been any left to threaten.

In rating terms, CBS had the most disastrous night of the year in October 1971, when it put three hours of public affairs

---

* A check of *Variety's* list of 272 specials telecast in prime time during the 1971–1972 season reveals that only one news and public affairs program made the top 50 rated specials. NBC's coverage of the president's return from his visit to the People's Republic of China was tied with the network's telecast of the All-Star baseball game for number 49. Of the bottom 50 specials, news and public affairs programs accounted for 35.

programming back-to-back, including hour-long essays on Picasso and the Chicano, and an edition of "60 Minutes." The sequence put CBS out of the running not only for the evening, but for the next week as well. The programs which had been replaced by CBS' block of public affairs specials, "Bearcats!" and "The CBS Thursday Night Movie," were still suffering the week after the specials were aired, while the competition showed a healthy gain (see the table on the next page).

ABC, whose nightly news had increased its audience and clearances, was, as usual, without any prime-time commitment to news and public affairs. Plans were announced for a new weekly half-hour Harry Reasoner show to be produced by Ernest Leiser * in February 1973. But the time set aside for it was Saturday evening at six thirty.

The will-o'-the-wisp relationship of news and public affairs to the Bible of TV management—the rating book—was dramatized by the fact that unless a program was sponsored, it was not rated. During 1971 about seventy-five news and public affairs programs in and out of prime time were not rated for that reason. Further, the networks had an irresistible urge to pack as many news specials and documentaries as possible into the "black weeks" (those weeks when, for administrative reasons, Nielsen did not collect numbers).

In the 1971–1972 season, there were five black weeks (one more than the year before), and in them there were nearly three dozen hours of prime-time network public affairs programming, including some of the best documentaries of the year. If they did get sizable audiences, no one would ever know it.

Usually the numbers or lack of them merely confirmed a fact of which most broadcasters were aware: the U.S. mass audience and the sponsors prefer fantasy to reality. There was a rumor that CBS had put its three-hour public affairs blockbuster on in a highly competitive spot simply to prove once and for all how unregenerate the TV audience was. How the networks could use such proof, beyond justifying actions long since taken, was unclear.

NBC News racked up one of the critical disasters of the 1971–1972 season, a distinction seldom earned by news and public affairs departments. Its "Quarterly Report" was an interesting idea, the summing up on prime-time television of the

* ABC continued to raid the other networks for top talent. Besides Leiser, who formerly had produced instant specials for CBS News. ABC acquired correspondents Herb Kaplow and Bill Matney from NBC and David Schoumacher from CBS.

| | % Total TV households | | |
Program *	Oct. 14 (week before)	Oct. 21 (week of specials)	Oct. 28 (week after)
Alias Smith and Jones (ABC, 8 p.m. EST)	14.4	18	17.4
Longstreet (ABC, 9 p.m. EST)	17.9	26.8	21.6
Owen Marshall (ABC, 10 p.m. EST)	12.9	29.2	17.9
Flip Wilson (NBC, 8 p.m. EST)	30.1	31.2	28.6
Nichols (NBC, 9 p.m. EST)	16.6	24.4	17.8
Dean Martin (NBC, 10 p.m. EST)	13.6	20.3	19.6
Bearcats! (CBS, 8 p.m. EST)	12.6	⎡ "60 Minutes": 9.7	11.5
CBS Thursday Night Movie (9 p.m. EST)	25.0	"Picasso Is 90" and "Chicano": 6.2 ⎤	15.2

* Source: A. C. Nielsen Co.

The above table indicates the impact of CBS documentaries shown October 21, 1971, on network ratings.

big, unusual, and significant stories of the previous three months. The program arrived on the air in mid-September—preceded by, according to *Variety,* a tangled history in the offices of its sponsor, Xerox, its ad agency, and at least two networks. A shapeless bundle of not-quite-good-enough features, presided over by John Chancellor, it received universal pans and was canceled by Xerox before the week was out—a particularly dramatic example of management's and sponsors' unwillingness to experiment or to give a good idea, even if poorly executed, a second chance—particularly in an expensive weekday evening hour.

Still, the fact that it got on the air at all seemed a hopeful sign to some TV newsmen. Less hopeful was the fate of public television's "The Great American Dream Machine," a critical success which treated news and public affairs with originality and, frequently, irreverence—disconcerting and informing at one and the same time. Before most of its fans had realized what had happened, it was cut back to an hour, and in February 1972 it closed down production with nothing remotely comparable scheduled to take its place. The explanation: insufficient funds.

Public television's documentary plans for the 1972–1973 season were even more uncertain than those of commercial television. Just two seasons before, PTV (public television) had set the pace in quality for the entire industry. Now the only producer of the formidable stable it had available who was signed up for more than one full-length documentary was the talented Frederick Wiseman, who was going to continue his remarkable *cinéma vérité* series on institutions. Morton Silverstein, producer of the controversial "Banks and the Poor" (see *Survey of Broadcast Journalism, 1970–1971*), was idle, as was his colleague Don Fouser, of "The Nader Report." None of the units that three years ago had turned out documentaries for the now defunct weekly "NET Journal" were still together. Instead the Public Broadcasting Service (PBS) was thinking mainly in terms of mini-documentaries done for airing in series such as "Behind the Lines" and "Bill Moyers' Journal."

The comment of Jim Lehrer, PBS' new coordinator for public affairs programming, had a ring familiar from his commercial counterparts: "The major problem with documentaries is getting an audience for them."

Network radio, with one conspicuous exception, reduced its news operations still further (see special report on page 178).

For yet another year, what the networks did best, they did least and least conspicuously.

The local news and public affairs scene in both television and radio seemed somewhat brighter. Of the news and public affairs directors participating in this year's Survey, 63 percent indicated that they had a larger budget, 47.5 percent had a bigger staff, and 39.7 percent had more time at their disposal in 1971–1972 than in the preceding year. Only 12 percent admitted to having less in any of these categories. The rest were holding their own.

Community by community, the reports received from DuPont correspondents indicated that the amount of time devoted to news was neither greater nor less than in the previous season. However, almost half of the cities reported on were seeing substantially more local documentaries and public affairs programming.

Some conspicuous cutbacks were reported. In Sacramento station KOVR sliced its local evening news in half and ran an ad boasting "Now—all the news—in half the time . . . no fluff, no repetition—just news" and announcing that the vacated half hour henceforth would be filled by reruns of "television's most honored detective series—'Dragnet.' "

WBAP-TV in Fort Worth–Dallas spent thousands of dollars in a promotion campaign announcing that it was offering "all the news in half the time," and managed to beat out the local competition which was still broadcasting a full hour of news.

Although WBAP said it had increased its budget and improved the quality of writing and editing, a local report from the DuPont correspondent did not indicate that all the important issues in the Fort Worth–Dallas community had received the time and attention from broadcasters they deserved.

That more rather than less time might be profitably used by most local news operations was indicated by DuPont correspondents' evaluations of the performance of stations on specific issues. Reporting of politics rated highest, with 10 out of the 65 DuPont correspondents indicating outstanding coverage in their communities. Law-and-order had 7 citations, and consumer problems 6. At the opposite extreme, regular coverage of such continuing big-city problems as poverty and urban decay was rated poor or nonexistent in 28 and 25 markets respectively. Poor coverage of women's lib was mentioned in 22; of consumer problems, in 25.

Whether the trend was up or down, both the networks and local stations had many impressive individual accomplishments to their credit during the year.

The Nixon trip to China was undoubtedly the story of the

year. Just being there and keeping the cameras in focus was enough to make it that. Pooled coverage may have limited network incentive to some degree, but still there was the impression that the American television viewer got a more superficial and predictable view of the most populous and least-known nation on earth than he need have. With a limit to the personnel they could send, the networks once again chose box-office names rather than knowledgeable journalists to represent them.

The one bona-fide expert present, Theodore White, who had an excellent book on modern China to his credit and who was there representing PBS, tagged along in total silence because the public broadcasters did not have the $300,000 required to get a signal out.

Walter Cronkite, John Chancellor, and Harry Reasoner, who were perfectly splendid for the moon, where they and their audience could all be surprised and amazed and proud together, were not quite up to a country which had the longest uninterrupted history of any on the globe and had arrived at a way of life almost incomprehensible to ordinary, well-heeled, middle-class, middle-aged Americans like themselves.

Even without the company of experts, however, the trip was well worth the dozens of hours and millions of dollars ABC, CBS, and NBC chose to spend on it.

Although the networks managed to make the 6,500-mile trip to Peking and send the story back live, none of them bothered to traverse the few blocks across Manhattan Island to perform the same service for an equally historic occasion, the vote to admit Mainland China to the United Nations. It was left to the local, municipal channel, WNYC, still staggering under last year's 50 percent staff and budget cuts, to do the full, live job on one of the year's biggest stories.*

Broadcasters paid closer attention to the disasters in Bangladesh—first the civil war and then the India-Pakistan conflict—despite the apparent unwillingness or inability of the two governments to give the press the sort of front-line service they had grown accustomed to in Vietnam. All three networks did a respectable job of covering the tragic conflict, ending with substantial prime-time documentaries. Of these, NBC's segment produced by Robert Rogers for "Chronolog" was outstanding.

Vietnam coverage, stimulated by the announced resumption

---

* To its credit, public television's National Public Affairs Center for Television (NPACT), a late arrival, was on live for an hour and forty minutes the evening of the vote.

of bombing of North Vietnam in spring 1972, followed by the mining of Haiphong harbor, was considerably more detailed and outspoken than it had been in the preceding months of "winding down the war." During the lull, however, CBS had aired in December a remarkable series on the continuing air war in Southeast Asia, which preceded by several months the revelations concerning the controversial air strikes ordered by General John D. Lavelle. NBC broadcast a two-part series called "Vietnam Hindsight," an attempt to put the record straight in the wake of the Pentagon Papers. These shows, aired on December 21 and 22, cleared just 162 and 179 of a possible 225 stations and went unsponsored.

The escalation of the air war in Vietnam brought indignant editorial responses from many broadcasters—most conspicuously, two New York stations, one radio, one television. WRVR, a radio station that for a year had been devoting its main attention to news in depth and a massive coverage of important local events in the hope of capturing a respectable audience of thoughtful New Yorkers, ran a twenty-four-hour editorial against the war. Five days later the station devoted more than four hours to replies. WNET/13, Manhattan's public television station, ran an antiwar telethon which lasted five hours and brought vehement objections from viewers, congressmen, and some TV newsmen who found it unprofessional. The program reinforced WNET's growing reputation as the nation's number one broadcasting maverick.

Despite their rough treatment at the hands of network schedulers and some local stations, the magazine shows "60 Minutes" and "Chronolog" continued to present some of the best journalism seen on the nation's screens during the year. The star performer again was CBS' Mike Wallace. His continuing series of dialogues with Americans who had something to hide and who, willing or not, found they were exposing themselves to Wallace in front of millions of Americans demonstrated that his historic interviews with Mylai army veterans Private Paul Meadlo and Captain Ernest Medina (see *Survey of Broadcast Journalism, 1969–1970*) were not just happenstance. In addition to virtuoso encounters with writer Clifford Irving and lobbyist Dita Beard, Wallace displayed his agile footwork in a number of "60 Minutes" reports: most notably "Company Town" and "An Enemy of the People," two harsh probes into the guts of big and middle-sized U.S. business, and a segment on the Law Enforcement Assistance Administration (LEAA), an inquiry into the expenditure of federal funds in the pursuit of law and order which brought cries of foul from both the Senate and the Department of Justice.

Among his best was "Not to *My* Kids, You Don't!," a twenty-minute essay on what schools the more liberal residents of Washington, D.C., chose for their children and why. Wallace made an embarrassing point and showed that busing in the North was obviously not the simple matter some would like to make it out to be.*

A great many other broadcasters handled the busing issue as it affected the nation and their own communities. Perhaps the most effective treatment of an infinitely complex and prickly subject was done by a unit which was neither strictly local or national in character—the Group W Urban Affairs Unit—which for four years had taken on major issues and presented them with great insight and skill.

Its hour-long show, "Busing, Some Voices from the South," was one segment of a three-part series entitled "The Search for Quality Education." *

Among those called upon to sit down together on camera were Ann Atwater, the black cochairman of the Durham, North Carolina, Save Our Schools Committee, and her fellow member, Claiborne P. Ellis, the local head of the Ku Klux Klan.

> MRS. ATWATER: I have never been afraid to work with anybody, and I've had questions thrown at me, you know, weren't you afraid to work with Mr. Ellis and I always said, no, because I wasn't here just to work with him. We were working on problems and he was trying to get some things changed for his son, I was trying to get some things changed for my daughter.
> MR. ELLIS: After I was elected and Mrs. Atwater was elected, I was uncomfortable to say the least. I remember reading in the paper where she tried to hit the Superintendent of the Durham city schools over the head with a telephone. I thought that was the meanest black woman I ever seen. But as I thought back on some meetings I had with him, I wanted to do the same thing because he's no more responsive to me than he was to her.

Producer Paul Altmeyer challenged Ellis: "Mr. Ellis, one of the tenets of the Ku Klux Klan is that the black as a race is inferior. Is Mrs. Atwater inferior?" It took three restatements of the question to get Mr. Ellis finally to admit, "As an individual, I don't know what her IQ is, but as an individual,

* See list of DuPont-Columbia Awards on page 159.

she's real intelligent. I'll have to give credit where credit is due, but the black race as a group are inferior to the whites."

Mr. Ellis explained his presence despite objections to "co-operating with the blacks and liberals" from many of his white friends:

> I said, I'll tell you what to do. You shut your eyes for about thirty minutes and when you open them you see if those black folks have gone away. They're not going anywhere and I'm not going anywhere so the best thing for us to do is just sit down and talk this thing over.

The program concluded with a statement read by Group W commentator Rod MacLeish behind a film montage of happily busing school kids:

> And there stands the South. For the first time since the days of Thomas Jefferson and John Marshall, the South leads the nation, Southerners, and especially, their children, with a lesson for all . . . the fear of busing is much worse than the reality. The days ahead could be as decisive for national desegregation as 1954 was for southern desegregation. But there must be a will to do it.
>
> One White House adviser has said, "the second era of Reconstruction is over. The ship of integration is going down." Yet public opinion polls indicate the opposite. Most Americans want integrated education for their children. But "the ship of integration" is stuck on the phony issue of busing.
>
> What is required is political leadership, the same type of leadership that fought the segregation of the South with passion and conviction. Today, the loudest and the angriest cries over integration come not from the South, but from the suburbs of the North.
>
> Integration in the states outside the South has come to virtually a dead halt in the last four years.
>
> Right now the North has more black students in segre-gated schools than does the South.
>
> But in the southern school districts we have visited, it's evident that integrated education, sensitively conducted and with community support, can mean better education for all children . . . white and black, rich and poor. The law of the land is very clear. School desegregation must be a fact of American life. And there stands the South.
>
> We must come to see that the de facto segregation in the North is just as injurious as the actual segregation in the South.

The busing dilemma was not put more clearly during the year, nor did Group W leave it at that.

Another show in the series was "Class . . . and the Class Room," produced and written by Dick Hubert, which showed the school situation in Duluth, Minnesota, where segregation by income and social status rather than race (only 2 percent of Duluth's population is black) prevailed, indicating other, perhaps deeper and more widespread causes for unequal schooling than the color of one's skin.

The third show, "A Chance for a Lifetime," done by freelance TV producer Susan Garfield, was a study of parent-run day-care centers and the threat to them in current state requirements and proposed federal legislation. With its plea for neighborhood controls, the program cut into education's problem from yet another direction. In the three shows nothing was simplified, and yet, thanks to the deep humanity of the approach, nothing seemed hopeless.*

Busing and desegregation was a big story in many communities this year. Perhaps the most ambitious job on the subject by a local station was that done by KWTV, in predominantly conservative Oklahoma City. It was the first really explosive story the station had faced since it had undergone a drastic overhaul and upgrading of its news operation in the fall of '71, doubling its daily news time, its budget, and its staff (from sixteen to thirty-five), and adding two hours a month in public affairs specials and documentaries.

KWTV's concentrated coverage began in February 1972 with a half-hour special the day that federal judge Luther Bohanan ordered massive busing of children to desegregate Oklahoma City schools. (It was one of two programs prepared and ready to go in case an alternate busing scheme was ordered.) This was followed two days later by the first of nine reports by the station's urban affairs reporter, Andrew Fisher, who had been dispatched to cities in the South and East that had been confronted by similar drastic court-ordered plans.

On his return Fisher edited his material into a one-hour documentary entitled "School Busing: The Trial of Two Cities," which compared local problems with the very similar ones which Charlotte, North Carolina, had faced and apparently survived.

Richard Townley, the station's managing editor, reported:

---

* Unfortunately, only eighteen cities in the country saw these superlative documentaries: thirteen in the North, five in the South.

In view of the growing public antagonism toward the busing plan and threats of mass boycotts, the program attempted to show that busing did not mean the destruction of a school system, that the court order was likely to be upheld, and that the community should use its energy in an attempt to make the court plan work instead of setting on a course of self-destruction. The documentary was aired on a Sunday. At the next day's School Board meeting, a resolution was passed by the Board (which was on record as opposing the busing plan) instructing the school administration to begin making plans to implement the court order.

In the summer the station aired three discussion programs, and on the first day of school it went on the air with a one-hour prime-time special.

KERA, the Dallas–Fort Worth public television station, followed the desegregation story in its community with unusual attention, assigning three reporters full time, with two weeks of advance stories prior to the crucial local court case and fifteen to twenty segments on the nightly "Newsroom" throughout the trial. The evening of the judge's decision, the station was on for two and a half hours, giving more than ninety minutes to a panel discussion by participants in the case. KERA also continued its coverage throughout the summer and into the school year.

The DuPont correspondent reports:

> Because of its format and time availabilities, [KERA's] "Newsroom" was able to communicate infinitely more information on this story than all the other broadcast outlets combined. The commercial television stations contented themselves primarily with getting film of the officials and participants entering or leaving the Federal Courthouse, brief, sound-on-film interviews, and short standups on the progress of the trial. The desegregation story was perfectly suited to "Newsroom's" format, and the quality and quantity of information provided by the reporters and in the interviews were exactly what the viewers needed.

Stations WSOC in Charlotte, North Carolina, and WVEC in Norfolk, Virginia, were also given high marks for helping defuse a potentially explosive situation by their intelligent coverage of busing in their communities.

An excellent example of a comparative rarity on the local TV scene, the instant documentary, which successfully combines hard news with a broader look at the larger issues involved, was KRON, San Francisco's sixty-minute special aired on the first day of court-ordered busing in the Bay Area. In addition to the events of the day, KRON camera crews followed the activities of three families with busing youngsters: one black, two white, two pro, one con. The station went on the air in prime time that evening with an hour-long program that was specific, thorough, and reassuring without losing its objectivity.

Not all stations did so well with what was probably the nation's number one controversy. The DuPont correspondent in Jacksonville, Florida, reported a consistent focusing by local newsmen on negative events.

> I know of no exception to the tendency of both TV and radio stations to give strong emphasis to violent incidents at integrated schools . . . nor do I know of any exception to the tendency to fail to provide in-depth coverage of positive aspects of black-white cooperation—by both students and teachers in the schools affected. . . .
>
> This is not to say that any station took a hostile attitude toward the integrating efforts—the problem was an old one. Any creature biting another has been considered more newsworthy than peaceful cooperation.

Directly allied to, although apparently light-years distant from integration, was one of the year's most perceptive and striking documentaries, CBS' ". . . but what if the Dream comes true?" * It treated a subject scarcely recognized on TV except in soap operas or situation comedies: the upper middle-class life style that de facto racial segregation helps perpetuate.

Produced and written by Robert Markowitz for "CBS Reports," it planted its cameras in the heart of an upwardly mobile Birmingham, Michigan, family (just fifteen miles from downtown Detroit) which had already achieved a standard of living that 99 percent of the human race, including most Americans, would consider stratospheric.

"You know what's in those houses," commented narrator Charles Kuralt as the camera glided between the sleek front lawns of the prosperous Detroit suburb, "a love affair with the obvious—good food, beautiful clothes, the best education. This is what America always said it wanted to become." It took four months of eavesdropping and kibitzing for CBS Reports to get its somewhat different story.

* See list of DuPont-Columbia Awards on page 159.

The Greenawalts—Sam, forty-one, a banker; Jane, his wife; and their children, Sheri, Tami, and Sani (the only boy); all healthy, all handsome, all happy—lived in a big glassy house surrounded by neighbors "with the same kind of values and goals we wanted for our children."

The picture seemed beautiful and enviable. Then the vigilant cameras and microphones began to pick up a little static and discover a few cracks.

"I've surprised myself lately in finding that by maybe, oh, eleven o'clock or so, you have actually broken a sweat. I don't think that my family understands that pressure. And I'm not anxious for them to understand it," says Sam.

"My children are now ten, twelve, and fourteen. I feel that I have very little actual responsibility for what they do," says Jane.

"I really don't know whether I will take drugs or not. It really depends on what happens in high school. . . . There's a good possibility that I will. It all depends on how the world will be in maybe two or three years from now," says Sheri, the fourteen-year-old.

"I worry about my son not being able to relate to a boy that has had nothing," says Sam. "I worry about him not being a true man and I think that money has a way of protecting him. My son's problem is that he goes with WASP's, with purebreds."

Sam sweats, Jane attends sensitivity sessions with her friends, and on weekends the family drives four hours north to their "cottage" where they can be "together."

There is a glimmer of hope for this quietly desperate family when three black boys arrive from Detroit's center city for dinner. "I felt like I was black," says ten-year-old Sani, "because they, they were really nice, you know, they talked to me and stuff and made me feel like I was, like I lived in Detroit, too. I felt like I was one of them, you know, like I was in on it."

But as surely as in the tragedies of the ancient Greeks, the opportunity is missed, the black boys depart, the fly sticks in the ointment, and the Greenawalts move on and up five miles cross-county to Bloomfield Hills, an even richer suburb than Birmingham.

Charles Kuralt reads Ecclesiastes and Clarence Day as the movers jockey the family belongings:

> Farewell, my friends, farewell and hail,
> We're off to seek the Holy Grail
> We cannot tell you why.

Remember please, when we are gone,
'Twas aspiration led us on,
Tiddly-widdly, toodle—oo
All we want is to stay with you,
But here we go Goodbye.

"I try not to look back," says Sam. "I'm sad that I'm leaving this house. It's a—it's a terrific house, beautiful house. But we're moving on. It's like the camel driver going to the next oasis."

"It has a library for Sam," says Jane. "It has a rec room in the basement for the kids so they can play in it. And it has a beautiful kitchen, a family room off of that, and a dining room. And, of course, the fireplace that you can see through from the living room to the dining room, that's nice. And it has a swimming pool. It has a diving board. And I suppose it has some other rooms that I've forgotten."

Without one drop of blood being shed, without the whine of a siren or a flashing red light, a garbage-strewn gutter, a smoggy sky, or any other obvious sign of the tribulations most modern Americans are becoming accustomed to, ". . . but what if the Dream comes true?" had to be one of the most depressing, and provocative, shows of the year.

The American Dream got a going-over by several other documentarians, notably Martin Carr and Fred Freed, two of the best complacency shatterers in the business.

Before giving up his berth at NBC, Carr turned in an outstanding sixty-minute documentary entitled "Leaving Home Blues" which explained where some of the urban blight was coming from. It offered no solution, and only implied what lay in store for the armies of youngsters who were setting out from rural America to seek their fortunes in the big city. Still, it showed quite clearly that the poor boy from the sticks who in Horatio Alger's time could hope to become a hero and a millionaire was more likely in our day, multiplied a thousandfold, to become a lemming. Nor, considering what was happening to the small towns and farms of America, did he (or she) have much choice but to head for the big-city abyss.

Fred Freed's "The Blue Collar Trap" * was perhaps even more chilling, since it told the story of four intelligent, personable young men who had gotten jobs which the kids in "Leaving Home Blues" would have considered themselves happy indeed to be offered.

* See list of DuPont-Columbia Awards on page 159.

Regularly employed at substantial wages in the Ford Pinto plant at Milpitas, California, with plenty of money and leisure at their disposal, they were, at the same time, textbook examples of all the dissatisfactions and doubts today's youth is heir to. While doing their bit on the assembly line, they were into drugs, offbeat religion, open marriage, motorcycles and headbands, beards and acid rock. Without exception they hated their jobs, and expressed it in chronic absenteeism and sloppy work—on occasion deliberately damaging the expensive hardware they were engaged in turning out.

The show was probably the year's most notable example of the new generation's coolness toward the medium. If there were occasional flickers of self-consciousness, Freed's camera obviously turned no one off. The four subjects said things about themselves and their lives which their parents would have hesitated to tell their doctor or their priest. And the expressions on their faces in some cases were as revealing and frightening as the words themselves.

Revealing humanity, without shame or reticence, was perhaps the most frequent achievement of television this year. If the medium was short on the unmasking of human cruelty, corruption, or just plain stupidity which characterized such past documentaries as "Harvest of Shame," "Hunger in America," "Banks and the Poor," and "Selling of the Pentagon," it was long on revealing the results of such lapses. The viewer, shown the end product, was allowed to figure out the cause.

"Suffer the Little Children," Robert Northshield's beautifully observed essay on the children of Northern Ireland, could not have been more telling in its revelation of the adult futilities that had created their tragic world had he been given full access to the activities of the IRA or the British army.

Death, old age, poverty, addiction, mental and physical ills, the obscenities of our affluent society, were all treated on television and radio with unparalleled candor and sensitivity.

"Who Has Lived and Not Seen Death," done by WNBC, New York, had the rare courage to show dying people on screen, confronting their own death and accepting it without sentimentality or bitterness. A second outstanding show to WNBC's credit was "Children of Poverty." Producer Tom Shachtman's cameras, with little or no evidence of a distracting presence, went into the crowded slum quarters of three impoverished New York City families and for an hour let the viewer share their crushing problems, and the realization that although in these grim surroundings the parent had perhaps more of a sense of responsibility to his offspring than his affluent counterpart, he had only the slimmest hope of living up to it.

Drug addiction, the bane of poor and middle-class alike, has been more frequently and effectively treated on the air in recent years than death or poverty. ABC network's best documentary of the season was "Heroes and Heroin," an unblinking look at the problem of drug abuse in the war zone which brushed aside nervous official explanations and presented the alarming and nasty facts.

Locally, "A Seed of Hope" by WTVJ, Miami, was an original and encouraging treatment of drug addiction among the middle-class young which managed to combine shock, sentiment, and uplift in its report on a drug program in Fort Lauderdale which has claimed more than 1,700 cures in less than two years.

WTVJ's news department also demonstrated its versatility and initiative when it went abroad for another in its season of thirteen hour-long documentaries, "The Swift Justice of Europe." An intelligent study of criminal justice in Britain and France meant to raise provocative comparisons to procedures at home (it was followed by an hour called "The Slow Justice of Florida"), it succeeded in every department—script, photography, editing—and became one of the few examples of the sort of serious journalistic excursion which many prosperous local stations could afford to send their newsmen on but seldom risk.*

Mental health, and particularly mental retardation, was the subject of at least two outstanding local station efforts during the year. WABC, New York's "Willowbrook—The Last Great Disgrace," which followed a series by Geraldo Rivera on WABC's nightly "Eyewitness News," was perhaps the most sensational, involving surprise visits to New York State facilities for the mentally retarded on Staten Island (Willowbrook) and on the Hudson River (Letchworth Village). Rivera, in his follow-up, was not satisfied to leave the viewer with the shocking memory of these discards of an affluent society, naked, befouled, bewildered, frightened, and frightening. He took him across the country to California to show how well retarded children can be treated, and for no additional cost, and left him with the uncomfortable knowledge that "it needn't be so."

More remarkably, Rivera went back again, and still a third time, to point out to the audience of WABC that despite all the

* See list of DuPont-Columbia Awards on page 159.

brouhaha, conditions remained unimproved. Finally, thanks in great part to Rivera, they did improve. Such persistence is rare in TV journalism.

An even more exhaustive treatment of the subject of mental retardation was aired by WRC in Washington, D.C., which first did a half-hour show on the local situation, then expanded it in an additional hour covering the state of Maryland. Reporter Clare Crawford had the satisfaction, not given to Rivera, of being able to report to her viewers that the state had begun to improve matters a little even before she had completed her program.

The single subject which received the most consistent and exhaustive attention from local documentary units seemed to be jails and penitentiaries. Undoubtedly triggered by the horrors of the riots at Attica and San Quentin during the summer of 1971, local penal institutions were subject to minute and disapproving scrutiny from coast to coast. A few among the many who turned in reports were WLW, Dayton; WJZ, Baltimore; WVUE, New Orleans; KPLR, St. Louis; WIIC, Pittsburgh; and KOVR, Sacramento.

One of the most imaginative treatments was done, as it had been for a surprisingly large number of topics in its brief two-year existence, by "The Great American Dream Machine," which took its cameras and actor Stacy Keach to a towering red brick prison outside Montgomery, Alabama. There they wandered down the echoing corridors and into the grim and empty cells, examining the graffiti, quoting the words of the prisoners, and finally abandoning the vast edifice to the wreckers, who razed it to the ground a few days after the TV team departed.

Another interesting approach was used by KQED, San Francisco, in its "Scan Goes to Jail," a live show from the controversial San Francisco County Jail which involved inmates stating their grievances directly to the county sheriff and various other dignitaries gathered in the KQED studio.

But Attica was undoubtedly *the* story, and the best treatment of it was unquestionably done by producer Richard Thurston Watkins and reporters Gil Noble and Geraldo Rivera for WABC's weekly minority show, "Like It Is." * The ninety-minute "Attica: The Unanswered Questions" took an unabashedly minority view of what, after all, was an affair of prime concern to blacks and Puerto Ricans, and it made its points indelibly, marking the consciousness of whites as well.

* See list of DuPont-Columbia Awards on page 159.

Toward the end of the grim and very disturbing show, Noble leveled with the viewers, an estimated 70 percent of whom were white:

American history is dotted with what are classified as riots, racial disturbances, and confrontations. We've had Newark, Watts, Detroit, Jackson State. Now there is Attica. They've occurred all over the country in so-called ghettos, on the campus, and even in quiet little towns. But they all had a series of common characteristics. It took place on Black turf, not White. It was a Black group or community versus a mostly White police agency. The police charged the existence of snipers, but those charges proved false. Police charged the presence of outside agitators, but none were ever produced. Police charged that they had to shoot first. But investigations proved that this was a bold-faced lie. Few police or guardsmen have been punished despite the condemnation of endless investigations. First reports from police, the National Guard, and the press have later turned out to be false. And there seems to be a constant inability to get the facts straight by all three. And the reaction or the retraction, the correction is always weaker than the accusation. In each instance, the Black grievance was made clear long before it hit the fan. Yet in each instance, after the explosion conditions remained the same. What happened at Attica, Watts, etc., must be regarded as pus. Pus indicates a deep-seated infection underneath, and if the infection isn't attacked, you'll continue to have pus until the patient dies. The infection is White American racism in all its institutions, legal, political, and penal, not Black snipers or Puerto Rican revolutionaries or outside agitators. And finally, to those viewers who don't like the positions that we've stated and feel that there should be more balance from a White viewpoint, let me say this. "Like It Is" is the only program this station airs that is an expression of the Black and Puerto Rican opinion. Everything else on Channel 7 comes from a White psyche. This single hour can hardly be called equal time because at least 30 percent of our viewers are Black and Puerto Rican. So it then follows that it would be indeed foolish to divide this already inadequate hour between our opinions and those of Whites. We view "Like It Is" as in itself a rebuttal.

At Attica, as at so many other scenes of disorder and violence, television became an active force *in* the events rather than an observer *of* them. The TV cameras were pointed to as a tragically distracting and disruptive presence, particularly during the delicate negotiations between prisoners and officials. According to some present, the simple fact that the prisoners knew they were being televised encouraged them to think that they would prevail. At the least, it turned the negotiations into a public performance and rendered compromise on either side unlikely. The most successful segment of WNET/13, New York's ambitious but uneven weekly journalism review, "Behind the Lines," described the impact of the press on the small town of Attica which gave the prison its name. The press did not come off well: "I don't believe anything I read or see on TV anymore," said one shocked woman. "I always did before." The program gave several good reasons why she might feel that way.

Later WNET performed a conspicuous public service by carrying 57½ hours of the McKay hearings which inquired into the causes and circumstances of the Attica uprising. This followed an earlier example of the station's enterprise, nearly 60 hours of the Knapp hearings on police corruption in Manhattan, which were carried live during the day with a 60-minute prime-time summary each evening. Not only did the station carry both hearings, but it furnished the premises for the official state-sponsored Attica investigations, which conveniently turned out to be one of its own studios.*

Experiment and controversy on the nation's public TV stations was at an all-time low because of short funds and sagging morale, to be discussed in a later chapter. There were exceptions. WNJT, the public station in Trenton, N.J., put together a half-hour documentary, "Towers of Frustration," that any network could have been proud of.† The problems of the Stella Wright housing project in Newark were indeed national in application, shared as they were by dozens of instant high-rise slums, coast to coast. There was rough talk from both tenants and management, whom WNJT conscientiously canvassed and put on the air. If anyone in Washington wanted proof of a local public TV operation doing top-quality work, worthy of network distribution, this well-edited, thoroughly reported half hour done by producer-reporter John Drimmer was it.

Another example was the Iowa Educational Broadcasting Network's "Take Des Moines . . . Please," which, although on a strictly local subject, gave indication of talents anything but provincial. The sixty-minute program was a witty and intelligent dissection of the traffic problems of the capital city of Iowa, which, surprisingly, are considerable.

---

* To help WNET out, WPIX, a New York independent, carried the public outlet's educational schedule during the day.
† See list of DuPont-Columbia Awards on page 159.

Perhaps the single most impressive accomplishment by a local public TV station again belonged to the new, free-wheeling, non-broadcasting team which had taken over WNET/13, New York. With nearly $2 million from Ford and other foundations, it set out to develop a new news format for public television and greater New York. After a shaky start "The 51st State" became the liveliest, if not the most professional, operation in town, often succeeding in getting a sizable chunk of the audience away from its ten o'clock commercial competition.

The format was loose and open-ended, tending to ignore the big news stories in favor of one or two local items done in considerable depth. To amplify a subject, the producers were not averse to inviting concerned people into the studio for a loud-mouthed free-for-all, which could result in chaos or real illumination.

The single most successful example of the technique and one of the year's most effective examples of local TV journalism was an hour-long inquiry into the youth gangs of the South Bronx undertaken by staffer Tony Batten.*

Opening with straightforward interviews with some of the principals concerned—teen-agers, teachers, and advisers—the program took off when the cameras were permitted to stay at a closed meeting where two hundred representatives of gang "families" discussed the killing of a member of one gang by another, obviously a situation of which deadly rumbles have been made. The colloquy which followed was spotted with expletives and obscenities seldom, if ever, heard on television. Much of the talk was incomprehensible. However, intent and mood were crystal clear, and the speakers had a conviction and eloquence lacking in older and more conventional urban leaders.

The participants and other members of the South Bronx community came together in the studio to watch the film and round out the program by rapping with its makers on camera. By the end of the hour the attentive listener had an insight into a world which, although a short subway ride from his home, usually was as invisible to him as the far side of the moon.

Another local experiment in public TV news, less ambitious and well-heeled but still, according to the DuPont correspondent in New Orleans, "the most refreshing instance of local broadcast journalism," was "City Desk" on WYES-TV. On the debit side, WETA, Washington's "Newsroom," which began as a one-hour weekday program two years ago, was cut back to a half hour, and finally left the air in October 1971.

* See list of DuPont-Columbia Awards on page 159.

The original "Newsroom" at San Francisco's KQED, which had been cut back to a half hour nightly last season, was scheduled to go back to a full hour in October. "The key goal will be to become far more public, with emphasis on news not now covered in other media, investigative reporting, a broader geographical base, and a real effort to cover such groups as blue collar workers and native Americans, whose interests are often ignored elsewhere," said a station spokesman.

The appearance of the youth gangs in WNET's downtown studios, in full regalia and with their pride, belligerence, and eloquence intact, dramatized a trend which had been growing throughout the country both on radio and television for several years. Actually the idea for the South Bronx show was born on another WNET regular, "Free Time," which allowed disaffected members of the community an opportunity to sound off. Thanks to a flourishing new trend there were dozens of similar programs across the country. What was known as public access, the right of the common man to use the air waves, which for decades had been declared to be legally his, was finally becoming generally recognized and indeed welcomed as a new source of programming.

Cable television was one reason for the new awareness of this possibility. Written into all new franchises in the top one hundred markets was a requirement for one public access channel, which sooner or later had to be made available to anyone who agreed to follow very simple ground rules: no obscenity, no personal attack, no incitement to riot. By the latter part of 1972 four such channels, all in Manhattan, were in operation. New York City's TelePrompTer had opened its public access channel on July 1, 1971, and celebrated its first birthday on July 1, 1972, by activating a special storefront studio in Harlem to facilitate the appearance of members of that community who wished to be heard. By that time it was averaging seventy-five programs per week.

Nearly half of the respondents to the DuPont Survey listed on their schedules special programs to give the public access to the air. The commonest and oldest form, of course, was the radio phone-in show. This variety, which began with late-night disc-jockeys accepting calls from lovesick teen-agers, had come a long way. Last year, at the time of Mainland China's admission to the United Nations, KABC, Los Angeles, went on the air with twenty-four hours of steady talk about the event which involved phone connections with Peking, Taiwan, the UN, seven senators, three congressmen, and any listener who could get through.

"Involvement," another Los Angeles phone-in on KGBS, devoted two hours each Sunday evening to specific subjects. One, "Crisis in the Courts," had a panel made up of four superior court judges and a justice from the court of appeals. "The People Talk" began on KFWB, Hollywood, in February 1972. Aired twice a month, it involved reporters going out into the community and talking to individuals about specified subjects. It differed from the classic man-in-the-street format—nearly as old as radio—in that the sample was scattered geographically, experts were employed, and a twenty-five-minute summary was offered at the end of each segment which put the subject into some sort of perspective.

On radio the most satisfactory phone-ins were those which employed a well-informed talkmaster (still few and far between) who, not content with his own knowledge, invited an expert in to discuss some timely subject with himself and any listeners who chose to call. In this way the discussion was channeled, crackpots were discouraged, and the misinformed and prejudiced stood some chance of correction. However, if the talkmaster himself were badly informed, prejudiced, or a crackpot, there was little to contain the discussion or keep slander and error off the air.

As for over-the-air TV, on which access shows until recently had been comparative rarities, our St. Louis correspondent reported: "I believe that the most important trend in St. Louis broadcast journalism during 1971–1972 was an effort to involve the audience more directly in newscasts . . . . Each of the five major television stations here . . . took some step in the way of encouraging audience participation." One was a thirty-minute weekly show on KPLR, which put studio facilities at the disposal of individuals wishing to sound off.

KTLA-TV, Los Angeles, actually opened up its ten o'clock newscast, presided over by George Putnam, to an audience, who after thirty minutes of news each evening were permitted to put in their two cents' worth. The experiment succeeded in bolstering ratings in a competition with three other non-network TV news hours at the same time. Not to be outdone, KTTV, one of the competitors, instituted a "secret witness" feature on an anticrime series in its ten o'clock news, paying people who phoned in with usable leads up to $5,000 in bounty money.

In Salt Lake City all three TV stations and KSL radio responded favorably to a group calling itself the United Front to

End the Bombing which demanded on-air discussions of the mining of Haiphong harbor and demonstrated on the street outside the stations to get them. At the end of its program, KCPX pointed out that mass demonstrations were not needed to get on the air—a simple request would be adequate. However, the demonstrators, in the process of demanding time, had managed to get on the news programs as well.

One of the oldest and most conscientious efforts to give the public access to the air was "Feedback" on WJCT, the Jacksonville, Florida, public television station. A daily one-hour show, it was built on specific questions from the audience. Also tied in with WJCT's access program was the station's Department of Community Involvement, a team of nine people which covered local meetings and devised new program formats to answer the needs of specific groups.

Other forms of public access included the "action line," on which disgruntled consumers aired their grievances, followed up by reporters' investigations that frequently resulted in substantial features on regular newscasts.

These shows might be considered the simplest form of investigative reporting, a respected type of journalism which seemed to be just holding its own on radio and television. Of those answering the DuPont-Columbia Survey, more than half said they did investigative reporting, but of those only half felt any specific investigative story worth mentioning. Correspondents reported an increase in investigative reporting in ten markets; only a handful of stations, however, had done things which the correspondents felt worthy of the jurors' attention. These included Richard Angelico's investigative reporting on WVUE, New Orleans; a WLS, Chicago, series on deplorable conditions in halfway houses for mental patients in that city; a series by KYTV, Springfield, Missouri, on meat packing; and an excellent series on the Jewish poor done on his own time by producer Dan Cooper for WCBS, New York.

Although several network programs from earlier seasons were still making waves—notably "Migrant," "Hunger in America," "The Selling of the Pentagon," "Banks and the Poor," and NBC magazine segments on chemical and biological warfare and the Atomic Energy Commission, there was little this year that promised to set up such reverberations. One of the few was the well-researched "Business of Blood" (on "Chronolog"), which was followed at the end of the summer by a new Food and Drug Administration ruling regulating the commercial sale of human blood.

One answer to the investigative problem was reported by WDIO, Duluth, which

> . . . found production of documentary reports too expensive for the amount of exposure they received even in prime time. Instead, we have expanded our news format to include regular investigative reports, sometimes in a "series" format, frequently creating measurable and important community reaction. We have a full-time investigative reporter, who is responsible only to the News Director for his time and materials. He generally originates his own investigations or does so at the instigation of the News Director, or a joint decision within the news department. We are finding that a newsroom consensus frequently produces the most meaningful areas for investigation.

The hiring of a full-time investigative reporter was rare enough to warrant praise. However, the sacrificing of full-scale documentaries to newscast investigations or mini-documentaries did not seem an ideal solution. The fight for time on nightly newscasts and the prevalent conviction that no news watcher could tolerate an item longer than ninety seconds militated against any investigator who had a lot to tell. One alternative was building-block documentaries, which packaged findings in four- or five-minute parcels that were later put together into a thirty- or sixty-minute program which, as in the case of "Willowbrook," added up to considerably more than the sum of its parts.

Instances of news manipulation, or attempts at it, continued to pile up, most commonly in the field of politics. The publicity release and staged event still dominated local news. Public relations men for public and private agencies were permitted not only to do a lot of the reporters' work but frequently called the shots for news directors who might be lazy, complacent, or overworked. Some broadcasters were objecting:

> It's when a TV station thinks for itself, begins to probe, to criticize, to examine the record, that it gets into trouble. I'm fed up with the complaints of elected officials, bureaucrats, and self-serving publicity hounds. Let the newsmen make the decisions, and let the public decide who is right and who is wrong.—*WDIO-TV, Duluth*

> I find myself having more and more guidelines imposed by newsmakers on how I can cover stories. Public agencies are getting public relations representatives to speak to broadcasters so the top man need not make himself avail-

able, and, if the PR man gives an answer that backfires, the top man can disavow any relation to it.—*WJZ-TV, Baltimore*

An alarming variation on the printed press release, or the friendly telephone call, was reported at some length in *The Wall Street Journal* by William McAllister, who had rounded up several instances of corporations with an ax to grind sending finished news items to TV station news directors to be inserted in their regular newscasts. The most flagrant was an item showing how pipelines could be accommodated to caribou on the Arctic tundra, with local newsmen from coast to coast assuring viewers that such successful safeguards would be a part of the controversial trans-Alaska oil pipeline. The feature was filmed, and the words, read by the newsman, had been written by the Alyeska Pipeline Service Company, a highly interested party. A local story, containing a plug for Wells Fargo Bank (which paid for it), got air time on three out of four of San Francisco's commercial TV stations. One film maker, according to McAllister, claimed that twenty out of thirty top California TV stations would accept a well-made outside film. "Another advantage for the public relations men," said McAllister, "is that the film can't be readily edited by the local stations, whereas a newspaper can easily rewrite or edit a printed release, eliminating the puffery and adding balance."

According to the DuPont correspondent in Charleston, West Virginia, WHIS-TV did not even bother to rewrite unsubstantiated releases from the Surface Miners Association about land reclamation and other controversial subjects, which it put on the air verbatim and without attribution.

Another subject of inquiry in the DuPont survey was, once again, the treatment of major local stories by stations in the community. One out of three DuPont correspondents saw these stories handled on television in a better than adequate manner. On radio, it was one in six—not an impressive score for the nation's top news purveyors.

One of the most flagrant examples of local newscasters turning their backs on a top story taking place on their own turf was the treatment by Harrisburg, Pennsylvania, broadcasters of the trial of the Harrisburg Seven last winter. Almost without exception, the only material that got on the air locally was furnished by wire services and the networks. When the next big story arrived, the floods brought on by Hurricane Agnes, many of the stations, unfortunately, had no opportunity to prove their mettle since they were flooded out.

However, WHP stayed on the air from 4:20 A.M., June 22, to 1:00 A.M., June 28, without interruption, discontinuing commercial programming for nearly half of the period, beginning with flood warnings and continuing with a variety of service announcements required by the emergency. WCMB was on the air for 157 consecutive hours, transmitting more than 70,000 flood messages.

On the other hand, station WABF in Baton Rouge, Louisiana, was reported to have completely ignored a hurricane and tornado going on outside its studio door, doggedly continuing its regular programming.

Station WTVT, Tampa, Florida, lost an item of considerable local interest on "The CBS Evening News" when, on Friday, June 2, 1972, according to the news editor, an engineer accidentally dropped a stack of tapes, and the tapes hit a button which blacked out a part of the telecast at the very moment it was being alleged that Santo Trafficante, Jr. (described by law enforcement authorities as a chief of organized crime for central Florida), was involved in Southeast Asian drug traffic.

The rise and fall of Senator Edmund Muskie's presidential aspirations were, according to the DuPont correspondent in Maine, skimpily handled on local radio and TV.

> Once Muskie's demise was complete, the Maine broadcast media displayed no interest at all. On the day that Muskie rejected McGovern's bid for him to be the vice-presidential nominee, one of the largest radio stations in the state led its most important newscast of the day with a benefit golf tournament . . . and no mention of the Muskie story was made—in spite of the fact that Muskie had made his announcement right here in Maine.

An amusing inversion of the big-story-overlooked took place at WTMJ, Milwaukee, which passed over NBC's "Projection '72," a ninety-minute network special using the talents of the network's top news personnel, in favor of a local basketball game. When the same news team arrived in town on a promotional tour a few days later, the NBC correspondents were conspicuously featured by the same station as visiting celebrities.

If profitable big-city stations sometimes did less than seemed required, more than one small-time station did more. KCFW in Kalispell, Montana, a town of approximately ten thousand inhabitants, gave full live color coverage to the community's big event of the year: the two-and-a-half-hour stopover of the President of the United States at Kalispell's Glacier International

Airport. "We used three Sony color cameras, mobile trailer unit, special effects generators, and a prayer or two in making Montana Broadcast History with our live coverage of this historic event." KCFW was also proud of "The Pasquinizo Story": "a continuing series of news stories and editorials (10) on a child being deprived of an education through geographical segregation. KCFW's coverage resulted in school board being forced to change its policies and admit the child (a boy of nine)." Besides the bureaucracy, KCFW also took on big business with "The Economy vs. the Environment," a series of reports on Anaconda Aluminum Company's fluoride process, which had resulted in the destruction of trees in Glacier National Park.

The Montana Television Network, serving one of the nation's most sparsely populated states, reported:

> A unique regional network put into operation in September of 1971 enables statewide news and public affairs programming to be originated in Great Falls and fed simultaneously to MTN stations in Billings, Butte, and Missoula.
>
> All MTN News programs have local news inserts allowing for local-importance items while freeing the small station news staffs from production responsibilities of half-hour programs. In addition, each station newsman contributes to the MTN portions of the programs. And, station news departments cover important state capitol stories on a rotating basis for network.
>
> Under the MTN concept, Montanans in many areas are seeing the workings of state government for the first time on television, they are seeing how residents in various areas of their state are coping with problems common to the entire population, and they are at the same time finding their local TV newsmen better able to cover local items.

The trend toward lightening the news and making it more palatable, which had apparently leveled off last year, showed up again in this year's survey, with over half the correspondents reporting an increase in emphasis on humorous items, short jazzy items, or good news. In New York, San Francisco, Los Angeles, St. Louis, Milwaukee, and San Antonio, this increase was linked to heightening competition, which had not only led to fluffier stories, fancier sets, and better-looking and less professional anchormen, but also in some instances had accounted for the elimination of all serious documentary and investigatory projects. The correspondent in Los Angeles reported:

The basic trends are evident: (1) a panic shift to the so-called "happy news" format, and (2) a panic flight from genuine investigative reporting of hard-to-dig-out, significant original local news . . . . Everyone seems to be . . . uncertain what it is that wins audience. What they never seem to consider is original reporting of significant news.

The specifics of the competition in some instances were gruesome indeed. The DuPont correspondent in Milwaukee reported:

The star newsmen, weathermen, and weather puppet (Albert the Alleycat) and sportcasters function first as public relations men, second as journalists . . . . Newspaper ads . . . for Channel 6 . . . picture the star of the late movie beside the anchorman for the 10:00 P.M. newscast. Television promos are even more crass. WISN runs a promo telling how a world-famous photographer came to Milwaukee just to do portraits of Ron Scott, their news star. The portraits were donated to a downtown bank building and hang there. . . . None of the advertisements promote the journalistic excellence of any of the stations . . . they promote the personalities.

KETV in Omaha had its weathercaster wear funny costumes and report in varying ethnic accents in a desperate attempt to put more humor in its newscast. The scheme was dropped after three months. Even "The CBS Morning News," perhaps the best of all the network newscasts, resorted to puppets during the year. They were dropped.

Possibly the worst example of inappropriate means to gain questionable ends came from San Francisco, where competition between the network affiliates for the early news audience continued to be fierce. One station, KGO, required its news staff to dress up as cowboy poker-players for a full-page newspaper ad slugged, "Feel like you're getting a bad deal from poker-faced TV news reporters? Then let the Channel 7 Gang deal you in. They're not afraid to be friendly." Whereupon a competitor, KRON, felt obliged to counter with its own full-page ad showing its news staff sitting for their portraits in enormous dogs' heads, with the headline, "The Bay Area's pet news team tracking down the news 24 hours a day. Watch the Newshounds of News-watch 4." Both gimmicks, unfortunately, paid off with ratings.

As in previous years, the Survey's news-director participants expressed their hopes and apprehensions about the future of their vocation.

I am hopeful about broadcast news—less hopeful about public affairs programming. We have begun to incorporate more investigative and interpretive reporting into regular newscasts at the expense of the traditional weather and sports segments in order to catch a large potential audience for community problems and issues. We are also experimenting with new formats and approaches to public affairs programs in an effort to attract larger audiences.

Our own local surveys have demonstrated that television viewers are demanding more substance in news coverage, more variety of subject matter, and more field reporting—and less of the newscasters as "star."—*KCPX-TV, Salt Lake City*

I believe much of the "boondocks" suspicion of national news programming can be related to the fact that many provincial daily newspapers are following this same tendency—i.e., to cast out that which simply cannot be allowed to be true. Local television news must increase its role of being an alternative voice.—*WFTV, Orlando, Fla.*

I believe we have been able to help destroy some TV myths. We have shown that a local station can increase its staff and its budget in hard times; we have indicated that controversy is not hazardous to broadcasting's health; our experiences have shown that even when sponsors bluster and threaten they usually come back; and I hope we have shown that a vigorous news department can be important to an entire community.—*KWTV-TV, Oklahoma City*

We think we are a part of a trend in broadcasting to provide the listener with more "listenable information" that goes to the heart of community problems and what is being done to deal with those problems. Our experience has been that every time we increase the amount of news and information on our station, we get more listeners and our "credibility rating" also increases.—*KTOK, Oklahoma City*

Support of television news by both broadcasters and the audience may have already peaked—by broadcasters, because of cost, and by the audience because of general apathy.—*KPIX-TV, San Francisco*

The audience is sometimes "irritated" by substantive in-depth reporting. Seem to prefer superficial "quick and dirty" reporting . . . . Only the elite comment on our investigative reports and our monthly documentaries.— *KVAL-TV, Eugene, Ore.*

The letter-writing public is becoming more and more abusive and exercising more "muscle" all the time. We find we are being tarred with a brush marked for the network. We also find public affairs broadcasting under more and more attack.

At this all-news station, we face the dilemma: should we be content providing news in brief, sprinkled with features—or should we go "in depth," even though the longer report seems to drive away listeners?—*WBBM, Chicago*

The dilemma was a real one, not only to a network owned-and-operated, all-news radio station like WBBM, but to every radio and TV station and network in the nation which had any sort of commitment to news. The choice before the nation's electronic newsmen sometimes seemed to be: Do what you know you should and, for the moment, lose listeners and cash; or ignore your own best instincts—make money—and risk, perhaps a long way off, a well-deserved oblivion.

2 • No News Is Good News (I)

IN THE BEST of all possible worlds, there would be no conflict between government and broadcasting. Their goals would be identical and they would proceed toward them in an orderly fashion. Unfortunately, in America, in the early 70's, the men who governed were still first and foremost politicians, and those who broadcast were still primarily businessmen. And even in an election year, the best interests of the public did not come at the top of either's list of priorities.

This bitter fact was nowhere more apparent than in the alternate punching and sparring which went on in and around broadcast journalism. As the elections of 1972 approached, the punching subsided somewhat. In place of Vice-President Spiro T. Agnew's roundhouse swings (see *Survey of Broadcast Journalism, 1969–1970*) there were jabs from him and lesser officials, followed, customarily, by denials of hostile intent. For the broadcast journalist there was no real time out.

In an address to the Association of Life Insurance Counsel in mid-December 1971, Agnew listed his Christmas gifts for a select group of "friends." Among them: "A news desk with legs cut on the bias so that documentaries will come out straight," to Richard Salant, president of CBS News; "for *The New York Times,* Daniel Ellsberg's unlisted telephone number, and for Daniel Ellsberg, a lifetime subscription to *Look* magazine; and finally, to the Public Broadcasting Corporation, a collector's item—a piece of videotape which reveals Sander Vanocur, in an unguarded moment, making an objective statement."

Two months later he told the Boy Scouts of America that he "wouldn't trade you one service-oriented Boy Scout for all the publicity-seeking environmental dilettantes the news media can dig up between now and Halloween." In April he added yearbooks, encyclopedias, and history books to his list of media which, as he put it, were increasingly tainted with clearly unobjective accounts of politically related events and personalities and guilty of "anti-intellectual Yahooism."

However, the vice-president's attacks had obviously lost their sting. The day of his wide-open assaults on the media seemed over, at least temporarily.

In many ways the second-string adversaries were just as troublesome as the first. The most obviously belligerent among them was, probably, the least effective. Representative Harley O. Staggers of West Virginia, spurred on by his colleagues' rebuff in connection with his earlier investigations of the CBS documentary "The Selling of the Pentagon" (see *Survey of Broadcast Journalism, 1970–1971*), held his hearings on alleged network "news staging." The testimony, frequently repetitive and inconsequential, produced no startling revelations or action beyond Staggers' own testy recommendation that the Federal Communications Commission lay down guidelines for filming news reports and documentaries, an expedient the networks themselves had already anticipated. Still its nuisance value was considerable. And in the fall of 1972 the FCC sent out requests to ABC and CBS for additional information on individual cases cited. And Staggers was a Democrat. The spokesmen for the Administration, coming in relays and avoiding eyeball-to-eyeball confrontations, flailed less and hurt more.

Senator Robert Dole, chairman of the Republican National Committee, continued his attacks on network newsmen, accusing unnamed television commentators of attempting to "sabotage" national policy.

The implication that any questioning of the Administration's actions in Vietnam amounted to treason was made explicit by top presidential aide H. R. Haldeman when he told "Today's" Barbara Walters, in his first network TV interview, that critics of Nixon's January 25 peace plan were "consciously aiding and abetting the enemy of the United States." In the uproar that followed, Senate opposition leader Mike Mansfield commented: "The First Amendment still stands and freedom of speech is still allowed."

The Republican National Committee's weekly newsletter, *Monday,* followed up with a blast at NBC and the United Press for transmitting photos and films supplied to them by North Vietnam.

> MONDAY: In showing Communist propaganda film, is the question of what gives aid and comfort to the enemy ever discussed; is it a consideration?
> WALLACE WESTFELDT [executive producer of "NBC Nightly News"]: We try to put on what is news.

MONDAY: When showing such enemy propaganda film, does the question of whose interests are being served ever come up?

WESTFELDT: It's not a question of this. We're trying to report a story that is going on. That is the principal question.

MONDAY: Do you consider the question of whether or not the Communist film shown grinds the enemy ax a relevant one?

WESTFELDT: No, we try to put stuff on the air that is informative to the American people.

In the same issue *Monday* editors accused CBS of inaccuracies in their Vietnam reporting.

NBC got it again when Governor Ronald Reagan told an NBC affiliates' meeting in Los Angeles that broadcasters were "irresponsible . . . pander to the drug culture, allow obscenity on the air, and turn over their facilities to those who shout 'revolution.' "

J. L. Robertson, vice-chairman of the Board of Governors of the Federal Reserve System, in an address to the Independent Bankers Association of America, took the opportunity to talk, not on the economic but on the credibility crisis, stating that the media were "being used to undermine the credibility of everyone who represents authority." Doing his best in turn to undermine the credibility of the media, he stated:

> The media agree that you bankers should be scrupu-lously honest in informing your customers about your interest charges. At the same time, some of them contend that "freedom of the press" gives anyone who has access to a printing press or a microphone the right to lie and deceive, even if those lies are part of an effort to incite people to perform illegal acts, such as blowing up banks.

Other adversaries of broadcast journalism ranged from Supreme Court Justice Lewis F. Powell, Jr., and the acting director of the FBI, L. Patrick Gray, III, to Jesse Helms, vice-president of WRAL-TV, Raleigh, North Carolina, and a candidate for the U.S. Senate.

In a 34-page confidential memorandum to the U.S. Chamber of Commerce written in August 1971, Powell, two months before his nomination to the Supreme Court, recommended that the Chamber launch a counterattack against the voices in American life which were antipathetic to what he called "the system." The voices came, according to Powell, from perfectly respectable elements of society; from the college campus, the pulpit, the media, the intellectual and literary journals, the arts and sciences, and from politicians. In most of these groups, the movement against the system is participated in only by minorities. Yet, these often are the most articulate, the most vocal, the most prolific in their writing and speaking.

Moreover, much of the media—for varying motives and in varying degrees—either voluntarily accords unique publicity to these "attackers," or at least allows them to exploit the media for their purposes. This is especially true of television, which now plays such a predominant role in shaping the thinking, attitudes, and emotions of our people.

Justice Powell seemed to see a conspiracy proceeding from the nation's colleges and universities, which he described as follows:

As these "bright young men," from campuses across the country, seek opportunities to change a system which they have been taught to distrust—if not, indeed "despise" —they seek employment in the centers of the real power and influence in our country, namely: (i) with the news media, especially television; (ii) in government as "staffers" and consultants at various levels; (iii) in elective politics; (iv) as lecturers and writers; and (v) on the faculties at various levels of education.

Many do enter the enterprise system—in business and the professions—and for the most part they quickly discover the fallacies of what they have been taught. But those who eschew the mainstream of the system, often remain in key positions of influence where they mold public opinion and often shape governmental action. In many instances, these "intellectuals" end up in regulatory agencies or governmental departments with large authority over the business system they do not believe in.

Among Powell's recommendations to correct this imbalance:

The national television networks should be monitored in the same way that textbooks should be kept under constant surveillance. This applies not merely to so-called educational programs (such as "The Selling of the Pentagon"), but to the daily "news analysis" which so often includes the most insidious type of criticism of the enterprise system. Whether this criticism results from hostility or economic ignorance, the result is the gradual erosion of confidence in "business" and free enterprise.

This monitoring, to be effective, would require constant

examination of the texts of adequate samples of programs. Complaints—to the media and to the Federal Communications Commission—should be made promptly and strongly when programs are unfair or inaccurate.

Equal time should be demanded when appropriate. Efforts should be made to see that the forum-type programs (the "Today" show, "Meet the Press," etc.) afford at least as much opportunity for supporters of the American system to participate as these programs do for those who attack it.

Radio and press are also important, and every available means should be employed to challenge and refute unfair attacks, as well as to present the affirmative case through these media.

Gray, speaking to the Orange County Bar Association in Santa Ana, California, excused himself from remarks more appropriate to the occasion (Law Day) and launched into a detailed attack on the press, particularly television, and specifically a "60 Minutes" segment on the Law Enforcement Assistance Administration (LEAA), of which he said:

So here again we perceive the stiletto at work behind the scenes, but the viewer is not aware of the depth and breadth of the emasculation. Only the reporters and the editors involved in this program know that they have led their audiences to believe that another one of the institutions of Government is inefficient or corrupt or both, regardless of what the facts may be.

In commenting on this gross travesty, I can do no better than to quote the distinguished Senator from Nebraska, Roman Hruska, who placed the whole revolting performance in the *Congressional Record.*

"Such deception," cried the Senator. "The cunning thus displayed would do credit to a burglar."

. . . Is the other side of the coin—the free press that should keep the electorate informed—now stepping into a new role—that of controlling the electorate by controlling the information it receives? Instead of the public using the press as the source of its information, is the process now being reversed, so that the press will be using the public in the same way that a programmer uses a computer?

. . . the basic decency—the sense of fair play—in the hearts of Americans will bring a rebirth of journalistic standards in areas where they have now become only an empty shell . . . there is a crisis of confidence in the press.

Helms denounced "distorted" newscasts and suggested that network evening news programs be dismantled and affiliates supplied with film to make their own.

The credibility issue was far from one-sided.* If Washington attacked the press, the press reported instance after instance of the government's apparent involvement in deliberate misrepresentation. Vietnam seemed to be the main breeding ground for these alleged deceptions. Within less than a year, there were the affair of General Lavelle; the Peers report, which gave additional damning evidence concerning the Mylai affair; and the apparent suppression of reports on drug abuse among GI's in Vietnam.

James Reston, commenting on the Lavelle affair in the June 14, 1972, *New York Times,* wrote:

> The whole Vietnam policy has been seething with deception . . . under Presidents Kennedy, Johnson and Nixon, and the astonishing thing is not that there has been some deception by generals on the battlefield, but that there have not been more Lavelles.
>
> Still, there is a fundamental question of public policy here. The Government has been caught once more in an obvious deception, which it tried to cover up. And this may be the most important issue before the people of the United States today. Nobody in either party has the answer to all our problems, but it would be reassuring to feel that the Government was telling the truth, even if its policies were wrong.

The Wall Street Journal, perhaps friendlier to the Administration than the *Times,* found other reasons to object:

> The President says he isn't going to change economic policy when he is already working on sweeping new controls; he insists he's not going to devalue the dollar when he knows he will. There may be good reasons for these deceptions, but they still make it hard for the average person to know just what he can trust.

* In October the Harris Survey reported a drastic decline in "public respect for the leadership of most major U.S. institutions." Only one profession—medicine—commanded a "great deal of confidence" from a majority of Americans, and it had dropped 11 percentage points from 72 to 61 in the preceding five years. The score for "major companies" dropped from 55 to 27, organized religion from 41 to 27, organized labor from 22 to 14, the U.S. Supreme Court from 51 to 23. Advertising, which was lowest in 1966, remained at the bottom of the list in 1971, dropping from 21 to 13. The military had the sharpest decline, from 62 to 27; television showed the least change, dropping from 25 to 22. The executive branch of the federal government, dropping from 41 to 23, rated one percentage point above television; Congress, dropping from 42 to 19, was three points below.

The atmosphere of credibility was not enhanced by the revelations of Jack Anderson, who embarrassed the Administration twice—deeply and in quick succession: first, by printing the transcripts of backstage White House discussions, masterminded by presidential adviser Henry Kissinger, which confirmed, Pentagon Paper style, that while the official line on the India-Pakistan conflict was supposedly neutral, the real feelings of the Administration were emphatically partisan; and then, three months later, with his columns concerning Dita Beard, International Telephone and Telegraph, and their alleged attempts to influence high-level Republican officials by campaign contributions. Although Anderson's own credibility suffered from his faulty reporting on Senator Thomas Eagleton in August, the doubts roused by his earlier revelations were never completely stilled.

Other Kissinger maneuvers led to considerable agonizing over the venerable Washington tradition of the backgrounder, which permitted high government functionaries to plant items, frequently untrue, in the press without being held accountable. *The Washington Post* blew Kissinger's cover, pinning him with a patently false item concerning the possible cancellation of the president's visit to Moscow. In a column in *The New York Times,* Bill Moyers, an ex-presidential press chief under Lyndon Johnson, commented:

> The backgrounder permits the press and the Government to sleep together, even to procreate, without getting married or having to accept responsibility for any offspring. It's the public on whose doorstep orphans of deceptive information and misleading allegations are left, while the press and the Government roll their eyes innocently and exclaim "no mea culpa!" . . .
>
> It is when the press becomes a transmission belt for official opinions and predictions, indictments and speculation, coming from a host of unidentified spokesmen—when the press permits anonymous officials to announce official policy without accountability—that the public throws up its hands in confusion.
>
> Mr. Kissinger's *sotto voce* threat to the Soviets, which, in true Orwellian fashion, had to be denied when its source was identified, is only the latest revelation of the ease with which public officials have come to use the backgrounder as a primary instrument of policy, propaganda, and manipulation. "The interests of national security dictate that the lie I am about to tell you not be attributed to me." . . .
>
> Reporters will be there to report dutifully what isn't officially said by a source that can't be held officially

accountable at an event that doesn't officially happen for a public that can't officially be told because it can't officially be trusted to know.

In the same column Moyers told the story of a college girl who came up to him after a commencement address and said, "Mr. Moyers, you've been in both journalism and Government. That makes everything you say doubly hard to believe."

Dishonesty in politicians and statesmen unfortunately tended to be taken for granted. The dishonesty of broadcasters, and particularly broadcast journalists, whose vocation pledged them to pursue the facts, was properly considered a very serious matter.

For many, substance was given to the attacks on network bias when Edith Efron, on the staff of *TV Guide,* published her book *The News Twisters.* Purporting to be an objective analysis, it monitored all network nightly newscasts for seven weeks in the fall of 1968. During these weeks just prior to the presidential election, Ms. Efron found sixteen times more anti-Nixon than pro-Nixon material. Pro- versus anti-Humphrey material was in the ratio of 1.1 to 1. Similar evidences of a liberal bias were tabulated in relation to ten "issues," including "U.S. Policy on the Vietnam War," "U.S. Policy on the Bombing Halt," "Viet Cong," "Black Militants," "White Middle Class," "Liberals," "Conservatives," "Left," "Demonstrators," and "Violent Radicals." Among Ms. Efron's conclusions:

> On the basis of these descriptive statistics, it is clear that network coverage tends to be strongly biased in favor of the Democratic-liberal-left axis of opinion and strongly biased against the Republican-conservative-right axis of opinion . . . .
>
> It is this monopolistic system which must be altered— a system which exists in defiance of the full-fledged political spectrum in this country and which mocks the very concept of a free competitive market of ideas. It is a system in which the American public has *neither* the First Amendment "dollar vote" control over the ideological material which is flooding into the nation . . . *nor* the political representation on the airwaves guaranteed by the Fairness Doctrine.

Two of the three networks chose to remain mute. CBS News president Richard Salant, as usual, spoke his mind.

> CBS News has a continuing interest in any suggestion or studies which can lead toward more perfect achievement

of the fairness and objectivity with which it presents the news. Regrettably, Miss Efron's book does not contribute to this goal.

It purports to be a scholarly, objective analysis, supported by graphs and word-counts, of the fairness with which the television networks covered seven weeks of the 1968 Presidential campaign. In fact, it is nothing of the sort. It examines only a limited part of the network coverage. It does so with a distinct bias which produces gross distortions of fact. It uses statistical procedures which are seriously flawed. And it draws erroneous, prejudiced and unsupportable conclusions.

CBS set its own researchers to work and retained two independent agencies to investigate the validity of Ms. Efron's claims. All three groups found them without substance. Ms. Efron promptly set up her own panel (including some "radical journalists"), who backed her up. Whichever side was right, *The News Twisters* got on at least one best-seller list and into paperback. Ms. Efron became a popular guest on talk shows around the country, where her opinions gained even wider currency.

Salant and his independent researchers were not the only ones to be critical of Ms. Efron's methods. Some, like Nelson W. Polsby, a political scientist writing in *Harper's,* refuted her position but had some harsh things to say about the media on their own:

> To my mind, the performance of the American news media does leave something to be desired. And their worst sins are these: *incoherence,* stemming from a style of news coverage and reporting that is highly mechanical and tailored more to the techniques of presentation than to the needs of citizens or the contours of events; *sparseness,* a characteristic that is mostly a consequence of the pressures on reporters to converge and concentrate on a narrow range of phenomena; and *inexpertise,* a quality that has its roots in journalistic craft norms that value amateurism, the general ability to turn out an undifferentiated product (the "story"), and egalitarianism ("we write for the man in the street"). I think these sins are increasingly the enemy of truthfulness, and certainly of an informed citizenry . . . .
>
> And so while I am prepared to entertain the proposition that network news programs are in some ways deficient, Edith Efron's criticism seems to me wide of the mark as well as questionably supported by evidence. More im-

portantly, I suspect that the simple mindedness and crudity of her address to this complex issue, by coddling the paranoia of hard-hats and eliciting self-righteous responses from the networks, will make it much more difficult to conduct sensible conversation about causes and cures for deficiencies in the presentation of the news.

As Polsby indicated, the question was not one of bias or balance, although it was hard for the politicians to see this, but of how well and thoroughly the journalists were doing their job, and whether their facts were straight and sufficient.

Another book, *President Nixon and the Press,* by one of the president's top speech writers and a former executive editor of *Time,* James Keogh, gave, according to the author's own description, "an insight into the controversy about the news media's coverage of the national Government" from the White House point of view, with numerous examples of apparent error and distortion.

The broadcasting fraternity, in responding to all the criticism, gave indication that the Administration, if it was trying to do damage, might have succeeded.

Morley Safer, co-host on "60 Minutes," one of the few network shows which attempted regularly to dig beneath the surface of things, told the annual awards dinner at the Overseas Press Club:

> This Administration has carefully planted doubt in this country about what we print or show or say. It has not been a casual, accidental thing, but a carefully planned program of misinformation . . . . The Truth? Agnew and Richard Kleindienst and Melvin Laird have done for the truth what the Boston Strangler has done for the door-to-door salesman.

Larry Israel, chairman of the Post-Newsweek stations, told a gathering at the Missouri School of Journalism that there was "a growing tendency to view broadcasting itself as a cause of America's ills . . . . Broadcasting thus is being whipsawed as never before in its history."

John Wicklein, who had been fired as news manager for WCBS, the flagship station of the CBS-TV network, said of the situation there before he left: ". . . the network would like very much to get out of the area of controversy and into nothing but entertainment. In fact, there are some people there who think the network would like to get out of news altogether. I think the hard news has been destroyed there."

Walter Cronkite told the Greater Boston Ad Club:

> . . . this Administration . . . has conceived, planned, orchestrated and is now conducting a program to reduce the effectiveness of a free press, and its prime target is television . . . .
>
> There are and there will be moments when the problems seem insurmountable, the challenges, unmeetable; when we are beset by self-doubts.
>
> In those moments, we shall cling to one certainty which shall sustain us.
>
> And that is that we are all *professional* journalists, dedicated to truth, honesty, to telling it as it is without fear or favor—and that there is no politician or bureaucrat who can make that claim. *

John Hart, Cronkite's counterpart on "The CBS Morning News," told the Midwestern Radio-Television News Directors Association that its members had perhaps allowed the "healthy suspicion of power in the hands of other men flawed as ourselves" to die. "That is the proper role of the adversary. It may be we are misunderstood as to that proper role because we have not been adverse enough. It may be that we have glorified the President and made stars out of politicians, and put them beyond the accountability that the Republic requires to remain responsive and alive."

Coming close to the central problem, Reuven Frank, president of NBC News, told a conference of electronic journalists in Virginia:

> The biggest difference between newspapers and television is that newspapers existed at a time when adventurous men with faith in their fellow-citizens laid down principles for a new society to live by. Television exists in a frightened time when this faith is honored either by lip service or by a frantic determination that freedom must be enforced. I think if Benjamin Franklin had invented television, its

* In a survey of the degrees of trust in public figures dated May 1, 1972, by Oliver A. Quayle, III, Walter Cronkite led the field. In 8,780 interviews in eighteen states across the nation, rating individuals on a scale from 0 to 100, the results were:

Walter Cronkite	73%	Edward Kennedy	54%
Average senator	67%	John Lindsay	54%
Edmund Muskie	61%	Eugene McCarthy	51%
Average governor	59%	Spiro Agnew	50%
Richard Nixon	57%	Wilbur Mills	50%
Hubert Humphrey	57%	Shirley Chisholm	47%
George McGovern	56%	George Wallace	36%
Henry Jackson	55%	Sam Yorty	35%

informing functions would have been included in the First Amendment.

Perhaps the most depressing evaluation of all came from Sander Vanocur, whose switch from commercial to public TV news had set up one of the major controversies of the year (see page 69). In an article entitled "TV's Failed Promise" in *Center* magazine, Vanocur wrote:

> The kind of self-limiting factor that prevails in government is not different from that which prevails at the networks. In either case, if you play the tactical game and smooth over the fundamental issue, you can buy time, but you wind up losing in the end. Perhaps such failure is built into both systems. More and more I see a parallel between government and network journalism: both concentrate their primary communication effort on purveying to the public illusion passing as reality . . . .
>
> If we accept the premise that we exist to help people deal with reality, not compound illusion, then we simply are going to have to find new techniques for dealing with the flow of news and information . . . .
>
> My personal dilemma arises from my belief that the inadequate manner in which we present television news is to a great extent responsible for the inability of our society to dispense with the myths that prevent it from coming to grips with realities. We cannot continue to shoehorn all those items into a half-hour evening news show without making it into a wire service budget with pictures. Nor do we get anywhere by adding another half hour, for we simply fill it up with the same staccato fare. Just because we have been doing it that way for the first fifteen years is no reason why we have to continue doing it for the next fifteen. Events have become too complex to be explained away in a minute and thirty seconds: we must be aware by now that the pictures we put up every night do not necessarily portray reality.

A suspicion of more specific pressures arose when it was revealed that an FBI check was being run on CBS Washington correspondent Daniel Schorr, not noted as particularly friendly to the Administration. The explanation given for the grillings Schorr's friends and broadcasting associates had been subjected to was an unlikely one—that Schorr was under consideration for a White House job. Schorr's comment:

> Job or no job, the launching of such an investigation without consent demonstrates an insensitivity to personal rights.

I think most Americans would feel more comfortable if there were legal safeguards against such arbitrary intrusion into their lives.

Concern was just as deep on the local level, contradicting the Administration's assumption that station owners and news directors had no interests beyond the parochial:

I think we will survive all political efforts to intrude into journalism. But it will be difficult. The problems of broadcast journalism have just begun . . . . Whereas we could once look to one political party or another to champion the cause of free broadcast journalism, we now find ourselves being strangled by both political parties, the courts, and so-called intellectuals who would spoon-feed the public their own political and sociological pap. If we continue to fight as a unit, it is our one chance for the survival of broadcast journalism. We must continue to be aggressive, factual and non-condescending. We must keep the subtle and open pressures in the open and we must meet them head on by practicing First Amendment journalism until it puts fear into the hearts of our enemies. I think we can win if only because we cannot afford to lose. Nor can the public.—*WCKT, Miami*

I think the government has backed us into a tight little box of regulations and fear that could squelch what little innovation is allowed or fostered now. Everywhere you turn, broadcast executives are afraid of anything different . . . . They mention the "commission" or "minorities" or "the White House" as though it were impossible to do anything new. Public broadcasting gets its hands slapped by Congress right when a lot of us are turning to PBS as an alternative to the restrictions in commercial broadcasting. The real "journalism" seems to be at the very top . . . and at the very bottom of the broadcast ladder. The networks are willing to fight and so are the rag-tag east and west coast independent operations. But the rest of us line up and do what we are told.—*WWDC, Washington, D.C.*

The carefully orchestrated anti-media campaign by the White House (taken up by sympathetic elements in Congress) is having its effect. More and more as one circulates amongst the public, attends meetings—one senses that a growing number of people are accepting the nonsense that the media are causing the problems of contemporary society, rather than just reporting them. An alarming number of citizens are firmly convinced that there is a credibility gap in media, rather than in government.— *WSBA, York, Pa.*

John Chancellor, anchorman for "NBC Nightly News," saw it as an even more deeply rooted problem.

> What . . . distresses me, is that people are dissatisfied with television news. Many middle-aged people who are opposed to television news are people who had not been subjected to serious news, seriously presented, until they got a television set and until television in the mid-fifties began to develop serious news programs. Before that, people read daily newspapers. They read the sports page, the comic page; they glanced at the front page. If people didn't want to read about the ax murder, they didn't have to read about it. If they didn't want to read about the race problem, they didn't have to read about the race problem. Then came television and the problem with television is that to see any news you pretty much have to see it all. It's a very brutal way to get the news. You can either accept the news that comes off the tube or turn it off entirely. You can't pick and choose. I think this has bothered people because they have been exposed not only to dull and serious news, but also to news that is embarrassing to them as Americans or embarrassing to them as Southerners, or embarrassing to them as liberals or conservatives. People around the country don't like news the way they're getting it. The only problem we have is that we don't know any other way to give them that news on television.

All these charges and countercharges might have been dismissed as hypersensitivity or paranoia on both sides if a pattern of attack, and a base of operations, had not emerged quite so clearly. Operation Central was not the FCC, nominally charged with the regulation of broadcasting, whose attitude toward its industry tended to be erratic and more inclined toward indulging than punishing broadcast management. Nor was it the courts, which, if they handed down some decisions that were annoying to broadcasters, scarcely pleased politicians with these decisions. Nor was it Congress, which controlled the FCC and initiated communications legislation, very few serious examples of which were proposed during the year. The negative vibrations beamed at the broadcast journalists emanated in most part from one source, the White House, where staff members concerned with communications matters were particularly active throughout the year.

Most visible was Clay T. (Tom) Whitehead, for two years head of the White House Office of Telecommunications Policy

(OTP), a bureau whose purpose and functions had never been made particularly clear. Whitehead, an earnest man with slick brown hair, horn-rimmed glasses, and a Ph.D. in management from MIT, was not known as a spellbinder and had kept a fairly low profile since his appointment in June 1970. However, in October 1971 the membership of the New York Chapter of the International Radio and Television Society was wonderfully surprised. In the course of a comparatively brief speech at one of the association's "newsmaker luncheons," Whitehead, one of President Nixon's acknowledged spokesmen, called for all the things the broadcasters had been clamoring for over the years and a few they wouldn't have dared mention: the deregulation of radio, the scuttling of the Fairness Doctrine, getting the government out of programming by revising the license-renewal process, and by implication, the rewriting of the Communications Act of 1934 and the dismantling of the FCC (see Appendix II).

Two weeks later in Miami, Whitehead made equally sweeping, if less welcome, recommendations to public broadcasters for public television.

It was a big year for the young man with the bland manner and the unlabeled portfolio. In something like thirty-five major addresses and dozens of other public appearances, he expanded and refined his thought on the above matters, attacked the FCC for its counter-advertising proposals, the Corporation for Public Broadcasting (CPB) for trying to establish a fourth network and ignoring its educational responsibilities, and public television in general for presuming to cover news and public affairs. In between speeches and public appearances he masterminded the new agreement between cable television, copyright owners, and broadcasters, and finally proved his ability to put his convictions into action by helping engineer the president's veto of the new and comparatively generous funding awarded by Congress to the CPB.

On December 18, 1972, Whitehead confirmed the worst apprehensions of already jittery network news departments in a speech delivered to the Indianapolis chapter of Sigma Delta Chi referring to new legislation which would benefit local broadcasters along with recommendations for more careful local screening of network programming, particularly news (see Appendix IV).

Midway into Whitehead's *annus mirabilis,* Senator Frank Moss asked his colleagues on Capitol Hill, "What is OTP? Did the Congress create it? Does the Constitution provide for it? Then what is its role? For whom does it speak?" Moss threatened to try to amend the executive budget "to preclude the expenditure of funds for the institutionalization of White House superagencies which interfere with the functions of the independent regulatory agencies." Moss had backing in the House, where Communications Subcommittee chairman Torbert Macdonald complained that OTP "had become the Administration's tool for attempts to muzzle the media and control the FCC. . . . OTP has a very clear idea of what it wants public television to be—localized, innocuous, impotent, without a national service that will attract enough audience to make it a factor in its 212 communities."

Macdonald's bid to cut the OTP budget by a third was supported by Representative Lionel Van Deerlin of California, who felt that the OTP "has gone beyond its depth somewhat in suggesting the deregulation of radio, in seeking to drive a wedge between the networks and their affiliates, and between local educational broadcasters and their Corporation for Public Broadcasting."

However, when the money was handed out, the OTP did considerably better, proportionately, than the FCC.

The contrast, if not the clash, between the OTP and FCC was particularly evident in their approach to the much maligned Fairness Doctrine, of which Whitehead said scathingly:

> Kafka sits on the Court of Appeals and Orwell works in the FCC's Office of Opinions and Review. Has anyone pointed out that the Fiftieth Anniversary of the Communications Act is 1984? "Big Brother" himself could not have conceived a more disarming "newspeak" name for a system of Government program control than the Fairness Doctrine.

Whitehead's cavalier dismissal, predicated to warm the cockles of any red-blooded commercial broadcaster's heart, hardly did the same for his friends at the FCC, who were soon to launch an elaborate series of hearings and panels on how best to revise the Fairness Doctrine to make it more serviceable to public and broadcaster alike.

Not that the Fairness Doctrine was a great favorite at the FCC.* Dean Burch, chairman of the FCC, called it a "chaotic mess." Richard Wiley, general counsel to the FCC and later

---

* The Doctrine, according to one of many definitions, "requires that those given the privileges of access [to the air waves] hold their licenses and use their facilities as trustees for the public at large, with a duty to present discussion of public issues and to do so fairly by affording reasonable opportunity for presentation of conflicting views."

named commissioner, and thought by some to be next in line
for the chairmanship, told the Illinois Broadcasters Association
at about the same time Whitehead was making his attack:

> It seems to me that to chip away at the licensee's discre-
> tion on issues to be covered in his station's programming,
> on the time and format of coverage and the spokesmen
> for contrasting positions is to invite not wide open and
> robust debate on the great public issues of the day, but
> news and public affairs programming which is increasingly
> more and more bland.

Even Commissioner Nicholas Johnson, noted for his tendency
to take the opposite side from his colleagues at every opportunity, was willing to entertain criticism of the Doctrine suggesting that an "access package" for stations might be a "substitute for [the Fairness Doctrine's] more objectionable burdens"
and also might "give the people of this country the rights of
access now shared only by the likes of General Motors and
Procter & Gamble."

From the opposite direction, Tracy Westen, head of the
Stern Community Law Firm in Washington, commented, "Until
Whitehead is willing to deal with the *causes* of media mediocrity, his proposals to eliminate the Fairness Doctrine can only
generate greater blandness and tedium over the air waves."
Westen also commented about another Whitehead proposal,
the deregulation of radio:

> Whitehead assumes that radio in large markets will spe-
> cialize its programming for particular audiences—all talk,
> classical, rock, etc.—and that there is no need for FCC
> regulation to compel diversity of service. Even in large
> markets, however, most stations still compete for mass
> audiences and bypass minorities which are small in num-
> ber, or too impoverished to purchase the sponsor's prod-
> ucts. In smaller markets, Whitehead's proposal would
> result in disaster. Many small-town stations are run by
> businessmen who care or understand little about program-
> ming, and import hours of tapes a day from fundamental-
> ist preachers and right wing propagandists. Only the fair-
> ness and public service doctrines require these stations to
> devote even minimal service to the diverse needs of their
> listener-minorities. The Whitehead Doctrine would create
> a stifling uniformity of programming in these communi-
> ties.

The Office of Communication of the United Church of Christ,
for a long time one of the Fairness Doctrine's most enthusiastic

boosters, whom even Whitehead recognized as a past master in the use of the Doctrine to promote public interest, wanted not less but more of what it considered a good thing. The head of the Office of Communication, Rev. Everett C. Parker, said that the Doctrine should not only be retained but should be more explicit in requiring every station to air controversial issues, and easier forms should be worked out to facilitate public complaints. He also said that the Doctrine should be extended so that paid political spots would require free reply time to be given. In a written brief to the FCC, the Church of Christ said:

> The Fairness Doctrine has been a remarkably effective device to stimulate discussion of important issues. Under it, no broadcaster is denied the opportunity to present any discussion of any issue or any viewpoint. In fact, the Doctrine encourages multi-faceted debate by placing the premium on the diversity promised by the First Amendment.

The American Civil Liberties Union petitioned the FCC for a program to insure full public use of the Doctrine, asking for "common carrier blocks" in prime time; help for groups and persons wanting free, unedited spot messages; a letters-to-the-editor format; and a rule that stations had to help disadvantaged groups to prepare news and documentary material for airing.

Like most broadcasters, John Schneider, president of CBS Broadcast Group, was as diametrically opposed to the Doctrine as the Church of Christ and the ACLU were for it. Envisioning its widest possible application, he said:

> There isn't a product or a service or an issue that wouldn't in some way fall under these scatter-gun interpretations of the Fairness Doctrine . . . . If free commercial broadcasting is destroyed, it will be as a result of attempts to accommodate the interests and dreams of good and well-meaning people, but people who spearhead and speak for the [splinter groups] of our society. In attempting to make broadcasting meaningful to the few, they will succeed only in making it meaningless to the many.

Local broadcasters also saw a severe and increasing hazard in the Doctrine.

> I am concerned with the Fairness Doctrine. Not the intent but with the practice. The FCC is not only unclear as to how and when it is to be carried out but sometimes by nature of its decisions, confuses it with the equal time provisions of the broadcasting regulations. This, of course,

encourages misleading license challenges. It also inhibits aggressive journalism and serves to contradict the very announced purpose of the FCC to provide the public with representative broadcasting. Fortunately, we have not permitted the threat of license loss . . . of censorship . . . to paralyze concerned journalism. I hope we can withstand the pressure and threat of government oppression.— *WCKT, Miami*

The Fairness Doctrine is essential until a better approach can be found. But it can be used by some for its nuisance value. We sometimes are tempted to NOT do something simply because of the hassles we would have. The local newspaper could do the same thing and not be subject to harassment.—*KVOS, Bellingham, Wash.*

In reality it [Fairness Doctrine] does not so much protect the public as it does those who wield the power in our society. It is these people who have taken advantage of the Fairness Doctrine and forced broadcast journalism to quiver under, what I believe, is unfair interpretation of the doctrine.—*WCCB, Charlotte, N.C.*

No matter how fair you try to be, those who have biased viewpoints object to your presenting the side they oppose. They seem to think that only their side is worthy of public attention.—*WBAP, Fort Worth, Tex.*

The Fairness Doctrine has not been as much trouble as the public's misunderstanding of it . . . . No matter how hard we strive to achieve balance on controversial issues, it has become an almost nightly tradition that advocates on one or both sides call to demand "equal time" to tell the "truth." We had *no* actual Fairness challenges, but our awareness of public opinion that all television news is biased has inspired an even greater determination to be fair—a situation we feel is healthy.—*WFMY, Greensboro, N.C.*

The most surprising comment from a broadcaster was Elmer Lower's. The president of ABC News told the International Press Institute in Munich that the Doctrine is

. . . not a particularly onerous news burden . . . . We do not shy from controversy because of it. Controversy is the stuff of the social process, and journalists are duty-bound to report it, and to report it fairly. We journalists, by our choice of profession, have a commitment of fairness . . . most assuredly the Fairness Doctrine does not mean that the Government, whether the FCC, Congress or the courts, has the right to substitute its editorial judgment for that of the broadcaster . . . .

There is nothing wrong with fairness. There is a great deal wrong with intimidation of broadcasters under the guise of "enforcing" fairness. The broadcast press should not be made into a common carrier for others' ideas. Thus far it has not been, and thus far, I think, our surveys have shown we've lived up to our obligation to be fair while producing a strong, valid editorial product.

The surveys Lower mentioned were commissioned by ABC News to evaluate the content of its evening newscasts. Figures cited, apparently satisfying to Lower, were subject to more than one interpretation. They showed that while in 1970, 31 percent of the time devoted to news and 33 percent of the time spent on commentary were likely to please the supporters of the Administration, and 34 percent of the news and 36 percent of the commentary would displease, in 1971, 27 percent of the news and 33 percent of the commentary were rated pleasing, while 28 percent of the news and 18 percent of the commentary were likely to displease. The margin of neutrality had, according to their researches, widened, but most conspicuously at the expense of commentary critical of those in office. Nor was there any reference to the accuracy of the news reported.

The FCC hearings on the Fairness Doctrine, which included comments from twenty-eight interested parties and five days of testimony and panel discussions involving fifty additional participants, were finally completed in March. A preliminary statement from Chairman Dean Burch in June covered only that part of the Doctrine dealing with political matters. Recommendations were promised on other crucial aspects, but by fall they were still not forthcoming.

Along with his suggestion to eliminate the Fairness Doctrine, Whitehead's proposal to revise the licensing process was perhaps the most welcome to the nation's broadcasters. From zero challenges to their licenses before 1964, they were faced with dozens of such challenges in 1971–1972.

Thanks to these challenges and the FCC's ascertainment requirements instituted during the past three years, which dictated that all license holders interview members of the community to determine how best to serve it,* broadcasters as never

---

* In a special study of ascertainment procedures in the New York area, Seymour N. Siegel, former head of WNYC, found that WCBS interviewed nearly 1,000 people; WNBC, 350; and WABC, 371.

before were subject to public pressure or, as some preferred to think of it, harassment.

The challenges and petitions to deny licenses, threatened or under way in more than one hundred communities, had been instigated by as many different special-interest groups, ranging from large church and public service organizations to scattered dissidents. Under present FCC conditions these cases could drag on for years, with the challenged licensee continuing to operate the station. Nevertheless, the challenges were among the things most disturbing to local station management. Some comments:

> License challenge worries are troublesome since management is rightly concerned that these can come at any time and from any source, despite concerted efforts to do a responsible broadcasting job. The current climate for challenges often seems to make management understandably reluctant to be much of a crusader in certain areas with the sentiment that it's just not worth the exhausting effort to attempt a fight over an issue that can be left alone. The prevailing view seems to be that stations can be "blackmailed" into actions that are not in the best interests of the station or the community as a whole, just to get a vociferous minority off your back.—*WISH, Indianapolis*

> The volume of paper work and time consumed in preparing for license renewal or answering challenges takes away nearly all the time I would have spent planning news program changes or planning in areas in which we feel our coverage is weak.—*WSOC, Charlotte, N.C.*

> The current trend in license challenges, based on pressure group tactics, is something of dire concern. Not only could they create instability within the industry and reluctance to make sufficient financial gambles, but could stifle bold news activities, make management fearful of supporting hard-hitting news and editorial staffs.—*WTLV, Jacksonville*

> A small market station just cannot afford to risk a law suit, subpoena or license challenge and therefore they stick to shallow coverage of auto wrecks, fires, robberies and festivals.—*WITN, Washington, D.C.*

> While many citizen challenges can be defended in their philosophic basis, the proponents often would obliquely or subtly exercise prior or post censorship on either news materials, subjects, reporters, or story treatment. Generally challengers are extremely reluctant to admit to differ-

ing community views or standards which also require exposure. More often than not, they request programs to deal exclusively with their viewpoint to the exclusion of other or related ideas.—*KDKA, Pittsburgh*

Whatever the negative impact of license challenges and the ascertainment rules, it was undeniable that from coast to coast a whole new brand of programming for minority and special-interest groups was appearing on the air—programming which, without petitions for license denial, might still have been only "under discussion." Of all the news and public affairs directors answering the DuPont Survey, 81 percent claimed to do special minority programming: 63 percent programming for ethnic groups, 47 percent programming for women.

In terms of employment practices, another crucial reason for license challenges, 40 percent of the stations reporting had increased minority employment in their news departments and 44 percent had added women in the past year.

If Whitehead's recommendations for unchallengeable licenses of longer duration were to prevail, such techniques for instilling civic responsibility would obviously no longer be effective.

As for local station owners, there was not much question of their hearty endorsement of Whitehead's proposals. Following his October 6 speech *Variety* quoted one anonymous source in Washington as saying, "If I were at the Republican National Committee, I'd set up about 50 dummy committees to handle the broadcaster contributions that are going to be coming in."

At the fiftieth annual National Association of Broadcasters convention in April, the broadcasters had an opportunity to applaud Whitehead, along with two other White House spokesmen, secretary of the treasury John Connally and the president's director of communications, Herbert Klein, who in the middle of his speech read a special message from the president which reinforced the hearty pro-broadcasting sentiments of all three speakers. The broadcasters returned the compliment by voting their number one honor, the Distinguished Service Award, to the president's spiritual director and confidant, the Reverend Billy Graham, who responded in a highly flattering sermonette:

> I will tell you with the utmost sincerity that I believe your industry—for the most part—to be peopled with men and women of integrity and character and conscience. I say this despite the brickbats which broadcasting draws from some self-styled critics who chastise it for falling short of perfection.

In an imperfect world, American radio and television have performed with great honor and credibility.

. . . I don't believe anything short of a moral and spiritual re-awakening is going to heal the sickness of spirit which infects our nation, and I am not at all convinced that this re-awakening will occur without the positive support and leadership of the great voice of broadcasting. . . . You have been, and will continue to be, in my thoughts and in my prayers.

Meanwhile, back at the networks, they could have used Dr. Graham's prayers. Things had gone from bad to worse. Less than a week after the Administration-broadcaster love-in in Chicago, the Justice Department filed antitrust suits against ABC, CBS, and NBC, plus a former CBS subsidiary named Viacom, demanding that they divest themselves of entertainment-programming activities.

Internal evidence indicated that the suit had been on the shelf for several years. The networks and others instantly saw an effort at intimidation—particularly since the suit was launched in an election year and just before the controversial decision to mine Haiphong and to resume the bombing of North Vietnam.

This view seemed to gain weight, and the implications of the suit for news and public affairs deepened when another White House communications spokesman, Patrick Buchanan, surfaced on television. Appearing on reporter Elizabeth Drew's public-television show, "Thirty Minutes with . . . ," Buchanan criticized the networks for their "ideological monopoly"—a term he had borrowed from Edith Efron's book *The News Twisters.* Said Buchanan:

> Now, that to me . . . that an ideological monopoly might be determining what goes on in news and ideas, is of far more concern to me, frankly, in a democracy than whether say General Motors is making all my automobiles. Because the ideas and information you get in a democratic society is the basis for your decision-making. . . . my own view is I think—this is a personal view—is that a monopoly like this of a group of people with a single point of view and a single political ideology who tend to continually freeze out opposing points of view and opposing information, that you're going to find something done in the area of antitrust suit action.

When Ms. Drew brought up the antitrust suits recently launched against the networks, Buchanan answered, "Well, that's just testing out the theory, that's all."

Another Administration spokesman, Walter B. Comegys, acting assistant attorney general in charge of the Justice Department's antitrust division, quickly came forward to correct Buchanan. Said Comegys:

> The current suits are in no way designed to provide any basis of a later attack on network news content; indeed, the antitrust laws would not permit such action. No antitrust action relating to television news programming is under consideration nor has any such action ever been considered . . . [the suits] are aimed solely at elimination of alleged anti-competitive actions by the networks which involve the production of network entertainment programs and the network's financial interest in independent production of entertainment programs for network use.

This was less reassuring than it may have sounded. Buchanan had also mentioned the possibility of legislation to break the network's "ideological monopoly." Moreover, broadcasters were quick to point out that whether or not it was directly connected with news and public affairs, any action which reduced network profits was almost certain to affect the quality and quantity of news on the air. The FCC's prime access ruling of 1971, which removed a half hour every night from network control, was another such punishing rule, ostensibly designed to encourage high-grade non-network programming. It was generally conceded to be an abject failure.*

Buchanan later told Julius Duscha, director of the Washington Journalism Center, in an interview for *The New York Times Magazine:*

> My primary concern is that the President have the right of untrammeled communication with the American people. . . . In terms of power over the American people, you can't compare newspapers to those pictures on television. They can make or break a politician.

If this was true, he should have been a man at peace, for seldom in the history of the presidency had a chief executive had such untrammeled use of a medium of communication with the American people as had Nixon, thanks to television, in 1971 and 1972.

---

* The networks had a third blow in store for them in late summer when the president and Whitehead, in twin statements, announced support for proposed legislation to curtail the number of prime-time network reruns, which could cost the networks millions of dollars for additional productions every year.

Of the president's 78 appearances on television from his inauguration through the summer of 1972 (not counting regular news coverage of his Russia and China trips), 15 were between July 1, 1971, and June 30, 1972.* Although his televised press conferences were at an all-time low (2 in 12 months),† formal speeches, chats with network interviewers, etc., were at an all-time high—and that did not count massive coverage of extra-continental activities in Europe and Asia, notably China and Russia, both of which not only kept thé president before American audiences for hours on end, but actually permitted him to address them, along with the Chinese and Russian viewers, from Peking and Moscow.

Beyond that were the "entertainment"-style presidential appearances, which included two holiday specials: "Christmas at the White House" and "A Day in the Presidency." In the final ten minutes of "Christmas at the White House," Nixon made a surprise visit and delivered a pitch for his Vietnamese policy. "A Day in the Presidency" gave him an opportunity to say a few explanatory words about his economic policy.

During the year in question, NBC also did a series of programs called "The Seven Summits" devoted to Nixon's meetings with French president Georges Pompidou, British prime minister Edward Heath, Canadian prime minister Pierre Elliott Trudeau, West German chancellor Willy Brandt, and Japanese prime minister Eisaku Sato (with China and Russia added to make the seven).

Nixon's sensitivity to the requirements of television increased. On the China trip thirty-seven out of the eighty-seven precious media seats went to television. The president's returns from China and Russia were masterpieces of staging which would have done credit to a Roman emperor: the first in the vast hangar at Andrews Air Force Base, where the army and air force bands, a freshly painted deck, a reception committee of five thousand, and a dozen live television cameras awaited him; and the second in the House, where congressmen, senators, and others high in government had been invited to greet him. The fact that many were reluctant to act as supernumeraries in the big show did little to detract from the impressive TV picture.

---

* Of these, 16 were televised press conferences (there were 11 not televised); 5, TV conversations; and 57, addresses or other special appearances.

† According to John Chancellor, Truman had 322 press conferences; Eisenhower, 193; Kennedy, 64 in 34 months; Johnson, 126; Nixon, 23 in 39 months, going for a full 11 months without a full-dress televised one.

In February, having already aired his State of the Union speech on television, Nixon decided to keep his State of the World speech and his February 15 press conference off camera because "I think television has probably had as much of the President as it wants at this point."

But he was back on March 16 to read his controversial statement on busing.

Nixon also made a point of socializing with broadcasters, the non-network variety. In June he entertained a group of thirty local station owners and executives at the White House for dinner.* A week later he had 110 local on-air news broadcasters and talk-show personalities for a full-scale White House briefing, followed by a reception.

George Putnam, the conservative Los Angeles TV newsman who had been critical of Nixon's China visit, was granted the courtesy of a personal briefing by Nixon and Kissinger at San Clemente.

Julie Nixon Eisenhower was sent with greetings from the president on the occasion of the fiftieth anniversary of WBT, Charlotte, N.C., a CBS affiliate owned by Charles Crutchfield, an old friend of the president and archenemy of the CBS management. Crutchfield was reported to have attempted to launch a general station revolt against the network following the airing of "The Selling of the Pentagon" in 1970.

Not all of Nixon's free air time went unchallenged. The Democrats doggedly filed complaints but with very little success. During the year they were only granted reply time to the State of the Union message—a traditional gratuity on the part of the networks. They did have the satisfaction, however, of having federal judge J. Skelly Wright and two colleagues reverse an earlier FCC ruling which had granted the Republicans reply-to-reply time on a CBS program, "The Loyal Opposition," which was aired in 1970. The judge's ironic comment:

> In granting a right to reply to the "Loyal Opposition" telecast, the commission shunned all reliance on the traditional balancing principles of the Fairness Doctrine. . . . the commission's handling of this case does not mark its finest hour. Put to the test . . . it waffled.†

* At this meeting he was reported to have promised to support legislation stabilizing the license-renewal process and to have declared his disapproval of the more virulent attacks on advertising and counteradvertising (see Chapter 4), which he saw as an attack on business itself.
† Another example of FCC waffling was its conglomerate study of the

Lawrence O'Brien, responsible for most of the challenges, commented, "the commission seems to view its primary mission as keeping those opposing the President's policies and programs from gaining equitable access to television."

In February, the U.S. Court of Appeals ruled, "In matters which are non-political, the President's status differs from that of other Americans and is of a superior nature" and refused to require the networks to give reply time on an equal basis to all presidential appearances.

In sum, the president seemed to be having his cake and eating it too. Although he had made no secret of his distaste for much of the press, and particularly network TV, no one since Franklin D. Roosevelt had made such astute political use of its facilities or prevented them so effectively from placing him in a position he did not desire to be in. It was a paradox pointed out clearly by a *New York Times* editorial in the summer of 1972:

> During its three and a half years in office, the Nixon Administration has evinced undisguised hostility toward working reporters and has attempted by threats and by legal and economic reprisals to intimidate television networks, influential metropolitan newspapers and magazines . . . .
>
> Under cover of legitimate criticism, implicit threats are made to block the renewal of television station licenses or to take legislative action against networks . . . . He [President Nixon] has also virtually destroyed the White House news conference, an important forum in which reporters used to be able to force a Chief Executive to provide at least a partial accounting to the public of his policies and the motives behind those policies.
>
> The relationship of the Nixon Administration with the press, a critically important relationship in a self-governing society and one which receives special protection in the Constitution, can thus only be described as dismal. It is exactly the opposite of the "open Presidency" which Mr. Nixon promised four years ago.

The truth was that Nixon was not interested in making the sort of news that was likely to come from even a controlled encounter with the press. He preferred to imbed himself in an occasion which, as he was fond of saying, was "historic"; do

---

influences of big-business ownership on radio and TV properties which had now been in the works for nearly three years with no report forthcoming.

his bit, have his say, and then slip away before the journalist-intruder could get to him. In this the networks could not avoid being his accomplice. One of their principal talents, and one it was hard for them not to use whenever the occasion presented itself, was to broadcast history live to the American people. The presidency during 1971–1972 made such occasions, some genuine, others less convincing, in great number, and television, whether it was friendly or not, seemed always to be on hand.

3 • No News Is Good News (II)

O N T H E E V E N I N G of January 12, 1972, listeners to National
Public Radio could have heard the following comment:

> There is a real question as to whether public television,
> particularly the national federally funded part of public
> television, should be carrying public affairs, news com-
> mentary and that kind of thing, for several reasons. One
> is the fact that the commercial networks, by and large, do
> quite a good job in that area. Public television is designed
> to be an alternative to provide programming that isn't avail-
> able on commercial television. So you could raise the
> legitimate question as to should there be as much public
> affairs, as much news and news commentary, as they plan
> to do . . . when you're talking about using federal funds
> to support a journalism activity it's always going to be
> the subject of scrutiny. The Congress will always be
> watching it very closely. It just invites a lot of political
> attention.

The comment was remarkable for at least two reasons. First,
because it was made on a National Public Radio news and
public affairs show paid for by federal funds. Second, because
it was made by Clay T. Whitehead.

Many of public broadcasting's problems were touched on in
the course of the sixty-minute program, entitled "Politics and
Public Broadcasting." Most of the problems were political, and
the foremost seemed to be Whitehead himself. The program
pointed up Whitehead's chilling October address to the annual
convention of the National Association of Educational Broadcasters in Miami. Among other things, he said:

> To us, you are becoming affiliates of a centralized na-
> tional network . . . . Do any of you honestly know
> whether public broadcasting, structured as it is today and
> moving in the direction it seems to be headed, can ever
> fulfill the promise envisioned for it or conform to the

policy set for it? If it can't then permanent financing will always be somewhere off in the distant future.*

To insiders, there was no question as to what Whitehead meant. John Witherspoon, director of television activities for the Corporation for Public Broadcasting (CPB), circulated a memorandum to 212 public-television station managers across the country pointing out that Whitehead's comment

> . . . says in straightforward political language that until public broadcasting is what this Administration wants it to be, this Administration will oppose permanent financing. Until Miami, CPB could honestly say that our relations with government had been free of political influence in the affairs of public broadcasting.

Whether or not the last sentence was an accurate appraisal, from that moment on the importance of politics to public broadcasting was admitted, and Whitehead's most casual comment scrutinized by hard-up PTV executives for hints as to their future. Seen in that light, and put alongside his Miami remarks, Whitehead's statement on National Public Radio was discouraging indeed.

On the surface it was quite simple. Whitehead's and the Administration's point of view was that public broadcasting should and must be decentralized, that CPB (the national funding organization) and PBS (Public Broadcasting Service, the national distribution network) were corruptions of the original intent of the Public Broadcasting Act of 1967 and the Carnegie Commission report on educational television. Not everyone agreed. *Variety* brought up the Senate report accompanying the Act, which read:

> Particularly in the area of public affairs your committee feels that non-commercial broadcasting is uniquely fitted to offer in-depth coverage and analysis which will lead to a better informed and enlightened public. . . . The programming of these stations should not only be supplementary to but competitive with commercial broadcasting services. This competition will benefit both types of service.

Although its phraseology tended to be broad, the Public Broadcasting Act of 1967 itself stated:

> —That it furthers the general welfare to encourage non-commercial educational radio and television broadcast programming which will be responsive to the interests of

---

* For the full text of the speech see Appendix II.

people both in particular locations and throughout the United States, and which will constitute an expression of diversity and excellence.

—That expansion and development of non-commercial educational radio and television broadcasting and of diversity of its programming depend on freedom, imagination, and initiative on both the local and national levels.

To the suspicious, the real motivation for Whitehead's anti-CPB attack was not quite so high-minded as his lofty references implied. To them it had to do, as did the earlier Administration attacks on the commercial networks, with the supposedly liberal tenor of news and public affairs programming put on the Public Broadcasting Service and more particularly to do with the hiring, during the summer of 1971, of Sander Vanocur and Robert MacNeil, who were to anchor the new National Public Affairs Center for Television (NPACT) in Washington. Both Vanocur and MacNeil were considered unfriendly by the Administration.

The situation was further exacerbated for all concerned, sympathetic and otherwise, when it was announced on the floor of Congress by Representative Lionel Van Deerlin that supposedly impoverished public television was paying Vanocur $85,000, twice a congressman's salary, and MacNeil $65,000.*

Worse still, the public broadcasters had their funding bill due to come up before Congress.

With this in view, CPB and PBS had been doing everything they could to reassure their nervous supporters that there was nothing biased or even controversial about their operation. Despite early strong resistance from some production centers within its organization, PBS had adopted formal news and public affairs guidelines. They were not put in force soon enough, however, to affect the report on the FBI done by radical journalist Paul Jacobs for "The Great American Dream Machine." PBS attempted to quash the segment and finally permitted it to go on the air in two versions, with a two-hour panel discussion by nine experts tacked on. It was a messy affair, leading not only to displeasure on the part of J. Edgar Hoover and the Administration, but to anger on the part of one faction of public broadcasters over interference and on the part of another over bad reporting. Also there was a threat by Representative Torbert Macdonald of a congressional inquiry into undue PBS censorship.

* Actually, the bill for their first year's salaries was shared equally by CPB and the Ford Foundation.

"The Politics and Humor of Woody Allen," strongly anti-Nixon in flavor, was unceremoniously dumped in February 1972 because of "equal time" problems. Shortly thereafter Jim Lehrer of KERA, Dallas, was appointed coordinator for PBS public affairs programming "to make suggestions to improve the professionalism of the programs."

To assist Lehrer, PBS established a board of review consisting of ten outside journalists and two public TV newsmen, whose duties included passing on the suitability of all possibly controversial programming.

"This is not the U.S. Post Office," said PBS head Hartford N. Gunn, Jr.

> We do not just distribute the programs. We're here to decide what it is that goes on the scheduled service. We have taken the position that we would not deny any program to any station that wants it . . . . But the problem with a scheduled service is that a lot of stations can be walked out on a plank and dropped into impossible situations by irresponsible people.

Elsewhere Gunn explained further:

> It is our belief at PBS that the programming of public television should not be evaluated by the PBS staff or the individual producer alone. Rather, we believe it appropriate to have the advice and consultation of a body of the producer's and distributor's professional peers.
>
> We propose this professional panel as a means to help assure both the public and the producer that their interests are being protected to the degree possible from "timid" managements as well as from incompetent producers. We do not believe this arrangement to be an exercise of censorship but rather one of public and professional responsibility.

By fall 1972, the board had yet to meet.

James Day—former head of now-defunct National Educational Television (NET), and currently running WNET/13, the Manhattan public TV channel and production center—who was one of the prime targets for all attempts at toning down PTV fare, objected to the growing power of the local stations: "I don't believe in a system of national television where decisions are based on the votes, so to speak, of the majority of the television stations. The analogy is not an apt one, but it's a little like running a magazine with the vote of the newsstand proprietors around the country."

Representative Clarence J. Brown, a newspaper publisher and former radio station owner from Ohio, circulated a survey for the purpose of establishing as fact that local PTV station managers were against public affairs programming, thus backing up his proposed bill to fund local public television through the Department of Health, Education, and Welfare and to also outlaw programs "dealing in whole or in part with the coverage, presentation, discussion or analysis of current news events or current issues that are the subject of partisan political controversy."

To his surprise, he discovered public affairs programming was given top priority by the local managers. Furthermore, they took the opportunity to point out to the congressman that they felt a lot of people were horning in on their business: 41 percent of their financial supporters apparently tried to influence programming decisions; 38 percent cited private donors; 32 percent, private corporations; 30 percent, state agencies; 24 percent, local governments; 22 percent, foundations. The three who threw their weight around least were the national PTV organizations: PBS, CPB, NET.

Despite the efforts of public TV brass to be discreet, their unruly producers rolled on, particularly at WNET/13, performing as though there were no tomorrow in which funds might run out. In March WNET/13 put on "Wintersoldier," a controversial documentary devoted to the testimony of veterans who admitted being implicated in acts of violence against the civilian population of Vietnam. When Representative James J. Howard asked Channel 13 to kill a rerun—not for political reasons but for bad language—the station ignored the request and replayed the program.

In May it was WNET/13 again, with its five-hour telethon devoted to negative opinions on the mining of Haiphong harbor and the resumption of bombing in North Vietnam, which provoked considerable angry comment in Congress.

None of this would seem to have helped PTV's cause in Washington. Whitehead had stated earlier, "I think the federal government does have a role in talking about the mix of programming, the broad purposes of the programming . . . ."

John Macy, head of CPB, countered, "I think it would be very inhibiting if public broadcasting were put in the position where suggestions were to come from those who provide the funds for programming."

"We've got to sit on this public broadcast organization to control its involvement in partisan politics," said Representative

John Anderson. "We need a little more congressional oversight."

Lyn Nofziger, a deputy chairman of the Republican National Committee, commented that CPB was "a victim of fiscal irresponsibility and partisan non-objectivity in its hiring practices and programming."

Bill Moyers, one of PTV's most highly paid performers, said, "It would be a painful irony if in trying to get out of the poorhouse, public broadcasters convinced themselves, privately, of course, not that it's dangerous to take risks, but that it's wise to avoid them."

In April, in another gesture of economy pleasing to the Administration, CPB cut back NPACT's budget by $400,000.

By December PBS had already announced that "The Great American Dream Machine," public TV's most controversial, expensive, and popular program, was going off the air. In one of the season's prime examples of double-talk, Hartford Gunn explained in a letter to *The New York Times* the program's imminent departure:

> "The Great American Dream Machine" . . . has not been cancelled by PBS. The 19 programs for this season which the producer, WNET, Channel 13, and PBS announced last summer have been presented. Unfortunately, it does appear that the "Dream Machine" will not return next season because WNET/13 like all the organizations in public TV is experiencing a severe financial squeeze.*

CPB's politically appointed board at one point actually considered a proposal to get out of public affairs broadcasting altogether. To its credit, it voted it down.

Some details could be marshaled in favor of more money for public TV. It has been estimated that possibly 50 million Americans watch PTV on a "fairly frequent basis" and over 500,000 contribute cash to its support annually. WNET, the *bête noire* of PTV's Washington critics, in its most controversial year increased its audience and its public contributions by one third.

Hartford Gunn pointed out that public TV so far had cost Americans only 15¢ per person per year, whereas in Great Britain it cost each person $13.20; in Canada, between $6.00 and $7.00; and in Sweden, $5.00. The average cost per hour-on-the-air for a public TV broadcast was $20,000, as compared to

---

* The WNET/13 budget for national programming was cut back by a total of $3 million for 1972–1973.

Less popular public TV shows, including William Buckley's "Firing Line," which cost $725,000 for the season, did manage to remain on.

$200,000 for an hour of prime-time commercial programming. And, according to the Federal Trade Commission, the apportioned cost per household of advertising for commercial TV was $60.00 a year.

"Are we as Americans—public broadcasters, congressmen, the Administration, all of us," asked Gunn with a grim eloquence, "so intellectually bankrupt that we can't devise a federally funded national system of communication, devoted to the public interest in all its aspects—free of inappropriate and dangerous influence?"

Inappropriate or not, Clay T. Whitehead persisted and grew more determined. On Bill Moyers' show in January he said:

> There are, I think, serious questions of principle, as to whether Federal funds should be involved when funding public affairs, because here, you're taking the taxpayer's money and using it to express controversial points of view, which inevitably is going to be opposite to the point of view of many citizens. And that's what controversial programming is all about.

Despite all the negative emotions on both sides, on May 31 Torbert Macdonald and his committee cleared a bill which, in the first year, would give half again as much money to the Corporation for Public Broadcasting as the bill recommended by the Administration and Whitehead and, in the second year, twice as much.

Macdonald had said before he introduced his bill:

> Public broadcasting is being subjected to a new technique developed in Washington which can be termed "intimidation by raised eyebrow." While the current Administration certainly did not originate the technique, it has refined it to a real art. A well-placed phone call, a well-timed speech or a coincidental personal investigation can all apply that government pressure which we had hoped the media were protected from by virtue of the Constitution or an act of Congress.

To everyone's amazement the bill passed 254 to 69 in the House, 81 to 1 in the Senate. A week later it was vetoed by the president with the following words, familiar in import to anyone who had followed the story:

> There are many fundamental disagreements concerning the directions which public broadcasting has taken and should pursue in the future. Perhaps the most important

> one is the serious and widespread concern—expressed in Congress and within public broadcasting itself—that an organization, originally intended only to serve the local stations, is becoming instead, the center of power and the focal point of control for the entire public broadcasting system.*

Torbert Macdonald called the veto "an incredible sacrifice of the public interest on the altar of partisan politics."

A month later a bill similar to one suggested by Whitehead was introduced in the Senate and eventually passed. It funded CPB for one year and raised its total allotment by $10 million, but made sure that the bulk of the extra money was passed on to the local stations.

Despite the approval and sympathy of the Administration, local and statewide public TV systems reported considerable financial trouble. In 1971–1972, KQED, San Francisco, one of the nation's foremost stations, had cut its news and public affairs staff by nineteen and its "Newsroom" by thirty minutes.

The local public TV stations in Washington, D.C., and New York both combined their operations with national programming facilities (NPACT and NET) to become GWETA and WNET/13. This might have been an attempt to insure the perpetuation of two highly professional production organizations whatever the Administration did. The California, Pennsylvania, and New York legislatures cut back appropriations to public TV. New York and Pennsylvania restored them after a last-ditch battle by PTV supporters.

The Mississippi educational TV network reported: "The Board of Directors for the Mississippi Authority for Educational Television has squelched most attempts at public affairs programming. We are a state-owned agency and the board feels our primary duty is to schools and should stay away from controversy as much as possible." Complaints by the Jackson, Mississippi, public TV station resulted in canceling all public TV news. A special program on highways and a weekly newsmaker show were both canceled, and in 1971 Mississippi PTV was prohibited even from airing election returns.

WJCT, Jacksonville's PTV station, reported that its documentary "Come to Florida . . . Before It's Gone" had angered some local businessmen to the point that they withheld items promised for the annual fund-raising auction. However, WJCT added:

* For the complete text of the veto message, see Appendix III.

Our public is responding extremely favorably to our brand of community involvement programming. The audience seems to be expecting more action-oriented media and basing more decisions on facts as presented by the most responsible elements of the local press. The direction is clearly toward participatory media in Jacksonville.

Whether the local public TV would suffer from the attacks on PBS and CPB—as with Mississippi—or prosper in spite of them, as the president seemed to intend, there were immediate signs of demoralization and rout in PTV's Washington offices. The resignation of Frank Pace, head of the corporation trustees, a Johnson appointee, came first; it was followed quickly by that of John Macy, the original head of CPB, also a Democrat.* The departures continued deep into the ranks, supposedly not susceptible to political prodding—most notably the author of the memorandum commenting on Whitehead's Miami speech, John Witherspoon.

At the end of the summer Pace's and Macy's replacements were announced. Thomas Curtis, a former Republican repre-. sentative from Missouri and counsel for the Encyclopedia Britannica, was named to replace Pace. Macy's successor was Henry W. Loomis, a physicist who served as second in command to Nixon's United States Information Agency head, Frank Shakespeare, who had himself been rumored to be in line for the job.

Neither man was likely to counter the Administration's wishes, nor did the appointments do anything to brighten the picture painted by Fred Powledge in his ACLU pamphlet "Public Television . . . A Question of Survival," published before the disastrous summer began. Said Powledge: "Public TV is being run by people who know very little about television, about journalism and its traditions, and about the creative side of communications . . . and people who stand in inordinate fear of politicians and therefore have no place in public broadcasting."

---

* Mr. Macy had been quoted as saying: "Four more years of the Nixon Administration with its impregnable resistance to what holds the best progress for public broadcasting would be the death blow for public broadcasting as I envision it."

4 • Who Pays?

"I INTEND TO TALK only a few minutes this morning, and you'll be on the beach or golf course in about fifteen minutes," said the final speaker at the 1972 meeting of the American Association of Advertising Agencies at the Boca Raton Hotel and Club in Boca Raton, Florida. What followed from the lips of Edward M. Thiele, vice-chairman of the Leo Burnett agency, was enough to put the most thick-skinned ad man off his game.

> As we look at our industry over the past 12 months we must agree that it has been an arduous year for all of us in the agency business. The harassments from government and from pressure groups have compounded the problems of running an agency as never before. Not only is our own agency world being attacked, but by the nature of our business, we are heir to the problems of each of our clients and the industries in which they compete. We feel like targets in a shooting gallery, knocked down, picked up, again and again—six shots for a quarter—until someone wins the stuffed panda, and then behind him comes another customer to start shooting all over again.
>
> We have seen in the past twelve months, the culmination of several years of consumerism . . . . Politicians have been listening to the many discordant carping voices of the consumerist movement with most sensitive ears. Perhaps the reaction—or should I say over-reaction—of the Senate, the House and chain reaction as the echoes bounce off the FTC, the FCC, the FDA, and other government agencies, to these often irresponsible voices may be accounted for by the fact that this is an election year. Let us hope so.

Mr. Thiele went on to quote public opinion researcher Daniel Yankelovich:

> In the minds of the public, the consumer protection issue and the pollution/ecology issue have merged into a single whole. In the public mind, the consumerist issues of product health, product safety, and truth in advertising are closely linked with pollution. Although these two burning issues—consumerism and ecology—are different from

a technical point of view, they form a single whole in the mind of the public.

The consumer/ecology movement has had an enormous impact on the public.

In effect, business is engaged on two battle fronts simultaneously. One is the familiar competitive market-place, the focus of most corporate policies and decisions. The other is represented by the new process described above. Let us call it "the public sector," where by public sector we mean the pressures on business that emanate from government, the general public, the consumer/ecology movement, the youth movement and similar sources. The great flood of demands directed at the corporation from the public sector have one common denominator: they all call upon business to make decisions which do not have the profit maximization of the company as their objective.

Earlier at the same meeting Dan Seymour, ex-broadcaster and presently head of J. Walter Thompson, the world's largest advertising agency, had spoken words that had a familiar ring to them.

Credibility, it seems to me, is the most important word in our business in 1972.

The concept of credibility recognizes the real world, the real customer, instead of some fictional, mythical creation existing only in Adland, and the minds of old-fashioned brand managers. . . .

That's where the so-called Fairness Doctrine lives and works—in the twilight area around credibility. It is hard for me to say the words Fairness Doctrine without choking a little; never was anything so misnamed, for there is nothing fair about it. We should have our own Fairness Doctrine; let us demand equal time against the FTC every time they indict by innuendo, every time they convict without trial, every time they make a McCarthy kind of mistake, as in the Zerex case, or with phosphates, or whatever—all those brutally damaging accusations which are shown to be false a year later. Just think of the beautiful commercials wc could do about the FTC.

The alarm and bitterness in these speeches were justified. As Thiele had said, it had been an arduous year for advertisers. The most arduous part of it was the critical attention they received from the regulatory agencies in Washington. In the fall of 1971 the Federal Trade Commission held a series of hearings on modern advertising practices involving the testimony of ninety-one different individuals and organizations.

In January the FTC sent a communication to the FCC stating

that it supported the concept of "counter-advertising," i.e., "the right of access in certain defined circumstances to the broadcast media for the purpose of expressing views and positions on issues that are raised by such advertising."

Submitting its suggestions as a contribution to the FCC's inquiry into the Fairness Doctrine, the FTC indicated that it felt advertising fell under the FCC's and the Doctrine's jurisdiction. For the FCC's guidance, the FTC had listed "certain identifiable kinds of advertising particularly susceptible to, and appropriate for, recognition and allowance of counter-advertising." They were:

> *Advertising asserting claims of product performance or characteristics that explicitly raise controversial issues of current public importance.* Claims that products contribute to solving ecological problems, or that the advertiser is making special efforts to improve the environment generally.

> *Advertising stressing broad recurrent themes, affecting the purchase decision in a manner that implicitly raises controversial issues of current public importance.* Food ads which may be viewed as encouraging poor nutritional habits, or detergent ads which may be viewed as contributing to water pollution.

> *Advertising claims that rest upon or rely upon scientific premises which are currently subject to controversy within the scientific community.* Test-supported claims based on the opinions of some scientists but not others whose opposing views are based on different theories, different tests or studies, or doubts as to the validity of the tests used to support the opinions involved in the ad claims.

> *Advertising that is silent about negative aspects of the advertised product.* Ad claims that a particular drug product cures various ailments when competing products with equivalent efficacy are available at substantially lower prices.

The FTC magnanimously deferred to the FCC concerning precise methods of implementing counter-advertising, although it suggested that it was not necessary to use thirty- or sixty-second spots for the ads and that "licensees might make available on a regular basis five-minute blocks of prime time for counter-advertisements directed at broad general issues raised by all advertising involving certain products as a way of fulfilling this aspect of their public service responsibilities." It also urged that the following points be embodied in any final plan:

1. Adoption of rules that incorporate the guidelines expressed above, permitting effective access to the broadcast media for counter-advertisements. These rules should impose upon licensees an affirmative obligation to promote effectiveness of this expanded right of access.

2. Open availability of one hundred percent of commercial time for anyone willing to pay the specified rates, regardless of whether the party seeking to buy the time wishes to advertise or "counter" advertise. Given the great importance of product information . . . licensees should not be permitted to discriminate against counter-advertisers willing to pay, solely on account of the content of their ideas.

3. Provision by licensees of a substantial amount of time, at no charge, for persons and groups that wish to respond to advertising like that described above but lack the funds to purchase available time slots. In light of the above discussion, it seems manifest that licensees should not limit access, for discussions of issues raised by product commercials, to those capable of meeting a price determined by the profitability of presenting one side of the issues involved. Providing such free access would greatly enhance the probability that advertising, a process largely made possible by licensees themselves, would fully and fairly contribute to a healthy American marketplace.

The uproar that followed this detailed recommendation from one Washington agency to another was immense. The broadcasters were predictably outraged. One of the most elaborate responses came from a former Kennedy aide, Theodore Sorensen, who presented a brief on behalf of the Television Bureau of Advertising to the FTC. After a long, detailed argument Sorensen concluded:

Particularly affected would be commercial television's news, public affairs, and other public service programming. In 1970, the television networks spent over $115 million for news and public affairs programming, more than 10 percent of total network broadcasting expenses incurred in that year, which amounted to approximately $1.1 billion. . . .

These news, public affairs, and other public service announcements and programming, however, are largely unprofitable. As a result, the level of justifiable network and local station expenditures on such programming is necessarily sensitive to revenue fluctuations and profit constraints, and would surely have to be curtailed were even moderate losses of revenue to be experienced as the result of regulation discriminatory in purpose or inadvertent effect. Television news is the primary source of information on current events, politics and international affairs for more people than any other medium; and restrictions on the scope and quality of its coverage imposed by a serious diminution of advertising revenues would not serve the public interest.

These losses to the viewing public cannot be justified in the name of the consuming public. Inducing marketers to shift all or a portion of their advertising budgets to other media would not improve the overall quality of consumer protection. On the contrary, because television—in contrast to the print media—is almost entirely dependent on advertising revenues, it is particularly conscious of its need to maintain public confidence in its advertising. Television advertising is, therefore, privately regulated, not only by the National Advertising Review Board, but also by the Television Code of the National Association of Broadcasters. It is also subject to Federal Communications Commission supervision applicable only to broadcasting; and it is additionally subject not only to existing Federal Trade Commission rules applicable to all media, but also to special Commission rules . . . that are already but properly applicable only to TV . . . .

A determination to regulate advertising so as to compel advertisers in significant numbers to abandon commercial television is at the same time, and inescapably, a determination to diminish access thereto among the political candidates, their critics and the various commentators, writers, and artists. Stripped of its ability effectively to promote lawfully sold products, reduced in strength, diversity, numbers and independence, commercial television could not serve as well those other voices whose undiluted right to constitutional protection no one would deny. Such regulation would surely raise substantial if novel First Amendment and other Constitutional questions . . . .

Any actions which jeopardize the viability of nearly 700 commercial television stations—the country's most important and influential national and local forum for political debate, social-economic commentary and literary and artistic expression—cannot be sustained by the generous standards sufficient for conventional regulatory action.

Sorensen had, of course, hit the heart of the matter. Although the pattern of protest—that any step damaging to network profits must necessarily hurt news and public affairs first and hardest—was wearily familiar, this time, perhaps, it carried the authority of true desperation. As everyone, including Sorensen, was eager to point out, the FTC's counter-advertising program, if carried out, would involve virtually all of network TV's 427 national sponsors plus all the thousands who supported the nearly 700 local commercial TV stations across the country.

WMAR-TV, Baltimore, stated, "It is difficult to conceive of a single advertisement which has been shown on any television station which would not come under the content of any or all of the . . . aspects of the FTC's proposal."

The Television Bureau of Advertising figured out that if counter-advertising had been required in 1970 at the same one-to-five ratio originally used for anti-cigarette commercials, the networks would have had, instead of $453.8 million in pre-tax profits, an $86.6 million loss. And this was based on the unlikely assumption that under such adverse conditions all the current advertisers would have continued to use television.

Less concerned about the informational and cultural functions of television were two Administration spokesmen, Clay T. Whitehead and Herbert Klein. Speaking at the National Association of Broadcasters convention in April, Whitehead said that the FTC's counter-advertising proposal amounted to a government-controlled right of access to state personal opinions on anything. Carried one step further, it could be applied to programs as well as to advertising. Klein followed:

> I couldn't be more in accord with Mr. Whitehead in saying that counter-advertising is counter to the system. Counter-advertising would lead to the demise of the broadcast industry. Counter-advertising would lead, I think, to a great discredit to the United States because we lose the freedom which comes from the commercial values we have . . . .
> And, while I'm being critical of the FTC, I'll go into . . . whether or not children are looking at the television ads and buying things they don't need. That's not the American way.

According to reports from the president's off-the-record meeting with broadcasters in June, Administration disapproval of counter-advertising went all the way to the top.

However, the fact that powerful forces were against counter-advertising was less reassuring than it might have been. The broadcasters and advertisers had no trouble recalling the days not so long ago when anti-cigarette ads led, first to a drop in sales, then to a legislative ban against all cigarette ads on radio and TV as of January 1971, costing broadcasters over $200 million in annual revenue. Nor was there any comfort, at least to broadcasters, in reports that tobacco sales were on the rise again, without their help.

"We—at the FCC," said Chairman Dean Burch, "have a concern not only with the pure logic of whether there ought to be counter-advertising but whether this broadcasting industry can take the number of blows that are being administered to it by leaders of all stripes."

Besides its counter-advertising proposals, the FTC had had an active year. It instructed several firms, including Ocean Spray Cranberry Juice and Profile Bread, to go on the air with corrective advertising. According to Robert Pitofsky, director of the FTC's Bureau of Consumer Protection, corrective advertising, which meant broadcasting a message indicating that your earlier commercials had been lies, was a productive advertising tool as well as an effective remedy for consumer deception.

The FTC had also asked for documentation on advertising claims from more than one hundred advertisers,* including automobile and appliance manufacturers, tire makers, drug firms, and soap and detergent companies. Such documentation could lead to no action, or an order for corrective advertising,

---

* Just what sort of claims were involved was indicated by the list of detergent and soap claims ordered to be proven in summer 1972, which included:

Jergens extra dry facial cleanser is something new and contains moisturizers.

Easy Off oven cleaner effectively cleans dirty ovens, warm or cold, and has 33 percent more cleaning power than another popular foam spray.

Dial soap is used by many hospitals to bathe newborn babies and is the most effective deodorant soap on the market.

Arm & Hammer cleanser is pure, natural, has no chemical odors, and cannot cause scratches when used to clean counter tops.

A liquid bleach like Clorox kills more viruses and bacteria than any other type of household disinfectant.

Palmolive Crystal Clear effectively removes dried-on foods and is safe for fine china and delicate crystal.

Leon Fresh Down oven cleaner does everything better than old-fashioned oven cleaners.

Mr. Bubble cleans effectively and does not leave bathtub rings.

Lifebuoy soap is so lastingly active, its deodorant protection won't let you down.

Janitor-in-a-Drum is strong enough to effectively clean greasy stove hoods and mild enough to effectively clean wicker furniture.

Noxzema is greaseless, a moisturizer, and cleans as effectively as soap without drying as soap does.

Clothes that are so dirty they appear to be ruined can be effectively cleaned and restored by washing them in Tide.

Purex gets out dirt other bleaches leave behind.

A little Borateem rubbed into stains or added to a detergent effectively removes tough stains from clothes.

or an out-of-court agreement, or, in rare instances, a court injunction to the advertiser to cease and desist.

In the case of the automobile companies, the FTC, according to Bess Myerson Grant, New York City's commissioner of Consumer Affairs, had not released a study made at its own request by an independent engineering concern which found that substantiation for 65 percent of the ads was irrelevant or inadequate.

Among the claims considered to have inadequate substantiation were:

> Chrysler's contention that its torsion-bar suspension provides extra comfort, ease of handling, and extra safety.

> General Motors' claim that the Chevelle has 109 advantages to keep it from becoming old before its time.

> General Motors' claim that the front-wheel-drive Toronado provides greater smoothness, improved traction, and sure handling.

> Toyota's and General Motors' claims that their compacts, Corolla and Opel, need no lubrication for the life of the cars.

> Volkswagen's contention that its Super Beetle has more luggage space, is longer lasting, and stops faster.

> Ford's claim that its Pinto never needs waxing and that its LTD is quieter than some of the world's most expensive cars.

The courts seemed even less friendly to the advertisers in some instances than were the regulatory agencies. In the case of Friends of the Earth (FOE) against WNBC-TV, the U.S. Court of Appeals overruled an FCC decision denying a request by FOE that the Fairness Doctrine be applied to automobile and gasoline advertisements in New York City. The court said the FCC should require WNBC-TV to broadcast balanced programming on the auto-pollution issue.

In April 1972, while WNBC-TV was responding to an FCC request for documentation of its coverage of auto pollution, the parties involved wrote a joint letter to the FCC asking the Commission to discontinue its examination of WNBC's past coverage of the issue. The letter explained that the request was based at least in part on WNBC-TV's decision to begin giving "substantial treatment" to anti–auto pollution programming.

In May, shortly after the two parties agreed to an "amicable termination" of their dispute, WNBC-TV was broadcasting an average of two anti–auto pollution messages a day. Although the frequency of the spots dropped to less than one a day by the fall of 1972, WNBC-TV was still broadcasting such spots more often than New York's two other network-flagship stations, WCBS and WABC, whose licenses were challenged for failing to present balanced programming on the auto-pollution issue.

Another case perhaps more disturbing to the broadcasters was that of the Business Executives Move for Peace in Vietnam (BEM) against station WTOP in Washington, D.C., which went all the way to the Supreme Court, where it was scheduled to be argued in October 1972.

The last round had been won by BEM, when the U.S. Court of Appeals held that WTOP-TV was wrong in denying BEM paid commercial time to air its views on the war. According to the court, the First Amendment prohibits any broadcaster who sells time for commercial messages from having a policy against selling that time simply because the message contains controversial material. Set opposite rulings in favor of counter-advertising, this created a hall of mirrors at the end of which the beleaguered broadcasters might indeed disappear, with news and public affairs programming dropping out of the picture somewhere along the way.

To upset the broadcaster still further, counter-ads against everything from drugs and automobiles to strip mining were being prepared by such personalities as Burt Lancaster and Rod Serling in anticipation of the day when time would be allocated for their airing. Indeed, some of them had already been broadcast.

There were other more specific problems. Despite Herbert Klein's having labeled such actions as un-American (see page 81), the lucrative Saturday morning children's programming on all three networks came increasingly under fire.

A report from Action for Children's Television (ACT) indicated that children's programming was interrupted with a commercial message every 2.8 minutes on the average and that less than one minute in 15 could be classified as informational. Overriding a CBS objection, the National Association of Broadcasters voted to institute a code becoming effective in January 1973 which would cut Saturday morning commercials from 16 to 12 minutes per hour.

In the summer of 1972, three drug companies—Bristol-Myers, Miles Laboratories, and Hoffman LaRoche (Sauter Labs)—agreed to end vitamin advertising on children's TV programs in response to objections filed by ACT. The total amount of vitamin advertising on children's TV was approximately $4 million a year. Toy and cereal advertisers were also under fire.* The White House Conference Report on Food, Nutrition, and Health had urged that information be beamed at the public to correct deceptive advertising. "This action is necessary to counteract the tremendous counter-education of our children by false and misleading advertising of the nutritional value of foods, particularly on TV."

The content of children's TV came in for the most alarming analysis of all. An ACT report concerning four consecutive Saturday mornings on the major Boston stations, including the three network outlets, stated that three out of ten dramatic segments were "saturated" with violence, and 71 percent had at least one instance of human violence, with or without weapons. Of these, 4 percent resulted in death or injury. "Although there is an abundance of violence of all kinds," said F. Earle Barcus, the Boston University professor responsible for the study, "one is left with the impression that, after all, violence is harmless since very little permanent damage is done to the characters."

This finding was even more intimidating when combined with the surgeon general's report on violence, which, after preliminary attempts to soften its message,† came out with the news that as far as its five volumes of studies were concerned, there was a definite causal relationship between TV violence and aggressive behavior in children.

* FCC chairman Dean Burch, the father of three children, was one of ACT's most conspicuous supporters, publicly agreeing that it would be a good thing if all commercials were eliminated from children's programming and stating that networks which crowded their offerings for children mainly into Saturday morning should have a minimum of fourteen hours a week directed toward the nation's youngsters. "As to content," said Burch, "there really is little room for debate. We must crack down on the hard sell that shades off into downright deception and, if anything, err on the side of toughness."

† The story of the surgeon general's report was a typical instance of bureaucratic blurring rendered progressively fuzzier at each stage from basic research to committee to public, with the media doing its part in dulling the final impact. The twelve-man steering committee was allegedly rigged in favor of the TV industry (the networks had been given the right of veto, and NBC and ABC exercised it on seven out of the forty names of experts suggested); five members of the panel were or had been employes of the networks; the 279-page report issued by the panel softened the impact of the five volumes of research it was based on; the summary release given the press was even softer; and the media misread and softened it even further: the *New York Times* headline on its first story was "TV Violence Held Unharmful to Youth." Later stories corrected the impression.

One of the background studies stated flatly, "We aren't going to get rid of violence until we get rid of advertisers. The advertisers want something exciting with which to get the audience. Violence equals excitement equals ratings."

Dr. Jesse L. Steinfeld, the surgeon general, testifying before the Senate communications subcommittee, pushed the matter out of Saturday morning and into prime-time programming, where violence also was widespread and where viewing by children was high. "My professional response is that the broadcasters should be put on notice . . . there comes a time when the data are sufficient to justify action, that time has come."

Undoubtedly the strongest statement of all came from FCC commissioner Nicholas Johnson, who commented in his most quoted remark of the year that the TV networks had "molested the minds of the nation's children. . . . If you do it during the week on the school playground, to one child, you are driven off to prison in a police car. But if you do it Saturday morning, in the living room, to millions of young children, you are just driven home, by a chauffeur in a long black limousine." *

All the excitement did have some constructive results. The networks continued into the new season with low-rated informational shows for children which they might otherwise have canceled (and added a few to the lineup, among them a scattering of eight two-and-a-half-minute "In the News" items dropped into CBS' Saturday morning schedule).

There were still other potential dangers to TV advertising. AVCO Broadcasting president John Murphy, talking to the Chicago Broadcast Advertising Club in January 1972, called attention to one.

> Do we really expect anyone to recall eight different sales messages delivered in a fourteen-minute period? What about five messages in two minutes?
>
> It is entirely possible that if we continue to dilute the impact of his [the advertiser's] message by overcommercialization and clutter, we can render impotent the greatest instrument of communications the world has ever known . . . .
>
> We cannot continue to provide irritations for the viewer and dilution for the sponsor without bringing disaster upon all of us.

* Senator Howard Baker, who heard Johnson's testimony, commented that it was "one of the most violent statements I've ever heard made before any committee." Johnson's chairman, Dean Burch, said, "We get this kind of performance almost every day."

In June 1971 Murphy had effected a 10 percent reduction of ads below the NAB Code maximums on AVCO's five TV stations, hoping that others would follow his lead. When after twelve months they hadn't, Murphy abandoned his crusade, saying:

> The change we must now make has been forced upon us by the highly competitive atmosphere in which broadcasters, sponsors, and the advertising agencies operate. It is impossible for one company to do this alone and when the support we had hoped for from others did not materialize—with but rare exceptions—the handwriting was on the wall.

Still, anti-clutter sentiments remained common in the industry as well as among citizen groups. In May 1972 Kenneth Mason of Quaker Oats told the American Advertising Federation that a company survey discovered that 97 percent of the audience for its six highest-rated shows could not demonstrate any product recall. A study for the NAB showed that although. Americans still think commercials are an acceptable price to pay for free programming, nevertheless they would like to see them go. Foote, Cone and Belding announced it was endorsing a "lower clutter" policy and was adding 10 percent to the audience measurements of all spots offered to AVCO. The Katz Agency recommended that ads be cut by 13 percent in prime time and by 17 percent outside of prime time.

Although all these pronouncements constituted substantial threats to the prosperity of broadcasters, the threat most persistent and difficult to deal with was that from the broadcasters' own news and public affairs departments. More and more, in their function as journalists, these staffs had felt obliged to deal with the environmental and consumerist movements.

In the environmental field, television had been particularly effective in dramatizing the crisis. Although it appeared that on the networks ecological specials might have passed their peak, on local stations they persisted. After politics, the environment was the subject most widely reported, according to DuPont correspondents across the country. Nearly 70 percent of the radio and TV stations reporting to the Survey were doing consumer coverage—half of them on a regular basis. This growth in interest was all the more striking because the possibility of inflicting pain on advertisers and getting hurt in return was immediate.

On the networks, the case of the Bumble Bee tuna company,

which responded to coverage of a congressional hearing on the fishing industry on CBS News by boycotting advertising on that network, was probably the year's most flagrant example of sponsor retaliation to editorial content.

On the local stations, instances of attempted interference by advertisers reported to the Survey took a sharp upturn. Among the hardest hit was WCCO-TV, Minneapolis, which gave its recurring program "Survival Kit for Consumers" prime-time scheduling and in four half hours covering dozens of services and products managed to lose an estimated $150,000 in advertising. The programs also led to state government suits against offending parties, and revisions in policy by many of the companies reported on. To increase the series' resonance, the station published and circulated a follow-up booklet for each program.

WDIO-TV, Duluth, Minnesota, reported advertiser reprisals from its five-night-a-week Action Line report, including the loss of a major Honda account, and $25,000 from Coca-Cola because of reports alleging violations of the wage-price freeze.

KWTV, Oklahoma City, also reported trouble with Coca-Cola and with local car dealers. WWDC, Washington, D.C., reported a cancellation by A & P after the station pointed out below-standard products in its inner-city stores.

Although many broadcasters obviously suffered for their vigilance in behalf of the consumer, only one, WQWK in State College, Pennsylvania, was reported as taking it out on its staff. Jim Lange, a student newsman who on the air identified a number of local merchants for not posting maximum-allowable prices, was credited with losing the station a $200 account and fired "for not clearing the story with management." Lange was later reinstated, but the Consumer Federation of America persuaded the FCC to hold up the renewal of WQWK's license until an investigation was conducted to determine whether the station had discharged him for improper reasons.

Perhaps the most provocative of all gestures from a local TV station came from WMAQ-TV, the NBC-owned-and-operated station in Chicago, which not only broadcast frequent consumerist editorials but also published a booklet entitled *Share the Savings,* giving its viewers hints on how to save money. Among the suggestions which, if followed, would substantially reduce the profits of most of the station's major advertisers were:

> Plan meals and cook dishes from scratch rather than using boxed or canned items. It saves money and it's more nutritious.

Don't buy cereal with gifts and other "junk" inside. It adds to the cost as well as to the contamination of the contents.

Bake your own rolls and bread. A woman who wrote in says she can make 8 dozen rolls for $1.00. The same rolls cost 70¢ a dozen at a bakery.

Buy cut-rate gas. It is as good as that sold through major oil companies, although the service at discount stations is not as good.

Maybe you should save by not owning a car. Take public transportation, cabs, even rent a car when necessary. It still won't add up to the initial price, upkeep, insurance, parking, etc., of a car.

Soap companies recommend excessive amounts of detergent. You can use much less soap and your clothes will get just as clean.

Unknown brands are usually less expensive than advertised brands. The store's house brand is often identical and costs less.

Do not shop where there are give-aways such as free gifts or savings stamps. The prices of these things are added to the price of the items you buy.

Eliminate things like paper towels—a cloth towel can be re-used.

Lower advertising rates on TV might result in lower retail prices to the consumer.

Concerning the delicate relationship between advertisers and broadcasters, the policy of General Foods was of particular interest to friends of news and public affairs programs, since the corporation, alone of all the big advertisers, supported not only network but local public affairs efforts.

M. R. Bohm, executive vice-president of General Foods, told an Association of National Advertisers media planning workshop:

> Once upon a time an advertiser could stand back and say: "Quality is not my business. I merely buy time or space. It is up to the network or the station or the publisher to worry about media quality if he wants my advertising dollars."
>
> This is not true or feasible today. The advertiser must encourage and support higher quality in what media offers

to the public. After all, the advertiser and his agency are the primary sources of revenue that support the enterprise. It is naive to assume that the revenue potential is not taken into consideration in future planning by media management. The advertiser can't avoid having an impact, and therefore, must be sensitive in use of such leverage.

For one thing, it means sponsoring programs that will sometimes deliver lower ratings but will make a contribution to the improvement of the overall programming fare.

As one of the sponsors of "The Six Wives of Henry VIII" this past summer, we found some commercial benefits that cost per thousand could never reflect. In children's network programming we've done the same thing. Over 40% of GF's commercial messages this year in children's network will be in programs that are designed to do more than just entertain.

The emphasis must carry over to local programming as well. And here you may be surprised with a higher return on your media investment than expected. We have recently begun a project in local public service programming in several major markets and have been delighted with the tremendous local interest in the issues covered. And it is evident that our advertising dollars were anything but a neutral factor in terms of media quality.

So I suggest that it is a matter both of public obligation and of practical self-interest for the advertiser to recognize the impact of his dollars on media quality, and to work to see that the impact is a positive one.

We advertisers are going to have to bite the bullet on this one. It's unthinkable that we should not concern ourselves with encouraging—even demanding—more attention to the *quality* end of the scale.

Very few advertisers chose to follow the example of General Foods and bite the bullet.

According to some network news executives, their product had never been harder to sell. CBS News president Richard Salant, for example, anticipated a $20 million difference between money expended by his department and returns for 1972.

As for the basic problem of truth in advertising, and the credibility crisis in the advertising and broadcasting industries, few of those who should have felt concern showed it. Out of 1,275 marketing and advertising executives asked to participate in a "Truth in Advertising" survey by the American Management Association, only 150 were interested enough to answer in detail. Of these, 50 percent indicated some real concern about the issue; 31 percent felt it was "overblown"; 60 percent believed their advertising was always truthful, although only

18 percent would give their competition credit for the same integrity.

Perhaps the indifference of advertisers was justified. Of the 427 major advertisers on network TV, only a handful had yet been required to change or eliminate their ads. The anticipated time for the FTC to mount any sort of punitive action was still four years. The famous Geritol case had gone on for more than ten. FTC demands for documentation of ads were perhaps more immediately troublesome.

However, Senators Frank Moss and Warren Magnuson had introduced legislation to permit the FTC to issue injunctions stopping false or misleading advertising, which would shorten the four years required to bring an advertiser to heel and otherwise strengthen the commission's hand.

Self-regulation, the industry's own proposal for solving the problem, was greeted with skepticism by radio and TV critics, who pointed to the industry's efforts to arrive at some sort of cigarette code, only to be outflanked by the action of a single private citizen, lawyer John Banzhaf, III, who had successfully invoked the Fairness Doctrine to force radio and TV to carry anti-cigarette announcements. The National Advertising Review Board (NARB), set up with considerable fanfare in the fall of 1971, with former UN ambassador Charles Yost as chairman, had yet to find it necessary to initiate disciplinary action against offending advertisers.

Complaints for the NARB were investigated by the National Advertising Division of the Better Business Bureaus (NAD). In the first year, the NAD had received 337 complaints against national advertising. Of the total: 112 were dismissed as being without merit; 72 were found to be justified (in all of the 72 cases the advertiser agreed either to withdraw the ad or to modify it), and 153 were still under investigation as of September 1972.

Six cases dismissed by the NAD and appealed by the complainants had been brought before the NARB. In two of the six, the American Dairy Association (ADA) and Miles Laboratories were judged to present misleading advertisements. No action was taken because the ADA promised not to use its ad again, and Miles Laboratories said it was getting out of children's television.

The red tape and frustration involved in the self-regulatory process had already caused one "public" * member of the

---

* The membership of the board included ten from advertising agencies, plus ten agency alternates, thirty advertisers, and ten members representing the public.

NARB, LeRoy Collins, former governor of Florida and one-time head of the National Association of Broadcasters, to resign. In his letter of resignation to NARB chairman Charles Yost, Collins said that he doubted that the advertising industry was prepared to accept the kind of agency that was needed for effective self-regulation.

Another "public" member, attorney Benny Kass, complained about the length of time it took to render a decision. Kass was quoted in *Television/Radio Age* as saying: "I know for a fact that too many complaints are lost, left on desks, or not acted on."

Furthermore, in the experience of most, the one brief mention that most consumer items usually got on the evening news did not have to be taken too seriously. The inattention and short memories of most viewers could work to the advertiser's advantage as well as his disadvantage.

Still, the unavoidable fact remained that in the past year a situation which had existed for decades and been ignored was out in the open and seemed unlikely ever to disappear again. Nor was it television alone that was involved. As Sorensen untactfully pointed out in his brief for the Television Bureau of Advertising: "The list of similarities among advertisements in any and all media is endless. To treat them differently is to violate the Fifth Amendment by denying equal protection of the laws to broadcasters and television advertisers . . . ."

According to Donald Kendall, chairman of PepsiCo, Inc. (whose principal product was Pepsi-Cola, although the company was also into potato chips, Fritos, sporting goods, and moving vans), discontent with advertising reflected "a deepening misunderstanding or distrust of the whole American system of free enterprise."

Free enterprise was indeed the issue, and there could be no question that advertising was central to it. Advertising had been instrumental in giving America the world's "highest standard of living," and now that some of the fruits of that high living were being recognized as bitter, particularly by the journalists whose livelihood was completely dependent upon advertising, the dilemma seemed insoluble. Dan Seymour stated the case baldly.

> The young tend to believe what they are taught, that advertising is wasteful and immoral . . . . What the young people coming out of college do not know is that the media have two faces. One is the stern editorial face which denounces or misunderstands advertising; the other

is the friendly smiling face that takes us out to lunch to tell us all about the media . . . to explain why we should place advertising . . . this face understands and loves advertising.

Seymour might have added, if he had been less polite, that both faces of the media were equally dependent on the "immoral" activity in question.

Richard Salant contended that the lot of the broadcast journalist was hopeless so long as the medium he worked for was licensed and thus subject to reprimands from public and government alike: "Every complaint reminds us we can't tell anyone to go to hell. It is a brooding omnipresence. There is no way out." It seemed doubly hopeless when one considered that the same electronic journalist has his bills paid by a hand which, if he does his job properly, he is bound to bite more and more frequently.

If disaster seemed in store for commercial broadcast journalism, what were the alternatives? Public television, which two or three years earlier had seemed to offer a promising alternative, was itself in desperate trouble where news and public affairs were concerned. The print media were scarcely likely to satisfy the needs of a public now accustomed to getting its news the easy way, without the effort of reading, and free of charge.

There was, of course, cable TV. But if the new television of abundance, with its multiple channels and its vast prospects for serving the viewer, was going to inherit the responsibilities and rewards of over-the-air broadcast journalism, it had done little to demonstrate its capacity for the task in the year of this report.

Clay Whitehead, working in concert with broadcasters, copyright holders, cable people, and the FCC, had hammered out an agreement for importation of distant signals in all but the top fifty markets. The effect was to break, at least temporarily and partially, the logjam which had blocked cable development for several years.

To Dean Burch, the new cable policy was "perhaps an historic event." Nicholas Johnson called it a "much heralded dawn" which turned out to be a "cold and smog-filled day." Fred Friendly, former president of CBS News, described it as a compromise "secretly arrived at by a head-to-head tug-of-war between all the vested interests." Still, it represented a move toward freeing the new cable technology.

The Supreme Court also reaffirmed the FCC's jurisdiction over cable TV, and overturned a U.S. Circuit Court ruling that cable operators with more than 3,500 subscribers need not originate programming. Commenting on the decisions, Henry W. Harris, president of Cox Communications, Inc., which owned thirty-two cable systems and reported a 23 percent increase in subscribers and a record income for 1971, said: "I think the whole industry was hoping the FCC would win, for the security it gives them in regulating us. Otherwise, they might have wondered what their powers in cable were and held back from rules that would be beneficial to us."

The new deadline for cable systems to begin originating programs was not immediately set. However, it was inevitable that some of those originations would be news and public affairs.

The new FCC policy also required cable operators to set aside channels for schools, local government, and the general public. Of the three categories, the most exciting was the public access channel, which would permit local talents, journalistic as well as artistic, to test themselves. With the growing availability of cheap, easily portable equipment, the open channels promised exposure to a whole new generation of citizen reporters and commentators, who were already springing up on both coasts.

System-controlled channels were also beginning to use the products of low budget and underground tape producers. Tele-PrompTer, in a historic first, provided gavel-to-gavel coverage of the National Black Political Convention in Gary, Indiana, in March 1972, complete with a highly expert anchorman, Clarence B. Jones, editor and publisher of the *Amsterdam News*. Sterling Manhattan, the other New York City cable system, had given full coverage to the two-day A. J. Liebling Counter Convention for new journalists. TelePrompTer celebrated some sort of cable first when it hired a full-fledged Washington correspondent.

The Ford and Markle Foundations gave $3 million to establish a Washington information center for private citizens as well as local and state governments seeking advice on how best to set up and develop local cable franchises. The United Church of Christ, always vigilant in protecting the public's broadcasting interests, issued a booklet entitled *A Short Course in Cable*.

At the same time, pay-TV, one element which might give cable TV a giant push, and also the one reasonably safe alternative to commercial sponsorship of broadcast programming, was scheduled for trial in several cities including Sarasota and Fort Lauderdale, Florida, San Diego, California, and Harrisburg, Pennsylvania, despite the continued resistance of broadcasters and theater owners.

The total circulation of cable TV went from 5.3 million homes in January 1971 to 6 million in January 1972. Its income rose from $320 million to $360 million. In the first quarter of 1972, seventy-two new franchises were granted—a substantial increase over the first quarter of the previous year. During the year TelePrompTer announced a $55 million expansion, Cox, $60 million.

Experimental two-way systems, which gave the subscriber a limited ability to respond to programming through his set—another important step toward a full cable technology—were being tested in more than a dozen communities throughout the country. A report to the Office of Telecommunications Policy recommended spending $8,258,000 on an experimental government-industry "wired city" employing the most sophisticated hardware now available to see if the public would make use of it.

Several other reports on cable TV were issued during the year. The most prestigious was that of the Sloan Commission on Cable Communications, which estimated that within the next decade 40 to 60 percent of the nation would be wired. It recommended controlled pay-as-you-go TV but was ambiguous about common-carrier status for the new technology, which had a strong advocate in the American Civil Liberties Union.

Not everyone was pro-cable, of course, nor anxious for the early and unhindered development which would make it a possible custodian for whatever responsibilities over-the-air television might relinquish.

In a letter addressed to Senators John Pastore and John McClellan and Representatives Torbert Macdonald and Robert Kastenmeier, Dr. Frank Stanton, now vice-chairman of CBS, commented on the FCC cable policy which was later put into effect:

> What is at stake in the pending regulatory proposals is no more and no less than the question whether government policy should be directed at preserving and enhancing, or diminishing and destroying, free over-the-air broadcasting in this country. Those who see cable television as the wave of the future are not, of course, concerned about the consequences to free television from a policy favoring cable television. Thus, for example, the Sloan Commission on Cable Communications . . . blandly dismissed such consequences for free television in these words:

"But in any case, if over-the-air television is to fall victim, in some degree or another, to technological change, it is in no different position from any other enterprise in which investments have been made, and possesses no greater right than other industries to protection from technological change. It does not appear to the Commission that the industry needs or warrants further protection by regulatory agencies."

If the current threat posed to over-the-air television were only that of "technological change," we would have little proper concern. What does concern us, and what moves us to write this letter, is the risk that free television will fall victim not to technological change, but to a deliberate and, we think, mistaken public policy which would prevent free and fair competition between those media and favor cable television at the expense of free television. In this respect we urge, contrary to the Sloan Commission, that over-the-air television *is* in a "different position" from other enterprises. It is in a different position by virtue of the fact that it is the means by which the American public receives most of its news and information as well as its entertainment, and does so without distinctions based on ability to pay or geographical separation.

Over-the-air television, whatever its faults, is a means of communication which deserves much of the American people and should not be dismissed as merely another "enterprise in which investments have been made." It warrants if not "protection" in the narrow sense referred to by the Sloan Commission, every fair opportunity to continue and to strengthen its service to the American people.

In view of the events of the season in which they were spoken, Dr. Stanton's words had a heroic and desperate ring.

5 • The Broadcasting of Politics (I)

The Primaries

ON THE EVENING of January 4, 1972, fans of the "Glenn Campbell Goodtime Hour" were wrenched untimely from the last ten minutes of the taped hijinks in CBS' Hollywood studios and transported across the continent to a frigid Down East parlor in Kennebunk Beach, Maine, where a live, unsmiling Senator Edmund Muskie told them in measured phrases what they already knew—that he was planning to run for the highest office in the land.

The senator's remarks were televised from the same Maine cottage where some fourteen months earlier he had, on the eve of the 1970 elections, sat by the kitchen hearth and summed up the Democratic view of things in his own reassuring, slow-spoken style. The contrast, when placed alongside President Nixon's final law-and-order harangue delivered standing in a hangar on an Arizona airfield, had been credited with increasing the Democratic congressional margin of victory the next day. Ever since, Big Ed Muskie had been the favored candidate of his party and the press.

If Muskie's announcement came as no surprise, the manner in which he chose to make it was unique. Customarily, those hopeful of winning their party's nomination for president make their intentions explicit in the hectic atmosphere of a big-city press conference, where they are subjected to questions from all the media. A few modest headlines and ninety seconds on the evening news (all three networks) usually follow.

Senator Muskie, however, mindful of the success of his earlier appearance, chose to repeat the circumstances, facing the television cameras alone, in a homey setting, in prime time. It proved to be a mistake, the first of many in a long campaign, growing from assumptions which, if they weren't completely false, were tentative and premature. The most dangerous of these was that anyone, amateur or professional, clearly understood the political uses of broadcasting.

The congressional elections of 1970 had left most politicians confused.

There was no clear way to read the score. If Muskie's election-eve, full-color TV pitch for the Democrats was considered a triumph in comparison with President Nixon's ill-tempered, black-and-white scolding, it obviously wasn't a fact that one could base subsequent performance upon. The flatness of Muskie's reprise, reconstructing as closely as possible his original success, was proof of that.

And the other facts were just as difficult to apply. According to Roger Ailes, Nixon's television adviser in 1968:

> In the thirty-five gubernatorial races of 1970, nineteen winners did indeed outspend their opponents on television and radio, but sixteen men who also outspent the opposition on the broadcasting media lost. In winning in New York, Nelson Rockefeller spent more than three times the amount spent on broadcasting by Arthur Goldberg. In Arkansas, Winthrop Rockefeller outspent Dale Bumpers three to one on broadcasting—and lost, collecting only one-third of the total vote.

Such scores could obviously be better ascribed to chance than to any magic formula of cash, television time, and know-how.

Television blitzes seemed to work much better in primaries (where building recognition was an important factor) than in general elections (where issues and experience were of more consequence). This deduction, however, was of little comfort to such big spenders as Howard Metzenbaum of Ohio and Richard Ottinger of New York, who, between them, spent hundreds of thousands of dollars on television spots in 1970. Both won the primaries and lost the election. Norton Simon in California spent $1,900,000 to raise his recognition factor among the state's voters from 0 percent to 55 percent, but was swamped by George Murphy in the primaries.

Yet for all its unpredictability, the conviction persisted that television was of prime importance. As Ailes and most of his 150 fellow members of the American Association of Political Consultants contended, no candidate would ever again be elected to office without the medium's help.

Indeed, in January 1972 Congress finally passed legislation based on that premise, the Federal Election Campaign Act. Although it included all media in its strictures, limiting expenditures to ten cents per voter per election, the act revealed its true purpose by making sure that only six of the ten cents would be spent on radio and TV. The act, put into effect April 7, also put ceilings on a candidate's own contributions and broadcasters' charges, and it made elaborate provisions for reporting expenditures and identifying contributors.

The new law was intended to replace the Corrupt Practices Act of 1925, which had been notable for its nonenforcement during nearly half a century. Supporters of the new law were determined that it be promptly enforced, and by October 1972 a total of 285 violations had been cited by John Gardner's Common Cause, which had appointed itself monitor. Not everyone was so enthusiastically behind the act. In other quarters it was called "unconstitutional," "useless," and "unworkable," and dismissed as "The Incumbents' Protection Act."

Ad executive Allan D. Gardner, writing in *The Wall Street Journal,* said:

> In placing limitations on primary spending, Congress has deliberately made access to political office much more difficult. The legislation not only favors incumbents, but it shores up the waning power of the political clubhouse. Insurgent candidates often relied on advertising because they didn't have an army of bell-ringers from the patronage rolls. Now renegades will pose less of a threat to the regular party organization.

Gardner quoted Howard R. Penniman, professor of government at Georgetown University and author of a book-length study, *Campaign Finances:*

> The setting of uniform limits on campaign expenditures for incumbents and challengers fails to take into account the subsidization of the incumbent (the franking privilege, free phone calls, etc.) and the more severe the limit, the greater the handicap placed on the challenger. Money for campaigning does not ensure a real contest, but tight limitations on funds may distort the democratic process by reducing the opportunity for a serious challenge of the entrenched officeholder.

Journalist Michael Gartner attempted to give both sides:

> It is a widely praised law designed to prevent people from buying elections, to put the spotlight on "fat cats" and to ensure that in future a man needn't be rich to run for office.
>
> It is also a law that is dubious both logically and legally, a law that will work to keep in office the people who wrote it and to penalize the very people it alleges to protect.

As for the broadcasters themselves, of those responding to this year's Survey, only a handful singled out the political spending act as a special headache, but those who did were emphatic in expressing their frustration. Typical was the news director of KSL, Salt Lake City, who wrote: "The new political spending bills are written in Sanskrit! Not even the politicians who drafted the bills understand them."

In April and May alone, the FCC got four hundred calls from both candidates and broadcasters asking for interpretations. Nor was the matter considered solved by the nation's legislators. Among several bills introduced in Congress to attempt to correct remaining inequities in the use of television was one to provide federal money to pay for prime-time speeches by the presidential candidates, sponsored by Representative Thomas P. O'Neill, in May 1972, and a similar bill proposed by Representative Robert O. Tiernan a month later. Other proposals suggested limiting campaigns to the five weeks before elections, in order to save television time and money, and forcing all television stations to carry political speeches simultaneously, so that viewers would have no choice but to watch when they were on.

Again, an attempt to repeal Section 315 of the Communications Act, the provision which requires broadcasters to give equal time to all political candidates, regardless of their party, passed the Senate and stopped in the House, ostensibly because of President Nixon's stipulation that the repeal apply not only to the presidential races but to statewide and other national elective offices as well. Generous guarantees of prime time to presidential candidates in case of repeal were offered by at least two of the networks, but they seemed only to stiffen the resolve of congressmen and the Administration.

Because of the campaigns, the FCC made a special pronouncement in June concerning the Fairness Doctrine and its application to politics. It did little to clarify matters.

> We believe that increasingly detailed commission regulation militates against robust, wide-open debate. The genius of the Fairness Doctrine has been precisely the leeway and discretion it affords the licensee to discharge his obligation to contribute to an informed electorate.

Confusion about the Fairness Doctrine, equal time, and Section 315 still rated high on the list of inconveniences for both broadcasters and candidates mentioned in reports to the Survey this year. Erroneous application of the regulations was frequent. Complaints to the FCC during the campaign months from March to September reached an all-time high of more than 3,000—an increase of 50 percent over the entire 1968 political year.

There were recommendations for change from other quarters. Again the remarks of Roger Ailes, the political TV consultant who had helped put his client in the White House, were of particular significance:

> I firmly believe that the number of commercials shown on TV during a campaign should be limited and, in fact, would favor in any new bill a provision requiring that at least 35 percent of broadcast monies available to a candidate be spent for the purchase of *program* time as distinguished from commercial time. Further, I would suggest that stations make several hours of prime-time television available in statewide elections to major party candidates, free of charge. After all, these are the men we must rely on to govern this nation—men of vision who can lead and men of conscience who can act. We have a much better chance of finding those men within the intimate environment of live TV than we ever did by watching a candidate wave from the back of a train . . . .
>
> There is no doubt that money is needed to get elected today. However, it is important to keep the outcry against campaign spending in perspective. It is true, according to FCC reports, that all candidates and parties spent about $89,000,000 on radio and television in 1968. (This figure includes both time-buying and production expenses.)
>
> So $89,000,000 was spent to help us decide for whom to vote and to tell us something about each of the candidates and issues. However, last year Proctor & Gamble, one of hundreds of television advertisers, spent $179,276,100 on TV advertising alone.

The logic, although not perfect, was persuasive. Not all advertisers or broadcasters, however, were as philosophical as Mr. Ailes. For seventeen years Ward Quaal, head of WGN Continental Broadcasting Company, had banned all political spots less than five minutes long from his three television and two radio stations. In September 1971 John O'Toole, president of Foote, Cone & Belding, announced his support of the WGN policy and urged all other agencies and stations to follow suit. FCC commissioner Nicholas Johnson seconded the move, and John Gardner of Common Cause was enthusiastic enough to ask the National Association of Broadcasters to incorporate a five-minute-minimum rule in their code. Gardner was voted down.

Among those roused by the debate was Edward Ney, the president of Young & Rubicam, the nation's second largest advertising agency. Ney said:

> We feel so strongly that the whole system is wrong that on October 6 [1971] we announced to our employees that we would not accept any political candidates in the United States in 1972. It is a perversion of our skills to attempt to use the techniques of a 30-second or 60-second commercial to discuss an issue or the character of a candidate for high political office. We believe that such advertising should not be allowed on the air.

Mr. Ney's high-mindedness was not allowed to go without comment. Charles Guggenheim, television adviser to Robert Kennedy and to George McGovern, replied:

> Go back and look at Ney's list of clients. He's selling gas that pollutes, cars that are unsafe, cereals without nutrients or calories. He's so conditioned to being fraudulent that he thinks if you take a candidate you have to say something fraudulent, so the best way to handle what you believe in is to stay away from it.
>
> People who talk about 5 minutes instead of 60 seconds have missed the target. They've gotten on the wrong bandwagon. They should be concerned with the debasement of the political process on TV. By taking off the 30-second and 60-second spot perhaps they solve one problem; but they are creating a more serious one. That is frequency. You can't buy enough five minutes on the local stations. They just don't have it. That means the incumbent has an even greater advantage. Guarantee the challenger frequency, and I withdraw my objection, but how do you do it? Besides, these short spots can be additional pieces of information. They don't have to and shouldn't tell the whole story.

Carrying the argument one stage further, Dr. Frank Stanton, vice-chairman of CBS, said in the Edward L. Bernays lecture at Boston University:

> Prime time on television is between 7:30 and 11 p.m., a time span of three and a half hours per night or 1,470 minutes per week. If the 950 candidates for office in New England in 1968 were given open access to every bit of this time from September to election day, wiping out any kind of prime-time programming except electioneering,

depriving the audience of all prime-time entertainment or news or specials, not one candidate would have more than one and one half minutes per week.

We would have destroyed the entire prime-time schedule, driven the audience to distraction and accomplished nothing more than the creation of a modern tower of Babel . . . that is why every form of journalism rather than merely reporting in their entirety the utterances of candidates is called upon to summarize, to select, to sample.

Challenging WGN's spot ban in Chicago, Robert Lemon, vice-president and general manager of NBC's owned-and-operated WMAQ-TV, told the Chicago Rotary:

I do not want the power to decide for the viewers of my station that they are not intelligent enough to make up their own minds about a 30-second political announcement. If a candidate wants to associate himself with a shallow, offensive advertising campaign, if he wants to risk alienating that segment of the voters who find his campaign repulsive, then I say let the candidate have the freedom to do this, and let him reap the consequences.

In the end, a handful of radio and television stations, including WDIO, Duluth; * WBAL, Baltimore; and KOLO, Reno, followed the lead of WGN Continental Broadcasting Company. No political candidates, not even the most idealistic, apparently, were ready to give up the much-maligned spots. However, there were indications that the use of such spots by candidates, in proportion to the total time spent on television appearances, had declined. The reasons were pragmatic.

The Ticket-Splitter, a study by Walter DeVries and V. Lance Tarrance, begun on a Ford Foundation grant and done with the encouragement of, among others, the Republican National Committee, analyzed the behavior of undecided Michigan voters and ticket-splitters in the 1970 election. It found that although appearances by candidates on newscasts, specials, documentaries, and other public affairs programming rated number one in influencing voters to switch party allegiance, TV and radio commercials of any sort—short, medium-length, or long—rated twenty-fourth on the list, far below newspapers, editorials, magazine stories, and talks with family, friends, and neighbors.

---

* Before the campaign had run its course, WDIO reversed its policy under pressure from candidates who threatened the station with a lawsuit or FCC action if they did not sell time in less than five-minute blocks.

**Relative Importance of Factors That Influenced the Voting
Decisions of Ticket-Splitters in Michigan (May 1970) ***

Very Important	Important	Not Important
Television newscasts	Radio talk shows	† Magazine adver-
Television documen-	The Democratic Party	tisements
taries and specials	Radio editorials	Television enter-
Newspaper stories	Talks with work asso-	tainers
Newspaper editorials	ciates	† Billboards
Television educational	Magazine editorials	† Telephone cam-
programs	† Talks with political	paign messages
Television editorials	party workers	Movies
Television talk shows	The Republican Party	Stage plays
Talks with family	Magazine stories	Phonograph records
Radio educational	Talks with neighbors	
programs	† Newspaper adver-	
Radio newscasts	tisements	
† Contacts with candi-	† Political brochures	
dates	† Television advertise-	
Talks with friends	—ments	
	Books	
	Membership in profes-	
	sional or business	
	organizations	
	† Political mailings	
	Membership in reli-	
	gious organizations	

* Source: **The Ticket-Splitter: A New Force in American Politics** by
Walter DeVries and V. Lance Tarrance (Grand Rapids, Michigan: William B. Eerdmans Publishing Co., 1972).
    † Factors which can be influenced or controlled by the candidate.

DeVries and Tarrance concluded: "Any major campaign
communications effort directed toward the ticket-splitter must
go through media that cannot be completely controlled (i.e.,
purchased) by the candidates."

The impact of this and similar evidence was not felt by the
Republicans alone. As never before, both parties badgered networks and local stations to get their candidates or their surrogates on the air. Of all the special headaches listed by news directors responding to the Survey, this onslaught was cited most
frequently:

> Candidates seem more demanding of time, and have
> indicated a vested right to use the airwaves to contact the
> public. There was a great deal of critical evaluation of
> television's performance by politicians following the '68
> convention. Most of the politicians do not understand the

technical limitations of TV news, and the difficulty that surrounds the handling of visual material. The sophistication of TV journalism has far outstripped the current state of technology, and the demands placed upon the small and medium market stations are insurmountable.—*Mississippi educational TV network*

Politicians who demand some sort of "special coverage" of a non-event are still with us. And they frequently refer to the Fairness Doctrine, which I quickly point out does not apply to newscasts.—*WDIO-TV, Duluth*

We very patiently remind the complaining candidate that he must judge us over the spread of the campaign in that our overall coverage will be balanced, but one news broadcast can't be used as a yardstick of overall coverage.— *WJZ-TV, Baltimore*

The candidates' desire to receive as much air time as possible (frequent news conferences which say nothing, overwhelming amount of news releases) has forced newsmen to be judicious in their coverage of political candidates.—*KDKA, Pittsburgh*

Other stations pointed to the increase of public relations people clamoring for air time, which has grown out of all proportion to the number of candidates or offices, and to the fact that in the presidential primaries every candidate had a national, state, and local media representative, each of whom had to be dealt with in sequence. Some unique problems were reported:

An interesting development this year was the broadcast in August of a documentary on Congressman Ron Dellums, commissioned by PBS more than a year earlier. Just before the broadcast, Mr. Dellums was anxious to have the program canceled because he felt he had not been able to make his own selection of what he would say on the film. After the broadcast, the Dellums staff changed its mind and is now trying to acquire the film from us for use in the Congressman's campaign. Meanwhile, his Republican opponent is very unhappy with KQED, PBS, and CPB because, though he has been offered equal time, we cannot and are not required to offer a $30,000 documentary.—*KQED-TV, San Francisco*

The effects of this bombardment of broadcasters by candidates were not all negative. If the realization of the importance of spontaneous coverage led to a plethora of demands for free time, it also tended to make politicians, at least the challengers, more cooperative. Candidates made a habit of furnishing audio and video tapes to stations as never before. Round-the-clock beeper services for radio interviews and immediate media availability of candidates were not uncommon. Special cassettes of news conferences missed were rushed to TV and radio stations. More than one small-city news director reported his wonder and gratification at the friendliness of presidential candidates and their representatives in town for the state primary.

The incumbents and avowed front-runners were, of course, as cagey as ever unless stung or frightened into cooperation. Some appeared only after long negotiations and at virtually the last minute. Debates seemed particularly intimidating to them.

> The new breed of political advisor and image maker now so popular seems to have a deathly fear of having his man face his opponent. Candidates thus far this year have attempted to avoid uncontrolled news conferences and interviews—and debates have been impossible to schedule.—*WFMY-TV, Greensboro, N.C.*

If this manipulating and jockeying for position went on at the local level across the country, it was reflected even more dramatically in the race for the presidency, which began in earnest with the New Hampshire primary in March.

Four months before the official opening gun, Senator Fred Harris of Oklahoma announced he could not afford to persist in a contest which had already cost him more than $250,000 and promised to require at least a $50,000 monthly investment as long as he continued in the race. New Hampshire inflicted other wounds—some fatal. Although there were only two television stations of any consequence in the entire state, Senator Muskie arrived with his full video team, shot 100 minutes of color tape during his first day of campaigning, and had it edited and put on in a half hour of prime time the same evening, in the hope that citizens would accept it as they might an instant documentary done by a local news team.

The approach was unquestionably original, but there was no accurate way to measure its effectiveness. It was easier to estimate the effect of a later episode recorded by network cameras, in which Muskie wept over the mistreatment of his wife in the editorial columns of the *Manchester Union Leader*. This brief, candid shot was credited by some with beginning the backward slide of the Democrats' front-runner.

Muskie won New Hampshire, but by too small a margin, or so the pundits decided, in the peculiar mathematics of primaries.

Contributing to the negative impact of the New Hampshire experience was Muskie's refusal of, and then capitulation to, George McGovern's demand for a face-to-face encounter. Neither man won the five-man debate * which was finally arranged, but it increased McGovern's exposure and Muskie's reputation for indecision. Nor did the final score in New Hampshire do anything to clarify how best to spend one's money to get votes. Muskie, the odds-on favorite, was reported to have spent about $65,000 in all media, and he got 47.8 percent of the vote, far below his expectations. McGovern spent approximately the same amount and got 37.6 percent of the vote, far above what had been anticipated. To further complicate matters, a committee for Representative Wilbur D. Mills spent $80,000 and got 4.1 percent of the vote, and Los Angeles mayor Sam Yorty paid $15,000 to get 6.1 percent.

The Florida primary, with the full field of candidates on the ballot,† was even more confusing for observers and discouraging for Muskie.

The trick in Florida was obviously to try to challenge Wallace, the acknowledged favorite. Some of the candidates had spent as much as three months and tens of thousands of dollars in attempting it. Senator Hubert Humphrey even took on some of Wallace's coloration. One of his Florida radio commercials went: "Humphrey will stop the flow of your tax dollars to lazy welfare chiselers. He will put your tax dollars to work here at home before giving handouts around the world."

Mayor John Lindsay, who got the most day-to-day free coverage in local newscasts, also spent a lot of money on commercials, enlisting, among others, Carroll O'Connor, television's Archie Bunker, for a cigar-chomping endorsement. Senator Henry Jackson, the top spender, aired no fewer than three different half-hour paid-for telecasts.

With fourteen candidates to keep track of, stations gave up trying to maintain balance between them. Debates were obviously impossible, roundups of candidates even harder. The announcer of an ill-fated edition of WCKT-TV, Miami's "Florida

---

* The real winner of an otherwise bland encounter might well have been thirty-two-year-old Edward Dole of Connecticut, who wangled his way on the air and then created a small sensation by holding up by the tail what appeared to be a dead rat.

† Although they all did not actively campaign, a total of 14 candidates were on the Florida presidential primary ballot: 11 Democrats and 3 Republicans. *Democrats:* Shirley Chisholm, Vance Hartke, Hubert Humphrey, Henry Jackson, John Lindsay, Eugene McCarthy, George McGovern, Wilbur Mills, Edmund Muskie, Sam Yorty, and George Wallace. *Republicans:* John Ashbrook, Paul McCloskey, and Richard Nixon.

Forum" aired on March 12 opened the program with the following explanation:

> Before we begin, I must point out that all eleven candidates in the Florida primary have repeatedly been invited to appear tonight. All have been Forum guests on prior occasions. Senator Vance Hartke withdrew last week when he quit the Florida Campaign. Congressman Wilbur Mills has not campaigned in Florida and Governor George Wallace claimed other commitments. Former Senator Eugene McCarthy decided to campaign in Illinois. Senator Ed Muskie has not accepted nor officially declined to appear. Senator Hubert Humphrey said he would—but then decided he had other commitments. Congresswoman Shirley Chisholm, who confirmed her appearance on three separate occasions today, said she has laryngitis. Mayor Sam Yorty, who also confirmed, said a member of his staff was ill and then said he didn't think there would be enough time in which to give meaningful answers. And Senator Henry Jackson, who withdrew this morning following confirmation of appearance last Wednesday, was upset because he said representative candidates were not on the program. Several hours later his office said he was trying to rearrange his schedule to appear. Within the hour he decided against it.

The program went on with John Lindsay and George McGovern sharing the hour.

WTVJ-TV in Miami ran out of prime-time spots for advertising more than two weeks before election day, and several dozen nonpolitical commercials were eventually bumped to clear time for politicians.

When the Florida votes were counted, they added up to another disaster for Muskie (who spent $150,000 and earned only 9 percent of the vote) and others as well. John Lindsay, without question the most conspicuous candidate, had David Garth, one of the country's most prestigious TV consultants, to advise him. Lindsay got more free air time than anyone else, spent $170,-000, and racked up only 7 percent of the vote. Henry Jackson, who spent the most ($180,000), got 13 percent, and Shirley Chisholm, without any formal organization and with a campaign fund of less than $20,000, got 4 percent, running seventh in a field of eleven. The big winners were Wallace and Humphrey, who spent $60,000 apiece, barely 20 percent of the total broadcast expenditure by Democrats, and between them got 60 percent of the vote: 42 percent to Wallace and 18 percent to

Humphrey. McGovern spent an estimated $28,000 on radio and TV and got 6 percent of the vote.

The presidential primaries, more numerous than ever before and more extensively covered by the three networks and public TV's National Public Affairs Center for Television, seemed to bring out the best or the worst in newsmen.

In Florida it was Mayor Lindsay scuba diving versus stations like WTVJ and WCKT conscientiously making a day-to-day pursuit of a platoon of hard-to-pin-down candidates and issues.

In Wisconsin, according to the DuPont correspondent, two big-time reporters, NBC's David Brinkley and CBS' Ike Pappas, provided questionable examples:

> Brinkley . . . covered the 1972 Wisconsin primary from a desk in a corner of the NBC road-show newsroom in Milwaukee's Pfister Hotel . . . . Given that NBC's commentator saw no more of Wisconsin than about 12 hours of the inside of a hotel, it is not clear why the expense of flying Brinkley around at all. Perhaps the following sheds some light: Brinkley spent the early afternoon writing his "Journal" segment for the NBC Nightly News. About 3 p.m. he and a producer went out to record the segment in a park on the city's Lake Michigan shoreline. They returned without the piece recorded because of heavy snow. Instead, they taped Brinkley's analysis in the hotel. It appears that Brinkley's interpretation of the election was thought by NBC to project greater credibility if a location backdrop established his presence on the scene.
>
> Pappas . . . was in the state the week before the primary. He wanted to do a story on the alleged taxpayer's revolt, property taxes in particular. Wednesday before the primary Pappas phoned the McGovern press headquarters in Milwaukee. He explained that he had been looking for an angry property taxpayer but could not find one. Did the McGovern organization know of any?
>
> Some background is necessary here: In February the McGovern press agents had staged one of the more blatant stunts of the Wisconsin campaign. McGovern had gone to the home of one Richard Wysocki, a Milwaukee South Side "white ethnic" blue-collar worker. In Wysocki's 12 by 15 living room the candidate talked with the citizen while about 27 newsmen plus lights, cameras, cables and the rest obliged coverage. (Later Lindsay topped that by actually sleeping overnight on the living room couch of another white worker in the area. His limousine had dropped off the candidate and his pajamas.)
>
> So when the CBS newsman phoned McGovern press in

search of a citizen the hold button was pushed and a quick conference ensued. Of course they thought of Wysocki. Someone of higher rank on McGovern's staff came in and said Wysocki had been "used" too much already. Wasn't there another white ethnic South Sider for McGovern? With Pappas still on the line, a call was placed to the Milwaukee Tenants' Union. Someone there suggested one Richard Wysocki. In the end two names were given to the reporter, Wysocki and that of a widow. The reporter said he could not use her because widows were not "typical."

A few days later on the CBS Evening News there was Mr. Wysocki on his job with heavy machinery.*

Some local newsmen got higher marks, particularly the Milwaukee public TV station, WMVS. The DuPont correspondent reported: "In sharp contrast to the questions put to candidates by reporters from the commercial television stations, the interviews were investigative, informed, aggressive, unpredictable and useful."

The high point of the local coverage was reached, however, when a reporter from a station in Green Bay interviewed George McGovern:

REPORTER: Have you ever sinned?
McGOVERN: Well, uh, of course.
REPORTER: Could you name a few of your important sins for us?

McGovern cited his voting on right-to-work, Vietnam, and some other past indiscretions as his sins. It was, according to the DuPont correspondent, a good story.

Wisconsin, as it developed, became the turning point for George McGovern. For an investment of $68,000 on television, the senator from South Dakota won 30 percent of the vote. Muskie spent $75,000 to get 10 percent. The big spender again was Henry Jackson, who eked out 8 percent of the vote after spending $110,000 for television. Dollar for vote, the winner again was Hubert Humphrey, with 21 percent for $22,000. Wisconsin also saw John Lindsay run out of money and withdraw from the race.

The next cluster of important primaries—Pennsylvania, Massachusetts, and Ohio—only confirmed that Hubert Humphrey and George McGovern were drawing into the lead, with

---

* Pappas later explained that he had "tried out" several angry taxpayers suggested by nonpolitical organizations, but he decided that Wysocki, despite his previous appearances, was the most representative.

George Wallace running a close third. As for the part played by broadcasting, that remained as inscrutable as ever.

In Pennsylvania broadcast budgets were the lowest of the major campaigns so far, with the largest portion going into radio. No one had the advantage in terms of media expenses, and Humphrey took the vote handily.

In Massachusetts, where the primary was held the same day as in Pennsylvania, Muskie, with only $35,000, mounted a totally new and inexpensive TV pitch, the fourth so far of the campaign; McGovern, anxious to win the state, spent three times that much; and Wilbur Mills, still in the running, was the biggest spender of all. McGovern, as predicted, won by a big margin. George Wallace with a minuscule budget and little effort ran second in Pennsylvania and third in Massachusetts.

After his double defeat Senator Muskie, who had been considering withdrawing from active campaigning since the Florida fiasco, finally did so, followed shortly by Senator Jackson, whose money had run out.

In a last-minute TV and radio blitz in eight Ohio markets (two-thirds of $125,000 in television; one-third in radio), McGovern managed to put himself within a few thousand votes of Humphrey, considered a shoo-in, who had spent less than $18,-000 in his broadcast campaign.

In a new set of commercials, designed by Charles Guggenheim, McGovern tacticians, according to *Broadcasting* magazine, employed the "Ottinger Rule," * which states: ". . . there can only be a minor charisma gap between the candidate's broadcast commercials and his live appearances, or else voters will reject not only the ad but the candidate."

Two days after Ohio, George Wallace won his second Democratic presidential primary in Tennessee.

Before he could confirm his strength in the next major primary coming up in Michigan, Wallace was shot in a Maryland shopping center. Despite the fact that he was in critical condition when the election took place, Wallace won with 50 percent of the vote in Michigan. However, his injuries put him out of the running.

The California primary at the beginning of June was considered crucial, as it had been four years before when Robert Kennedy had won it and been murdered on the same night.

---

* The "rule" bears the name of former Representative Richard L. Ottinger, who lost his bid in the New York senatorial race when his ads proved more articulate than his live appearances.

Whoever came out on top would take, by prior arrangement, all 271 of the delegates to the national convention the following month. McGovern chose to sprint. He outspent Humphrey to the point where the former vice-president accused him of exceeding not only the five cents per voter limit that the Democratic candidates had voluntarily accepted early in the campaign, but the legal six cents per voter limit designated in the campaign spending act. Humphrey's charge was not sustained.

McGovern's blitz was not only in paid time (Guggenheim had made a whole new set of television commercials—the fifth of the campaign) but in free-of-charge news coverage. By outfitting a Volkswagen Microbus with compact TV taping equipment and dispatching daily ninety-second newsclips about his activities plus daily radio feeds, McGovern managed to get much more than his share of local station attention.* The tapes dispatched via four small planes no later than 4:30 each afternoon were ticketed for thirty-five television stations from Eureka in the north to El Centro in the south. McGovern staffers estimated that they were used by 80 percent of the recipients on a day-to-day basis.

Again Humphrey complained to Washington, this time claiming the stations were running the clips without crediting their source, thus violating an FCC ruling that films or tape supplied by any candidate to a station news department must be so identified on the air—although this is not required of printed news handouts or advances on speeches.

California, like Florida, saw invitations for debates, this time extended by the national networks. Both leading candidates were asked to appear jointly on the three Sunday news-panel shows: "Meet the Press," † "Face the Nation," and "Issues and Answers." This time neither candidate demurred. Before all three programs were aired, however, Representative Shirley Chisholm—still in the race—demanded equal time, claiming that the panel shows, by altering their format to accommodate Humphrey and McGovern, had lost their exemption from the equal-time rule. She was joined in her complaints by Mayor Sam Yorty.

---

* *The New York Times* took a four-day survey of the state's four largest media markets covering 85 percent of California's television audience and found that McGovern had 109 minutes of coverage to Humphrey's 70, which the *Times* attributed to the fact that "Senator McGovern, a very distant dark horse to most campaign analysts only three months ago had made his startling rise to front-runner the most newsworthy political story of 1972."

† In this instance, aired on a Tuesday evening in prime time.

The FCC turned down Mrs. Chisholm's request, but the U.S. Court of Appeals reversed the commission's ruling, granting her "interim relief," which amounted to a half hour on CBS and inclusion in the ABC Sunday program. (NBC had already given her equivalent time on its "Today" show.)

CBS vice-chairman Frank Stanton was heard from:

> This whole hurried preposterous series of events underscores the need for wiping Section 315 off the books once and for all. The fact that the FCC, which administers the Communications Act, unanimously held that the "Face the Nation" Humphrey-McGovern joint appearance was exempt from Section 315, while a few hours later the Court of Appeals unanimously held precisely the opposite, demmonstrates the uncertainties under which the broadcaster must live in this vital area of providing political information to the American voter. This ridiculous confusion and uncertainty will force the broadcasters to limit their efforts to inform the people.
>
> Worse yet, the Court of Appeals decision contracts rather than expands the political opportunities of the candidates. The American political process and the people's right to know are the victims of the vagaries of Section 315.

Nonetheless, Mrs. Chisholm took her two half hours.*

The election which followed gave McGovern a 5 percent victory margin over Humphrey. The fact that his lead was one-fourth the 20 percent projected by some polls was ascribed to McGovern's poor performance during the debates.

The California election had other dramatic facets, including some $1,500,000 spent in the media to defeat an environmental proposition on the ballot which (according to its well-heeled opponents) would have halted all transportation, allowed malaria to rage, and killed the economy.

The anti-proposition ads, which outnumbered political spots for any single candidate by a wide margin according to the DuPont correspondent, hit "a new low of bad taste, exaggerating to the extent of the famous 1964 Goldwater ads with the little girl and the A bomb."

Additional excitement resulted from a state law which prevented any election returns from being counted or announced on the air before all polls closed. A snafu in San Francisco polling booths put this time off until 11:00 P.M., which left

---

* Although he was not included in the Court's ruling, Mayor Yorty got his share of time on ABC's "Issues and Answers" and then withdrew from the race.

radio and TV reporters with a whole evening to fill and very little that they could legally say.

In 1972, overall broadcast coverage of the campaigns, including the twenty-three presidential primaries, reached an all-time high. Of the local stations reporting to the Survey, 59 percent stated that they had increased their political coverage this year. Only 2 percent had fallen back, and the remaining 39 percent were staffing and budgeting political news at approximately the same level as in 1968. Again, the results were mixed.

In Louisiana, where there was no presidential primary but where other important political events took place, the DuPont correspondent reported:

> The most reprehensible feature of the past year in local broadcasting was the poor coverage of the 1971–72 campaign for Louisiana governor. It had all the elements of a great story. The incumbent governor had served two terms and could not succeed himself; a power vacuum was there. About a dozen men entered the Democratic primary, six of them powerful politicians with significant constituencies. The state had gone through the turbulent 60's, changes in race relations, labor strife, allegations of Mafia influence on state government, more people living in urban areas. Change itself was an issue.
>
> What did the local stations do? Practically nothing.
>
> Through two Democratic primaries and a general election, only one station produced a prime-time special . . . . Coverage dealt mainly with personality profiles, films of handshaking and some snippets of speeches. The approach was generally who was ahead, not who was talking about what, who was appealing to what voters, who was getting money from whom. No analysis, no background, no insight, no in-depth coverage . . . . All that I'm saying is that if a citizen had to depend on the local broadcast media to get his information about these important state offices leading up to his having to choose in a voting booth, he may well not have been prepared to make a sensible choice.
>
> It was an important and exciting and in some ways historic race, which held the interest of the people of the state for several months. Stations would have been well justified and, I suspect, rewarded for spending the time and manpower to do more than they did.

On the other hand, outstanding coverage of local primaries was reported by KERA, the public TV station in Dallas, which between April 3 and May 6 provided fourteen evenings of prime-time television featuring more than two hundred Democratic and Republican candidates running for major local and state offices. All legislative candidates from the Dallas–Fort Worth area and all candidates for statewide offices were invited, and they appeared with their opponents before a panel of journalists. A three-hour telecast on April 26, which brought Democratic and Republican gubernatorial candidates together for the first and only time, was carried throughout the state.*

The University of North Carolina Educational Television did a special "Candidates '72" series in which it presented twenty-six out of twenty-seven candidates for U.S. senator and for governor and lieutenant-governor in individual full-hour, prime-time shows. Half of each show was devoted to a statement by the candidate (no film), and in the following half hour he was interviewed by a panel of professional reporters.

WFMY-TV, Greensboro, North Carolina—a commercial station—preempted three hours of prime time in the ten days before the primaries, during which four candidates for governor were interviewed for thirty minutes, as well as two candidates for the Democratic nomination for the Senate (the Republican nominee had already been selected).

Innovations in coverage were reported: among them, KTEN, Oklahoma City's coupling of news-film cuts of the candidates to provide comparison on issues. Some others:

> We are broadcasting more speeches than in 1968 . . . .
> It reflects my belief that a "live" speech carries more impact—in unedited form—than many "spots" on newscasts. We are averaging seven speeches a month, running in nighttime or midday slots. Listener feedback, critics' comment, and the ratings for the time periods—all are favorable.—*WBBM, Chicago*

> Two candidates for a sensitive Congressional seat were presented by the station in a format where they were confronted by questions from their constituents filmed on location by the station and presented without prior screening to the candidates for their live response. The effect was to create an atmosphere of face-to-face encounter which eliminated the possibility of distortion.—*WBZ-TV, Boston*

> Regular use of new format called "The Election Game." Candidates are given unpreviewed questions which they must answer in an extremely short time. The "game" style setting allows each candidate to respond, to the best of

---

* See list of DuPont-Columbia Awards on page 159.

his ability, to as many as a dozen questions in a half-hour. The admittedly gimmicky format catches a new political audience and allows candidates a chance for "humanization."—*WJCT-TV,* Jacksonville, Fla.

As for the candidates, they had learned, according to one DuPont correspondent, that

> . . . in campaigning it was wise to hit as many media markets as possible—up to three in a day. The most important event, and the one it was imperative to make visual, was likely to occur in late morning and could get you not only on the local evening news show but on the network news as well. Other events up to late afternoon could get you on the late evening news, and a big evening event could hope for exposure on the following morning news when the whole process began again.

The last primary of the year and quarter was held June 20 in New York, with McGovern winning the overwhelming majority of that state's 278 delegates. On July 9, the Democrats temporarily bound up their wounds and resolved their differences long enough to put television to brotherly use in an 18½-hour telethon on ABC, paid for by John Brown, president of Kentucky Fried Chicken, and starring, among others: Andy Williams, Carol Channing, Lorne Greene, Edie Adams, Lauren Bacall, Burt Bacharach, Groucho Marx, Shirley MacLaine, Tony Randall, and Milton Berle.

The purpose was to pay off as much as possible of the Democrats' $9 million debt still outstanding from the last presidential election. Pledges for an estimated $5 million came in. If somehow all the Democratic candidates had been able to forego the mixed blessings of television advertising, the money saved and given to the cause would no doubt have made the telethon unnecessary. However, the campaign was far from over.

On July 10, in Miami, the Democratic convention opened.

6 • The Broadcasting of Politics (II)

The Conventions

IN 1940, 50,000 New Yorkers watched an experimental broadcast of the Republicans convening in Philadelphia to nominate Wendell Willkie for president. Since then, the political conventions every four years have become the most important recurring event on television.

Not only has the marathon coverage of the conventions informed the public and put network news staffs to the test; over the years it has been credited with selling hundreds of thousands of television sets. Furthermore, tradition had it that the network whose news department won the convention audiences could expect to hold them for the next four years.

Nineteen sixty-eight changed all that. During the course of the four-day Democratic convention in Chicago, a sense that convention coverage and indeed television news had been dramatically altered, so far as the networks, the politicians, and a large sector of the American people were concerned, seemed to strike all three groups simultaneously. For the politicians, the liabilities as well as the benefits of massive wide-angle coverage were demonstrated as never before. As for the public, it realized that television had been rubbing its nose in things it would prefer to ignore, often making unpleasant comments while doing so. The networks felt the full force of this double resentment from the politicians and the public, and they became, in their turn, resentful and apprehensive.

Vice-President Agnew's remarks, the next year in Des Moines, did not create this alienation; they merely exploited existing feelings. In the succeeding three years these emotions had not subsided.

There were other reasons why the networks and the politicians approached the 1972 conventions in an uneasy and skeptical mood. After having first indicated that they would hold their meeting in San Diego, the Republicans selected Miami Beach. The decision was made in the shadow of allegations based on a memo sent by lobbyist Dita Beard to her bosses at the International Telephone and Telegraph Corporation. The memo, published by Jack Anderson and disowned by Ms. Beard, indicated that the choice of the California city had been connected in some unwholesome way with a sizable donation in cash and kind to the Republican campaign and a favorable settlement of a Justice Department suit against the huge conglomerate. At the time of the conventions the matter remained unresolved.

Nor were the city fathers of Miami—already chosen by the Democrats for their meeting in July—particularly happy at the prospect of a second national convention. Instead of rejoicing at the three more days of big spending and international attention the Republican meeting would inevitably bring to their city, those in charge of Miami's convention hall announced punitive charges for the storage of broadcasting equipment during the thirty-eight days between the two meetings, which canceled out much of the savings the networks realized by having the two conventions in the same spot.*

Miami took its share of precautions in anticipation of an influx of young dissidents which, some estimated, would reach a quarter-million. Manhole covers were sealed; a $24,000 chain-link fence was put around the convention hall and camouflaged with hibiscus bushes; 8,000 National Guard and federal troops were bivouacked in the vicinity; and a special Law Enforcement Assistance Agency grant of $573,737 was given the city— of which $354,000 was spent in sensitivity training for the police.

Among the network news teams, an atmosphere of anticlimax prevailed. Network earnings, if still substantial, were down from 1968. Total expenditures for convention coverage by the three networks in 1972 were estimated at $20 million, about half of that being earned back by commercial sponsorship, which sold out on all three networks before the conventions started.

News staffs, as well as budgets, for the 1972 coverage had been cut, by about 20 percent, at CBS and NBC.† Some of this was made up for by more compact operations, more effi-

---

* The city fathers' lack of enthusiasm was justified. Total hotel bookings for the summer of 1972 fell far below normal in the city, ostensibly because vacationers feared the violence and confusion which might accompany the political gatherings.

† The networks weren't the only ones to cut back. *The New York Times* had reduced its convention staff from sixty to thirty-five.

cient equipment, and the new rules initiated by both parties to streamline the conventions, which, among other things, limited each network to one camera on the floor and four floor reporters.

Although some individual budgets were cut, the total number of credentials issued to TV and radio groups and stations did not decline. And plans for individual coverage in many instances had never been so ambitious. Fifty-one percent of the stations reporting to the Survey mentioned special convention and campaign coverage aimed at their local audiences. Group W, as usual, had the largest number on hand after the networks. WTOP, Washington, D.C., and the other Post-Newsweek stations mounted one of the most elaborate operations, with five commentators—Hugh Sidey, Carl Rowan, James J. Kilpatrick, Martin Agronsky, and Peter Lisagor—on the scene. "This is Washington, D.C.," explained station vice-president Ray Hubbard, "and what may be national news for some stations is local news for us."

If Florida got a large dose of television politics in the coverage of its first presidential primary, the dose was even bigger for the national conventions. A report from WCKT-TV, Miami, showed the special effort made by one local broadcaster:

> Our convention coverage was thorough. . . . We elected to concentrate on our own delegation inside convention hall but felt it necessary to provide full coverage of all activities outside. This included demonstrations, riots and special candidate reports including the arrest of two men as suspects in the possible assassination attempt on George McGovern.
> We also staffed the streets 24 hours a day. Several of our camera crews were assaulted by both demonstrators and the police. One police assault was pursued, was strongly pursued by the news director until the City of Miami police made a written apology and volunteered to pay for our damaged photographic equipment as a result of an unprovoked assault.

KMPC, Los Angeles, put one of the Democratic presidential aspirants, Mayor Sam Yorty, on the air as a guest disk jockey for three hours every morning, live from Miami. California boss Jesse Unruh covered the convention for KABC-TV, Los Angeles, as did Dick Gregory for the Pacifica Radio stations.

Both parties had modified their convention procedures to facilitate television coverage. The Democrats eliminated floor demonstrations entirely, cutting back drastically on the number and the length of nominating speeches. Other Democratic schemes to accommodate, or to bend television to their own purposes, were devised with varying degrees of success. John Stewart, director of communications for the Democrats, told *TV Guide:*

> Obviously, television will still have to cut away from time to time to cover the news. But naturally we hope they will not seek out sensational things for their own sake, and that they will be balanced and fair. If a serious debate is underway on the floor, and a few dissidents take off their clothes to attract attention, we'd hope the networks will cover the serious debate. But if a major disturbance breaks out, the networks obviously can't pretend it isn't happening.

NBC News president Reuven Frank responded: "We will cut away from the podium as we see fit. We are there not to *carry* the convention: we are there to *report* the convention. You just have your meeting and I'll cover it."

It was, of course, nowhere near that simple. Before the conventions assembled, Julian Goodman, president of NBC, and Frank Stanton, vice-chairman of CBS, had made presentations to the platform committees of both parties, recommending planks concerning broadcasting. Their proposals included provisions relating to the First Amendment, counter-advertising, and public access. The Democrats responded with a section which read: "We are determined that never again shall government seek to censor the newspapers and television . . . . The Nixon Administration policy of intimidating the media and Administration efforts to use government power to block access to the media by dissenters must end, if free speech is to be preserved."

The National Association of Broadcasters added its representations, and was reported to have convinced the Republicans to come out against counter-advertising and frivolous license challenges.

At the last minute, however, the Republicans thought better of it. Ironically, the only mention of broadcasting in their document was a boast that they had increased funding for public television.

It was on a cautious and slightly defensive note, therefore, that on Monday, July 10, the television networks opened their coverage of what Max Frankel wrote in *The New York Times* was bound to be "one of the most dramatic evenings in the colorful history of American politics."

On television it was not quite that.

The men in the booths—John Chancellor and David Brinkley for NBC; Walter Cronkite, Eric Sevareid, and Theodore White for CBS; Howard K. Smith and Harry Reasoner for ABC— seemed, as usual, calm, and perhaps a bit supercilious. They had little reason to be. The first serious call on their expertise, the South Carolina credentials challenge, they flubbed.

Discussion of the challenge concerning the number of women in the South Carolina delegation began at 10:22. For a full hour the anchormen remained confused or convinced that a vote for the South Carolina dissidents was a vote for George Mc-Govern. The challenge was defeated, and the fact that the defeat was expertly engineered by the McGovern forces was first articulated by NBC's John Chancellor at 11:36. CBS' Walter Cronkite, who had dismissed the challenge as not overly important, finally admitted his mistake after 1:00.

Nor was it only the men in the booths who missed the point. The floor reporters pursued the story doggedly from delegation to delegation, racking up more than twenty-five interviews, some of them containing deliberate misrepresentations by the interviewees, before uncovering the truth.

The networks' slowness might have been more forgivable if it hadn't emerged later that Top Value TV, a commune composed of a few dozen young "video freaks" armed with two cheap portable video recorders, had attended a meeting of delegates where Willie Brown, cochairman of the California delegation, explained the South Carolina challenge strategy in lucid detail. The beginners had the whole story taped and in the can long before the old hands began their bumbling.*

Nor, after this first and major blooper, did the convention ever really come into focus. If the makeup of the convention had changed drastically, the makeup of the network news teams had not kept pace. Of the Democratic delegates in the hall, 80 percent had never been to a convention before, 40 percent were women, 20 percent blacks or other minorities, 21 percent under thirty.

Of the twelve network reporters assigned to the floor, only one—NBC's Cassie Mackin—was female. None were black and none were conspicuously youthful.† Ms. Mackin was a credit

* The sequence appeared in Top Value's lively sixty-minute convention "scrapbook" called "The World's Largest Television Studio," which was screened on cable TV later in the summer.

† The late Michele Clark, both black and under thirty, got on the convention floor as a small-hours replacement for the CBS first string on Tuesday night.

to her sex, challenging her male colleagues in both persistence and tact. But she and her associates seemed incapable of spotting and separating the new politics from the old and explaining their interaction. Some didn't try.

Furthermore, the Democrats' attempts at accommodating their meeting to the media failed miserably, contributing to the confusion. If the purpose of eliminating daytime meetings was to reach the bigger prime-time audience, they defeated that purpose by starting late and continuing their business so far into the night that the only major speech (after those of the keynoters) which caught the prime-time audience across the nation was George Wallace's—the one the convention managers might have preferred to skip. If the discussions of abortion and homosexuality, two of the most startling pieces of business ever to be seriously brought before a political convention, were relegated to the small hours of the morning, so were the acceptance speeches of the candidates.

The Democrats, as so often in the past, were their own worst enemies, but the networks ran a close second. Not that their disservice to the party was intentional. Time and time again, the floor reporters would unearth the beginnings of a story and tease it in multiple interviews, only to lose track of it in a new wave of interviews on an unrelated matter, which was left equally unresolved.

Lacking a large contingent of familiar political faces, the networks fell back on multiple interviews with candidate spokesmen like Frank Mankiewicz and Gary Hart (who were both past-masters at deflecting awkward questions) or developed their own cast of characters, which frequently were neither particularly representative nor illuminating.

A partial list of interviewees and the frequency with which they appeared on CBS and NBC, the two channels which undertook gavel-to-gavel coverage, is instructive. The fifteen people interviewed most frequently by CBS and NBC during the convention coverage, and the total number of interviews on both networks (outside regularly scheduled newscasts) were:

Frank Mankiewicz (McGovern staff)	11
Gary Hart (McGovern staff)	9
William Singer (Chicago alderman, anti–Mayor Richard Daley)	8
Frank King (Ohio labor leader)	7
Hall Timanus (Wallace supporter from Texas)	5
Dolph Briscoe (candidate for governor of Texas)	4
Rev. Robert Drinan (congressman from Massachusetts)	4
Senator Thomas Eagleton	4

Frances (Sissy) Farenthold (candidate for governor of Texas
   and vice-president)   4
Senator Hubert Humphrey   4
Shirley MacLaine (actress)   4
Lawrence O'Brien (chairman of the Democratic National
   Committee)   4
Pierre Salinger (McGovern staff)   4
Senator Adlai Stevenson III   4
Governor John C. West of South Carolina   4

NBC, whose floor interviews and reports averaged in the
neighborhood of 1.5 minutes per interviewee, logged almost
150 during the four days, which was approximately twice the
number aired by CBS. On the other hand, CBS' average interview or report from the floor lasted 3 minutes. NBC interviewed
more than thirty delegates whom CBS did not put on the air,
including some crucial figures such as Willie Brown, the California delegation cochairman; Jesse Jackson, the black leader;
and Jean Westwood, the future head of the Democratic National Committee. CBS pinned down fewer than five people who
were not also put on the air by NBC. They included Representative John Conyers, of the congressional Black Caucus, and
Senator Henry Jackson, whom CBS interviewed three times.

The floor was not the only place where the significant was
frequently ignored in favor of the inconsequential or inscrutable.
The booth men, cued by producers who were trying to placate
the floor people and satisfy the advertisers,* cut in and out of
happenings on the podium with a heavy hand. Except for a few
obvious party stars, the network score was not impressive in
spotting those on stage who might have something interesting
to say and getting them on the air while they were saying it.
Fannie Lou Hamer, the heroine of the Mississippi Challenge in
1968, and Allard Lowenstein, the man who was given credit
for the new look of the Democratic party, were both virtually
ignored by the networks when they seconded Frances (Sissy)
Farenthold's nomination for vice-president. Valerie Kushner,
the POW wife who seconded McGovern's nomination, had to
share her brief podium time with the candidate himself, whom
CBS and NBC both chose to visit in his hotel room while she
was on.

Most of union leader I. W. Abel's anti-McGovern seconding
speech for Senator Henry Jackson was passed over by NBC in
favor of interviews on the floor, and by CBS in favor of a long

---

* Actually, *GULF,* the sole national sponsor of NBC's coverage, did
not take as many commercial minutes as it was entitled to.

string of commercials, at the end of which Walter Cronkite cued the viewer in to Abel's last minute with the comment: "I. W. Abel is making one of the hardest speeches yet. Let's listen. I'll fill you in later."

Although their representation at the convention was at an all-time high, women delegates got short shrift on the floor as well as on the podium. Despite Ms. Mackin's active presence, CBS on the whole seemed friendlier to females than did NBC. Over a third of the CBS interviews were with women, while NBC talked to a woman one time in five.

One justifiable departure from the podium occurred early Wednesday evening, when CBS and NBC switched to the lobby of the Doral Hotel to cover the confrontation between George McGovern and a collection of hard-shelled dissidents. NBC's camera stayed tight on McGovern's face, coming away with one of the few human insights of the four days. However, it was a dramatic exception to the dozens of remote-live pickups, which consisted of a reporter on camera relating what had been going on in his vicinity before and what was likely to happen afterward. Whether it was at the campsite in Flamingo Park or in the lobby of the Fontainebleau Hotel, a human face or voice other than a reporter's was seldom seen or heard.

In one of these journalistic monologues, Jack Perkins of NBC chose to read selected portions of McGovern's acceptance speech four and a half hours before the candidate went on the air with it. Several viewers phoned in to object, leading to an on-air justification by John Chancellor of Perkins' questionable action. Chancellor himself was guilty of some lapses in judgment and taste, most notably his labeling of civil rights leader Bayard Rustin as "an uptrodden black" and his sign-off comment Wednesday morning, when he capped the ten-hour session by labeling George McGovern, the just-selected Democratic candidate, a "humble, self-effacing egomaniac."

This lapse was almost matched by the Democratic decision to follow up a prayer for the seriously ill former Senator Ernest Gruening by introducing the convention's principal sugar daddy, "Colonel Sanders" of Kentucky Fried Chicken.

Occasionally the politicians struck back. Most notable was an interchange between Garrick Utley and Rev. Robert Drinan, representative from Massachusetts, who dismissed the NBC floor man with the words: "My delegation is more important than NBC." Utley told his audience that Drinan did not "have time for us." Drinan, visibly annoyed, turned around and snapped: "No, I didn't say that. I said my delegation is more important than NBC."

Father Drinan's was obviously not the official opinion. Still, all efforts to accommodate the networks seemed doomed to frustration. McGovern's nomination came at midnight Wednesday night, and thanks to the delegates' insistence upon participating in the selection of the vice-presidential candidate, McGovern did not reach the television screen with his acceptance speech until nearly three o'clock in the morning on Friday.* All three networks had left the hall within thirty minutes of his final word.

Between them, they had spent 91½ hours in and about the premises. Whether the network coverage of the Democratic convention deserved all the air time it got was a matter for debate.

One of the harsher views came from columnist William V. Shannon, who wrote:

> . . . CBS and NBC pretend to give "gavel-to-gavel" coverage of each session. But, in fact, they put on a kind of journalism school demonstration of their own editing and reporting talent. It is as if they are trying to demonstrate how they can improve upon the reality of a convention by editing it, interpreting it, anticipating it, livening it up and distracting attention from it.
>
> On CBS the ordinary viewer trying to watch a political convention sees so much of the "anchorman" and his star reporters that the program might well be called "Walter Cronkite and His Friends." Likewise, the NBC coverage might better be known as "The David Brinkley Show."
>
> If the anchormen took a self-denying vow not to talk more than five minutes every two hours and if they had no reporters on the floor to conduct interviews, then the viewers could enjoy the game—excuse me, the convention —as it is actually played in all its sweet boring interludes, intricately knotted parliamentary tangles and lush wildly flowering speeches.

David Brinkley shot back:

> If we kept the camera on the rostrum continuously, never looking elsewhere for news, insights, sidebars, explanations and background, the television audience would hear a vast Niagara of speeches and partisan rhetoric. It would know who was nominated but not much else. If *The New York*

---

* Although his audience was measured in the thousands, rather than the millions, no network saw fit to rerun the speech in its entirety for a larger audience the following day.

Times reported a convention simply by printing the transcript of every speech, the bare figures on every vote and nothing more, it would be an inadequate job of journalism.

And we do see our job at conventions as journalism, not simply as coast-to-coast public address systems for the political parties. No doubt we could do that job far better, but if we took Mr. Shannon's advice, it would be done far worse, and in fact, not done at all.

Mike Dann, former vice-president in charge of programming at CBS and an informal adviser to the Democratic National Committee, said: "No political event has received more objective, detailed, and thoughtful coverage. It's been the shining hour of the American networks."

If not all the Democrats were as ecstatic as Dann, they had to admit that things were better than four years before. At least for a few weeks. Then the roof fell in—under the weight, in great part, of the media.

In late July the Knight newspapers uncovered the story of vice-presidential candidate Thomas Eagleton's hospitalization and shock treatment for mental illness. What followed was described variously as "hysteria," a "press riot," and "a mob scene out of Shakespeare." In a week Eagleton was off the ticket, but not before Jack Anderson had broadcast on radio an unchecked, apparently uncheckable story about his alleged arrests for drunken driving, and George Herman on CBS' "Face the Nation"—during a particularly grueling inquisition of Eagleton (Anderson was also on the panel)—called attention to the fact that the senator was sweating and trembling. In seven days vast amounts of newsprint and broadcast time were squandered on describing Democratic reactions and telling the party leaders what they obviously had to do.

Much of the drama was played out before the television audience, including apparently contradictory statements by George McGovern at various stages in his disengagement from his running mate and a crucial broadcast on "Meet the Press" immediately following Eagleton's CBS appearance, when Jean Westwood and her vice-chairman, Basil Paterson, contradicted Eagleton's assertion that McGovern was still 1,000 percent behind him.

When the sorry affair was finally over, both McGovern and Eagleton's advisers agreed that the turning point had come with the Anderson broadcast, which, the Washington columnist announced concurrently with Eagleton's resignation, he was finally "totally convinced was not true." It was one of the chief ironies of the campaign that the most conspicuous example of the instant power of the electronic press had to be the premature and highly unprofessional reporting of an unconfirmable but devastating rumor.

There was no question that the insistence of the press (and, to a great degree, the broadcast journalists) forced Eagleton's departure and magnified a personal tragedy into a national issue—McGovern's indecisiveness, which, as the media continued to drum away at it, probably cost the Democrats a great many votes, if not the election. Nor did the broadcasters, still harking back to the Eagleton affair as the election returns rolled in, seem to appreciate their own part in making it the focal point of a campaign where one candidate refused to confront the other in debating the real issues.

The "mini-convention" which was held in Washington in early August to nominate Eagleton's successor was covered in its entirety by NBC and PBS and partially by CBS and ABC. Despite a smaller hall and a fraction of the cast of characters, it looked remarkably like its full-scale predecessor. It contained also the campaign's most conspicuous example of rudeness, when NBC's Tom Pettit, after a brief interview with Eagleton, asked him to get out of the way so that the camera could be directed at the fully visible mother of his successor, Mrs. Hilda Shriver. Shriver himself performed one of the few acts of gallantry recorded at any of the year's conventions—mini or maxi —when he declined to be interviewed, suggesting that the camera might be better employed covering the not very interesting speech of the new Democratic national chairperson, Jean Westwood.

Finally, it was the Republicans' turn.

The Democrats' mistakes were not lost on the Republicans. Faced with a potentially boring convention, the Republicans relegated the housekeeping and parliamentary chores, which consumed so many of the Democrats' prime-time hours, to afternoon sessions or private caucuses and cut their total days from four to three. They revamped the podium, raising a three-panel rear-projection screen, which they used for the four party movies they managed to get on NBC and CBS in their entirety. The screen was also used to project television coverage of outside events, such as the arrival of President Nixon at the Miami airport, and his "spontaneous" appearance before a crowd of young people at the Marine Stadium after his nomination. When the screen was in use, the house lights were dimmed, and in most instances the television cameras cooperated by focusing on the front of the hall.

In fact, the Republicans seemed to make all things work for them. Every aspect of the convention was scaled for television. The speech of party co-chairperson Anne Armstrong was directed not to anyone in the hall but, as with many of the major addresses, to the Democrats in the television audience who might be inclined to vote Republican. The eleven one-minute and half-minute speeches seconding the nomination of President Nixon from the floor (representing every possible voting minority from housewife and hard-hat to astronaut) offered little opportunity for interruption. John Chancellor commented: "It is called the politics of leaving no stone unturned."

Chancellor, the convention's principal scold, made his snidest comment when, during a demonstration following the introduction of the First Lady, he compared the well-scrubbed Nixon Youth to a claque of Mayor Daley's Sixth Ward sewer workers in Chicago in 1968. The comparison probably drew more objections from viewers than any other single event at both conventions, and John Chancellor came on the next day saying, "I caused something of a ruckus last night," and giving his explanation:

> In the grand tradition of American politics, there have been organized political groups or claques at practically every convention since both great parties began meeting in convention halls. I didn't say they were sewer workers but they are a claque and they are about the youngest claque I've ever seen at a political convention and, I say, they are here tonight and there will be more of them and you'll hear them chanting.

The Republicans confirmed that none of what happened at the convention had been left to chance when they inadvertently circulated a script of the convention to the network news desks. Embedded in the schedule were breaks and musical interludes (intended to give the networks time for commercials), verbatim prayers, and informal introductions to speakers (kept brief to prevent unwanted commentary),* with time specifications for invocations to God, applause, and "spontaneous demonstrations." The Republican approach, involving big political and show-business names, insured that more time was spent on the podium or on scheduled floor events than at the Democratic

---

* A survey by the *Miami Herald* showed that 80 percent of the Republican delegates considered the television networks hostile.

affair, where faces were often new, young, black, or female. Democrats were able to hold the camera on scheduled events approximately half of the time; the Republicans, with few surprises, managed to keep the network cameras on the podium a remarkable two-thirds of the time.

The most striking moments of coverage at both conventions, however, were in no one's script. Mike Wallace spent a grueling nine minutes trying to get former secretary of commerce Maurice Stans to confess his involvement in the Watergate affair. Walter Cronkite dueled for ten minutes in the booth with Nelson Rockefeller, Nixon's former adversary and 1972's nominator. On the surface it was all Alphonse and Gaston, underneath more Tybalt and Mercutio.

However, these were the odd waves on an otherwise glassy-smooth surface. Although there were considerable disturbances outside the hall, the networks seemed at pains to play them down.

This was clear despite the claim by the networks that coverage was proportionately greater at the mildly inconvenienced Republican convention in Miami in 1972 than at the violently disrupted Democratic convention in Chicago in 1968. A minor riot, which resulted in the tearing down of Miami's new $24,000 fence, was filmed and aired only by ABC. NBC did not broadcast the film it took of the Zippies' attack on a Republican platform subcommittee meeting.

On the whole, CBS tended to point out more convention aberrations and bugs than NBC or ABC. Apart from the interviews with Rockefeller and Stans, they talked to a fair number of dissidents—including the Vietnam Veterans Against the War —and produced a gently devastating essay on high life among the convening Republicans along Florida's Gold Coast.

One of the conspicuous innovations of the convention coverage came from the hard-up Public Broadcasting Service, which had given its viewers incidental if highly intelligent coverage of the Democratic convention. The National Public Affairs Center for Television (NPACT) decided to attempt genuine gavel-to-gavel coverage of the Republicans. This would be the first time in history, according to PBS head Hartford N. Gunn, Jr., that any television camera would stick with the podium from beginning to end.

Although there had been widespread complaints about the networks' short attention span in covering the Democratic convention, there were prompt cries of foul in some quarters. NPACT's president, Jim Karayn, replied that public TV didn't want to wait four years to test the premise that the television viewers desired and needed more podium coverage. Pointing to the full coverage of the Democrats' mini-convention, Karayn said both were "done as a supplement to—not a replacement for—our basic commitment to aggressive and innovative journalism." Karayn, however, did not convince his anchormen, Sander Vanocur and Robert MacNeil, to go along.

Vanocur explained: "We didn't feel it was journalistically right to have public broadcasting serve as a mere conduit for a political party's presentation; it's wrong to let a party present a one-sided case without outside analysis of what's going on." He and MacNeil provided special commentaries after the convention coverage. But they left the anchorman's chore to former White House press aide Bill Moyers, who, in the brief interludes allotted to him, did some of the most intelligent commentary heard at either convention.

Fewer than 50 percent of the nation's public TV stations cleared the PBS coverage on the first two days. The third day, for Nixon's acceptance speech, 65 percent plugged in. On the other hand, clearance for the much briefer Vanocur-MacNeil commentary—like Moyers' presentation, highly literate and informed—ran close to 90 percent. It was Vanocur and MacNeil who, all through the conventions, had had the final word, staying in the hall past the other networks, no matter how late the session. On August 23, as the Republicans still stood in line to shake their candidate's hand, Vanocur's last words were: "You can orchestrate a convention but not a campaign."

Where did the 1972 conventions leave the broadcasting of politics?

Obviously, as a TV spectacular, convention coverage was slipping. Although the numbers did not necessarily indicate it, the percentages did:

	1968	**1972**
Democrats:	50.2 million (89.7% TV homes)	53.4 million (86.1% TV homes)
Republicans:	45.5 million (81.2% TV homes)	50.4 million (81.1% TV homes)

These figures, however, referred to those who tuned in at "some time" during the entire length of the convention, whether it was for ten minutes or ten hours.

Although NBC claimed a ratings victory with its coverage of the Democrats, and CBS with the Republicans, both were losers when up against entertainment shows on ABC. On the evening of July 11, NBC's and CBS' coverage from 7:30 to 9:30 averaged a 20 percent share. Against them ABC had a 31 percent share with "Mod Squad" and a 38 percent share when "Marcus Welby" was on the air. Both shows were reruns.

The record low for prime-time convention coverage was set on the first evening of the Republican convention, when all three commercial networks accounted for only 28 percent of the total audience watching television.

At least two of the network news presidents had been heard to say things which could be interpreted as the beginning of the end. Richard Salant of CBS talked about "selective" coverage in 1976. Reuven Frank of NBC said, "I don't know whether we'll have gavel-to-gavel convention coverage again. The public tuned it off. If the public does not want it, it won't go on."

Variety called the Republican convention the "biggest commercial freebee since television began."

Of the Democrats, *Newsweek* said: "Rarely have so many TV news stars been asked to fill so much yawning air-time with so little of genuine substance." *Time* said: "Television was simply not the best reporter of what was essentially a business meeting." The most acerbic comment came from Anthony Lewis in *The New York Times:* ". . . the whole process of the [Republican] convention was an insult to public intelligence, a vulgar exercise by cynical men with a deep contempt for ideas. In a country facing difficult and at the same time exciting challenges, there was not a single thoughtful speech on any matter of substance."

For all their on-the-air boredom and offhandedness, the CBS and NBC anchormen still favored a continuation of the status quo. "I'm dead set against abbreviated coverage," said John Chancellor. "I tend to believe gavel-to-gavel is one of the most valuable services television provides the American public."

He was undoubtedly right. However confused or perfunctory the job sometimes seemed, however confused or contrived the quasi-events that were covered, whether the politicians or the public wished it or not, television still managed to reveal and inform.

In the final analysis, the network coverage had to be accounted a valuable service to the public; the way American politics now worked, it was indispensable.

7 • The Broadcasting of Politics (III)

The Campaign

THE PRESIDENTIAL CAMPAIGN of 1972 was possibly the longest and nastiest in recent memory. It was without question the most expensive. With a persistence seldom before seen, radio and TV magnified and frequently distorted these characteristics.

McGovern declared his candidacy in January 1971, and his campaign continued with increasing intensity for the next twenty-two months.

At the campaign's peak the senator was making as many as 11 scheduled appearances a day, and he made a total of between 300 and 400 in the final months. Although they varied from visits to shopping centers and old folks' homes to formal speeches before large audiences, most of them had one object in common: media, and particularly television, coverage—the hope that by talking to a handful or a few hundred Americans, thousands and millions might be reached.

The fact that McGovern's intended audience was, for the most part, quite different from his actual one imparted an air of unreality to many of these occasions—an unreality which frequently clashed with the senator's acknowledged sincerity.

Nor was the coverage of these appearances left to chance or the whim of local stations' news directors. As the campaign developed, McGovern's staff made its own audio and video tapes, offering them gratis to all stations who were interested. Many were. However, 67 percent of the stations or groups reporting to the Survey said that they had refused to accept such tapes, made in great abundance by the Republicans as well as the Democrats. The reason given by Sid Davis, the head of Group W's Washington bureau: "You can't question the tape. You are forced to accept something as true without the opportunity to face the source and ask questions and determine the validity of his statement."

On the other hand some stations accepted the tapes on their own terms. WSAZ-TV in Huntington, West Virginia, reported:

> Newspapers complained stations were using film material supplied by candidates. We did, on some occasions, but always with obvious early attribution of the source of the film . . . and two commentaries pointing out the limitations of such film or tape. I find it no different from a newspaper handout, if properly verified and attributed to the source, assuming newsworthiness.

Besides those appearances in which McGovern met the public face-to-face, with only a few microphones and cameras between, he made endless appearances on panel, phone-in, interview, and talk shows. How important the Democrats considered these activities was demonstrated by a report from the DuPont correspondent in Cincinnati, who stated that in two visits to his city, both McGovern and Shriver gave as much time to each television station as to all the print media together. Neither Nixon nor Agnew bothered to visit Cincinnati.

In the later stretches of the campaign McGovern resorted to telethons, money-raising devices popularized by comedian Jerry Lewis. The name indicated their inseparability from the television screen. On these regional shows, most of them an hour long, McGovern appeared with big-name politicians, answered phoned questions, and had star entertainers on tape asking for money. A total of ten of these occasions were held from New England to California.

Much of McGovern's television budget went for a series of fireside chats. The one on October 10, discussing Vietnam, gained some fame as the most highly rated paid political appearance in history. It also was credited with bringing $2 million into the party coffers, leaving a substantial margin after the $160,000 tab was paid and convincing the McGovern camp that the 7:30 to 8:00 prime-time slot in which it had been telecast was highly desirable. That half hour had been returned by the networks to the local stations under FCC orders a year earlier, with a special proviso allowing the networks to reclaim it for political broadcasts. The fact that in most instances the politician would be replacing inferior local fare and that he could pick his own network, eliminating and adding affiliates as he saw fit, made it particularly attractive to presidential candidates.*

---

* Oliver Treyz, former ABC president and now a New York–based television consultant, was the brains behind the 7:30 time slot on a

McGovern's performance was not lost on the Republicans, who hastened to book the 7:30 to 8:00 period for themselves, although they had not till then been eager to pick up their share of the $3.5 million worth of prime time in five-minute and one-minute spots the networks had set aside for both parties at bargain rates.

The rush for the early-evening half hour annoyed many local stations, who either had sponsors to dump or a policy against thirty-minute paid political speeches. The Republicans hit another snag when they attempted to put John Connally into the slot and were told that FCC rules permitted appearances only by bona fide candidates. At the last minute they got around this prohibition by slipping in a brief tape of the president in China, with voice-over commentary by Connally. Putting together a bigger hookup of stations, including independents and affiliates of all three networks (a feat accomplished, according to embittered Democrats, through presidential clout), Connally commanded an even larger audience than McGovern. Several of the important markets were virtually blanketed: In New York, five out of six VHF commercial channels carried it; in Los Angeles, five out of seven.

Although the networks lost no sponsors in the half hour and made a little cash, they were not as enthusiastic as they might have been. No matter how large the audiences, such evening political appearances would eventually pull down the network ratings in the all-important month-long Nielsen and Arbitron "sweeps" which began three weeks before the elections.

Scattered through all the hundreds of gratis appearances and the dozens of paid-for major segments of time were thousands of McGovern-sponsored TV and radio flashes, varying in length from thirty seconds to five minutes.

Beginning with the low-keyed *cinéma vérité* products of Charles Guggenheim's workshop, McGovern advertisements became less gentlemanly as the campaign progressed. They culminated in a series of one-two punches on corruption, tax reform, and law and order, done by Tony Schwartz. Schwartz, who had left the Muskie team after the early primaries, was noted principally for a television commercial he had created

"customized" network. The idea was to buy heavily in states where McGovern stood a chance and to forget about such lost causes as the South. After the strategy proved a ratings success, Treyz said he was bowing out of any further McGovern buys, explaining that he had accomplished what he set out to do: prove that any political candidate can get a share of the network prime-time audience if he knows how to buy. "Once it's done, any clerk can repeat it."

for the Lyndon B. Johnson campaign in 1964, which linked a small girl picking petals off a daisy with an atomic countdown. It was considered such strong medicine that Johnson canceled it after one network showing. Schwartz's services had been sought out by hard-pressed politicians ever since.

If broadcasting's interest in the campaign had been limited to the straight, event-oriented news coverage that McGovern strove to attract, to the usual talk and panel shows, or to the commercial time he bought for speeches, telethons, and spots, McGovern would have had little to complain of. But the attention paid the Democratic candidate was compulsive, focusing on his campaign troubles instead of the message in his speeches. Nor, with Nixon invisible, was there any chance for a full-blooded encounter.

In such a lopsided campaign the broadcasters were damned if they did (overcover the Eagleton affair, concentrate on the Democrats' inner-party squabbles and McGovern's changeability) and damned if they didn't (arrange debates, explore the issues, give full attention to McGovern's campaign pronouncements).

In the final days of his campaign, possibly because he came to accept his defeat as inevitable, McGovern recaptured a little of the directness and unflappability which had carried him from virtual invisibility to the Democratic nomination. But, by then, it was too late.

President Nixon, whose 1968 campaign demonstrated that he had learned to master the electronic media, continued this magisterial role throughout his first four years in the White House, as the earlier chapters in this book indicate. This made it difficult to say at exactly what point his campaign for reelection began.

The president's appearances throughout his first term were expertly constructed to increase his personal stature and enhance his prestige. Moreover, the trips to China and Russia, late in the term, were bound (thanks to the mediation of television) to make the events of a formal political campaign seem anticlimactic and insipid.

Nevertheless, the president, never one to leave matters to chance, ran an exceptionally astute campaign, which as much by omission as by commission celebrated the power and importance of the electronic media.

The official beginnings of this campaign can be traced to the so-called November Group which was formed to supervise the media operations of two "clients," the Committee to Re-Elect the President and Democrats for Nixon—two flanks of the Republican operation in the field. The group was put together in February 1972, almost a year after McGovern announced his candidacy.

Under the leadership of former attorney general John Mitchell, who had run Nixon's 1968 campaign, the team included few faces that would be familiar to readers of Joe McGinniss' widely read *The Selling of the President*.

The one-time, one-chore agency, headed by Peter H. Dailey, a California advertising man, with fifty members screened for loyalty, was dedicated to getting "the independent and Democratic votes that any Republican candidate needs to win." According to remarks made to WTOP media critic Edwin Diamond and printed in *New York* magazine, the November Group entered the lists in a sober mood. When it set up shop the polls showed Senator Muskie with a slight edge over the president, and Wallace with 12 to 15 percent of the vote spoken for. "We saw it as a three-way race," said Dailey, "with a Democratic centrist candidate like Humphrey or Muskie and a strong Wallace candidacy. We also thought that Vietnam and the economy would be issues adversely affecting the President. And we weren't sure how much the new Federal Election Campaign Act, which limited media outlays, would hinder our activities."

Elsewhere Dailey was quoted as saying: "I really think our job is dealing with the facts of this Administration rather than the personality of the President. This business of charisma is overrated. You don't go to your doctor because he has charisma, or pick a lawyer for charisma; what you care about is that you have competent professionals."

Although Dailey's analysis of the American psyche might be challenged, it clearly indicated what tack the Republicans were likely to take. Dailey and his associates were planning to keep Nixon out of sight and let George, and Melvin, and Spiro, and a few dozen assorted cabinet members, senators, and other party dignitaries do it.

"It was easier, cleaner for us to run ads on a man who didn't campaign actively," Mike Lesser, general manager of the November Group, explained later. "We had the opportunity to convey a message to the people without having to concern ourselves with the President making a conflicting statement, something that McGovern had happen a lot."

At the top of the first list of "surrogates," chosen in early spring to represent the president in the field, was the name of a woman, Martha Mitchell. According to a November Group member, she was so sought after as a spokesperson that she "could go to three different functions every day from now until the election."

Mrs. Mitchell did not stay the course—becoming, according to unconfirmed rumor, part of the fallout around the so-called Watergate scandal. Her husband left with her. Watergate, the arrest of five men * with bugging and microfilm equipment who allegedly broke into the Democratic National Committee headquarters in a fashionable Washington apartment and office complex, not only coincided with the departure of the Mitchells but became the red flag which the Democrats waved whenever other issues failed them.

It also indicated that, no matter how calm the president himself might seem, some of his underlings were taking nothing for granted, a conclusion which was reinforced by the last-minute scramble for anonymous donations before the deadline set by the campaign spending act.

If the November Group began the year in a sober mood, by the time the G.O.P. convention was over in August, its temper was one of ill-concealed jubilation.

Later the president admitted that he felt the nomination of McGovern had, to all intents and purposes, ended the campaign. Just the look of the Democratic convention, with its preponderance of women, young people, and blacks and its patience with such explosive issues as abortion, amnesty, women's lib, and homosexuality, did its part. And if a *coup de grâce* were needed, the Eagleton affair delivered it.

On television, the Republicans began their campaign two weeks after the Democrats and announced that they were spending considerably less money. The ads, done by the November Group in the name of the Committee to Re-Elect the President, were comparatively mild. In the first week of October a new cluster of commercials, also executed by the November Group and labeled "Democrats for Nixon," appeared. They were unpleasant enough for the Democrats to consider filing a protest with the Fair Campaign Practices Committee and the FCC. One spot in particular, on McGovern's defense proposals, quoted Senator Hubert Humphrey and showed a giant hand sweeping away toy representations of U.S. military personnel and equipment. Another of the commercials, showing McGovern's profile switching back and forth, was a Republican version of a Demo-

* Two more were indicted later.

cratic spot of Nixon as a weather vane, made for Humphrey in 1968 and never used.

Still the president did not appear.

The situation in late September was described by Warren Weaver, Jr., in *The New York Times:*

> While Senator McGovern is fraying his nerves and his finances out on the hustings, the President sits in the White House reaching just as many voters through the media and, what's more, reaching them in the role of a confident powerful leader rather than as a scrambling self-assertive office-seeker.
>
> But beneath this deceptive surface image of inactivity, the great Republican media machine has been whirring away pumping millions of dollars worth of propaganda into American homes, mostly through their television sets and mail boxes.

The reference to mail boxes was important. In the same article Weaver quoted a McGovern aide as saying: "Direct mail has made my candidate possible. Without direct mail, we would not have been able to afford paid television. Without television, we would have had no hope of reaching the American voters."

The flood of mail—pleading, exhortatory, inspirational—which poured over the American people in the 1972 campaign was even more startling than the radio and TV hammering to which the public had become accustomed. An estimated 15 million pieces went out in behalf of McGovern, raising nearly $15 million. Nixon's first mailing alone totaled 12 million pieces. Counting all the computer-directed activities of the candidates, including direct-mail appeals for votes and money together with telephone and house calls, the budgets exceeded those allotted to radio and TV. Furthermore, they were not subject to limitation by the campaign spending act.

Although Nixon moved around less than any presidential candidate since 1944, he was far from inactive. Major Administration news breaks of one sort or another had a habit of coinciding with major pronouncements by McGovern, frequently driving them into secondary positions on front pages and nightly newscasts. The most conspicuous example of this was Henry Kissinger's "peace at hand" press conference (televised in its entirety by CBS News), which proved the White House aide a masterful television performer and overshadowed McGovern's campaign for days after. Although peace did not materialize by Election Day, the expectation alone was sufficient to deprive the Democratic candidate of the principal reason for his candidacy.

The president also put radio to its most sophisticated and effective political use since FDR. In fourteen speeches on network radio, most of them at midday, he outlined his various positions. If the speeches themselves were heard by a relatively small number of Americans, they insured the president of important newspaper coverage as well as prominent mention in the nightly TV news in a way that press releases or formally released position papers would never have done. Nor was he risking, thanks to the variation in time and day of exposure, any form of audience fatigue, something that George McGovern was forced to consider and continually ignore.

In his October 6 press conference (not televised) Nixon gave his radio strategy away. In answer to a question concerning the possibility of other press conferences before Election Day, he responded:

> Well, I would plan to try to find ways to be as available for purposes of presenting my position as I can. For example, in the matter of taxes, how we avoid a tax increase, I know that Mr. Ehrlichman has represented my views, and Mr. Shultz, as have a number of others. I have tried to cover it here briefly this morning.
>
> But at Camp David, yesterday, I completed a speech that I had made on the subject and while I cannot get away this weekend, I am going to deliver it by nationwide radio on Saturday night. So for the writing press, you will have time for the Sunday papers. That is only coincidence, of course.

The assiduous attention of the White House to the media was demonstrated elsewhere, perhaps most strikingly in an ABC "Issues and Answers" hour, in which the following interchange took place between Frank Reynolds and the Democratic candidate:

> REYNOLDS: I thought you might be interested in what has happened here. It has been known, of course, that you were going to appear on this program and yesterday a White House official called ABC to be sure that we had a copy of John Connally's address. But he also said he had some questions that he wanted us to put to you.
>
> McGOVERN: These questions from the President?
>
> REYNOLDS: Well, I don't know. They are questions from the White House and what makes it interesting, I think, is, you know, they are phrased in question-type language.

Not just, "ask him about Vietnam or amnesty or something else." But I think I will read one if you don't mind.

> "You have likened President Nixon to Adolf Hitler. You have implied President Nixon is barbaric in his conduct of the war and you have repeatedly used personal attacks in your campaign against the President. How do you reconcile this with your views that issues should be rationally discussed and that harsh rhetoric is unproductive. There is a good amount of public opinion that you have used some of the most strident language of any Presidential campaign ever."

McGOVERN: Well, I think this is really an interesting development here, that I should come on a program to be interviewed and have questions submitted by the White House. Isn't it interesting that the President himself is afraid, apparently, to come on this program with me, or to come on any other television program and raise his own questions.

"Face the Nation," the CBS equivalent of "Issues and Answers," claimed the White House had made similar attempts to get questions to Sargent Shriver, the vice-presidential candidate, who had appeared the same afternoon. Producer Sylvia Westerman said: "I didn't even want to hear the questions. It's obviously a news management attempt."

However, rumors were current in the industry that CBS' exceptionally forthright treatment of the Watergate affair, which ran in two installments on "The CBS Evening News," lost some of its punch in the second installment thanks to an exchange of telephone calls between the White House and top network brass.

Relations between the White House and the media had supposedly never been better. The coverage of the conventions and of McGovern's campaign, particularly the Eagleton affair, had left the Administration little cause for complaint. "I think the treatment that the media . . . have been giving what's been going on lately has been very fair, objective treatment," Spiro Agnew told ABC correspondent Bill Wordham on one of the network's election specials.

Nixon was perhaps a little less enthusiastic. He expressed his disapproval in one of his few speeches during the campaign—given before the National League of Families of Prisoners of War and Missing in Southeast Asia.

Harking back to his order to mine Haiphong harbor and bomb military targets in North Vietnam, the president said:

But let me tell you what happened immediately after that decision. It is often said that when a President makes a hard decision, the so-called opinion leaders of this country can be counted upon to stand beside him, regardless of party.

Who are the opinion leaders? Well, they are supposed to be the leaders of the media, the great editors and publishers and television commentators and the rest. They are supposed to be the presidents of our universities and the professors and the rest, those who have the educational background to understand the importance of great decisions and the necessity to stand by the President of the United States when he makes a terribly difficult, potentially unpopular decision. They are supposed to be some of our top businessmen who also have this kind of background.

Let me tell you that when that decision was made there was precious little support from any of the so-called opinion leaders of this country who I have just described.

Toward the end of the campaign Senator Robert Dole, chairman of the Republican National Committee, was still insisting during an appearance on CBS' "Face the Nation":

> . . . the President, I think, is conducting the highest level campaign in history; he's never mentioned his opponent by name. He doesn't run around trying to depict his opponent as corrupt or some kind of knave. In fact, in 1960, Cardinal Cushing called candidate Nixon, who lost the election, the goodwill man of the year because of the campaign he conducted, so it has been a lofty campaign in the Nixon tradition.

Not quite so lofty if one listened to Clark MacGregor, John Mitchell's replacement as Republican campaign director, who began his summary campaign statement:

> As the campaign enters its final week, one persistent question is why Senator McGovern has so far failed to win the trust or confidence of the American people.
> I have, of course, heard several theories advanced:
> —He's radical;
> —He's wishy-washy, changing his position from one headline to the next.
> —He's running a dirty campaign;
> —And he's a weak figure.
> There's supporting evidence for each of these explanations, but in my own travels and in the soundings I receive each day from the field, I have found that the dominant

mood of the electorate today is simply this: they have heard George McGovern promise, promise and overpromise to the point that he simply can't be believed.

Soon after he seized the Democratic nomination, we wondered whether the Prairie Populist—the man of conviction on the far left—would try to weave artfully back to the center of the field. He has, indeed, but every time he picks up the ball, he brings back memories of "Wrong Way" Corrigan—the fellow who scored a touchdown at the wrong end of the field. One wonders why they don't send someone off the bench to tackle him before it's too late.

Perhaps someday he'll be kind enough to explain it all in his memoirs—"The Paper Lion, Vol. II," for instance, or, "The Face That Launched a Thousand Slips." *

The network coverage of the primaries had been persistent and well-intentioned, if usually uninspired. At the conventions, although there were few surprises, no one could fault the networks for spending too little time, money, or energy. During the campaign the networks seemed to give up, failing to provide the kind of steady, informed attention that could have extracted interest from an apparently barren situation.

Again, public TV's NPACT, as it had in the primaries and at the conventions, showed up impressively, airing four segments in prime evening hours during the campaign month of October, a month when the networks chose to devote not a single evening hour to substantial coverage of politics.†

This stunned silence, however, did not prevail across the country. Local radio and TV stations chose to spend more time on the coverage of politics than ever before. The League of Women Voters, reporting to the Survey this year on well over 1,000 stations in nearly 200 communities from coast to coast, found that since 1968 the free time given to candidates or their spokesmen had increased overall in 51 percent of their home towns, remained the same in 41 percent, and decreased in only 8 percent. News coverage of politics had increased in 73 percent of the communities, remained the same in 23 percent, and decreased in only 4 percent. Approximately the same proportions prevailed for radio.

---

* Mr. MacGregor himself made a slip, confusing Douglas E. Corrigan, the puddle-jumping flycr who in 1937 set out from Floyd Bennett Field in Brooklyn for California and ended up in Ireland, with Roy Riegels, center for the University of California, who in the Rose Bowl game against Georgia Tech in 1929 intercepted a pass and ran seventy-five yards down the field for a touchback.

† See list of DuPont-Columbia Awards on page 159.

The importance of television to candidates and constituents alike seemed also to have increased. Forty percent of the respondents indicated at least one instance when broadcast coverage was crucial to a candidate or ballot issue.

The DuPont correspondent in Iowa reported:

> In Iowa . . . there is much evidence that broadcast *news* coverage (specifically television) of the candidates continued to be one of the major factors in helping voters to arrive at their decisions. The upset victory of Democrat Dick Clark over incumbent Republican Jack Miller for U.S. Senate seems largely to have been a product of the increasingly favorable image of Clark, who started as an unknown. Much of this seems to have resulted from the dozens of times he was interviewed by broadcast newsmen and was seen on local-station TV newscasts, as he walked across the state. Here was an interesting phenomenon of a statewide image acquired through many individual station exposures in many towns.

League chapters in Maine and Idaho said flatly that radio and TV were essential in their states in all instances because of their small populations and large dimensions.

This despite the fact that League chapters reported fewer than 3 percent of the stations endorsing presidential candidates, and only 2 percent expressing preferences on local candidates or ballot issues. Eight percent were reported as displaying a bias in favor of one or the other of the presidential candidates.

A third of the League chapters found the broadcasters' coverage of politics to have improved since 1968, while only 2 percent found it to have deteriorated. Thirteen percent of broadcasters were reported braver, 16 percent more cautious.

The format most favored by stations (cited by 64 percent of the Leagues) seemed to be the appearance of the candidate interviewed by a single reporter. Among the formats least favored by station management were debates, individual appearances by candidates, and documentaries, either because of noncooperation by candidates or lack of staff and money.

KPLR-TV, St. Louis, ran a series of eight half-hour, late-night "Soap Box" shows which offered all political candidates, no matter for what office, four minutes opposite their opponents. The station reported:

> Television does a very poor job of acquainting voters with some of the elected officials who may be closest to them. Many complaints are heard about calibre of state legislatures, yet few stations even try to cover state legis-

lature races because of their number and the difficulty in highlighting "personalities." We had excellent response from viewers and a pathetic eagerness of candidates to appear. (Most had never previously been on television, although some were officeholders.)

The tremendous advantage, of course, is the opportunity to get a feel for a candidate through the immediacy of television, which can reveal hesitancy, dishonesty, immaturity, in a way not evident from printed statements.

According to the DuPont correspondent in Iowa:

The Iowa Educational Television Network and KRNT, Des Moines, both set up a series of programs in which major statewide candidates were questioned by a veteran newsman "live" in the presence of their opponents so that both, in effect, debated the questions raised although not in direct dialogue with each other.

The DuPont correspondent in Indiana praised WRTV, Indianapolis, for the attention it paid local political candidates:

The free time for legislative candidates was informative, if not amusing, inasmuch as many of the half-witted and inarticulate hopefuls proved their incompetence for office by their appearance on television. I feel this is an excellent method of exposing talent and no-talent candidates without the interference or influence of a smooth-talking commentator or news analyst. The cranking off of equal time in front of a camera is a highly informative exercise. I feel that perhaps the relentless eye of the television camera may have been cruel to some of the candidates, but that is the name of the game and I feel that WRTV here in Indianapolis did the voters a great service if only to interject some rude humor into the campaign by permitting fools to appear on television.

Although the largest number of League monitors felt that the best way for a voter to get a clear impression of a candidate was through a panel interview, panels and debates were reported broadcast far less frequently than individual appearances, the type of showcasing seen as most useful in getting the candidate votes. This would seem to indicate that candidates were still able to specify just how they would appear on radio and TV in most localities.

The League in Hillsborough County, Florida, reported:

Broadcast hard-news stories probably influenced the outcome of some elections locally but I question that programs devoted to issues or candidates did. Their impact could be multiplied significantly if the stations would "plug" the upcoming programs or put them in a regularly scheduled time slot. As it was, only a random dial turner would have found them . . . . This would seem to be an area where the FCC should try to refine its rules.

Although an increase in the number and length of political ads over 1968 was reported by seven out of ten League chapters, a minute being the favored length on television and thirty seconds on radio, there was no agreement as to the effectiveness of the ads in the general election. In an equal number of cases cited, excessive spending led to victory and defeat.

A League in South Dakota complained:

In the closing two weeks of the campaign, the sheer amount of advertising prevented viewers from getting their expected share of news, regular programming, etc. Nearly half of the 6 p.m. local newscast would be taken up by political ads. I also feel that 30 to 60 second spots do little to clarify issues or to tell people about a candidate as a person. These short ads are mainly designed to build images.

Spots of all lengths were found by the League chapters to be used for image making twice as frequently as for exploring issues. However, some of the most deceptive advertising had to do with ballot propositions rather than candidates.

According to one League in California, where there were twenty-two propositions on the ballot, "there was misuse of political advertising on at least five propositions—the most deceptive advertising I've seen. The encouraging fact is that not one of the propositions went the way the false ads directed."

Similar misrepresentations were cited concerning the graduated income tax issue in Massachusetts and the Olympics referendum in Colorado, where the challenged ads failed to win a pro-Olympic vote. A Nebraska League chapter reported: "Elected officials, while speaking to groups and organizations, were allowed to lobby against a ballot issue on *many* news broadcasts while proponents had little access to media and were frequently edited out after news conferences."

One of the most expensively fought local campaigns in the country was an attempt by the railroads to repeal laws requiring minimum train crews in Arkansas. The unions fighting to save the laws spent between $1.5 and $2 million, most of it on television, where they featured an ad containing the testimony of a railroad worker who had lost both legs in an accident. Later the victim was revealed to be an actor, and resentment at the falsification was given credit for the union's defeat.

Another deceptive policy was reported by a DuPont correspondent in North Carolina, who wrote:

> A campaign aide to a candidate for governor told me during a private conversation that his campaign's advertising strategy was to make their commercials look like news. He said that TV news in North Carolina was so "primitive" that in a sense it helped his candidate, because he could fashion his commercials to get his campaign message across by using a news film, action-type format.

This was not true, however, of some North Carolina broadcasters. Station WFMY-TV, Greensboro, turned down no less than one hundred tapes from a single gubernatorial candidate during the campaign and got denounced at a special news conference called by the candidate for that purpose. The station's stubbornness did not come from indifference to political matters. WFMY-TV devoted twenty prime-time half hours to candidates for state and national office during the campaign and accommodated no less than sixty-two candidates from five counties with half-hour morning segments, which included a brief biography of the candidate, who then made a statement and was questioned by a reporter.

On the Sunday evening prior to the election the station devoted three and a half hours of prime time to a special program, "Carolina Candidates '72," which had been in production for three months and which treated in depth the principal offices in the state and profiled the major candidates. It also went into detail on ballot issues. The audience response was greater than for any locally produced show to date, and only two viewers called to complain about missing such popular preempted fare as "Anna and the King of Siam" and "M*A*S*H."

The station news director commented on some of his concerns about local political coverage:

> I view with alarm the use by candidates of slick "selling" techniques insofar as relations with television news is concerned. (What they do with paid political time is their business.) More important, I think, is the fact that "newsmen" use the video and audio tapes which are prepared under tightly controlled conditions by the candidate's staff with no opportunity for interrogative questioning by a reporter. I reject the contention by campaign aides that the

tapes are only an electronic improvement over the traditional news release—for the simple reason that I never used printed news releases from candidates.

I am concerned also by the "newsmen" who openly supported candidates this year, displaying campaign buttons and bumper stickers. One of those explained to me that his activity was totally honest, in that it staked him out and warned his audience to pay more careful attention to his political stories. Hogwash! Newsmen who want to support candidates should get out of the news business and into the campaign, leaving the rest of us to try to report news fairly and with objectivity.

I am also informed by a press aide to one candidate that there were newsmen in 1972 who accepted fees for assisting with speech writing, newsmen who advised candidates on "hot" issues in their communities, and even one who "let it be known that he could get film used on his station if candidates would buy his services as a photographer to shoot news clips that would be shipped to other stations."

A station in Florida was cited for giving its favorite candidates free time in newscasts for political appearances; another in Idaho was reported to interview only "conservative" candidates; and one in Honolulu was said to habitually end its newscasts with unpleasant items about candidates.

Fifteen percent of all stations reporting to the Survey cited the Fairness Doctrine and equal-time rules as their principal headaches. Twelve percent of the Leagues reported that stations in their communities were using these rules—a familiar hedge in the past—as excuses for limiting political coverage or refusing political ads.

Instances of bias reported were remarkably low considering the suspicious temper of the times. Less than 11 percent of talk-show hosts were accused of voicing political preferences. The politicians themselves came off less favorably, with two in seven suspected of putting broadcast time to questionable use.

Nearly half the chapters reported the existence of cable TV in their communities, and more than half the cable systems mentioned carried political news, speeches, and advertising—striking evidence of the growing use of a technology which eventually could be of tremendous value to the political process of the United States. In several instances cable was the only source of information on local races. The TV Cable Company of Fort Walton Beach, Florida, reported:

We . . . are proud of our overall program of exposing political candidates to the new industry of cable casting.

Unrestricted by the limitations of broadcast TV, we were able to videotape and replay not portions but entire political addresses by visiting presidential candidates and their spokesmen.

We were able to arrange debates or discussions on vital local issues such as the proposed courthouse annex, ecological bond issues, and utilities increases. If there is an outstanding aspect of our efforts it lies in the fact that Okaloosa County has no local television and for the first time in history more than 50,000 viewers could see and hear their local candidates and issues aired on television. For the first time, they saw complete election returns in the primary, runoff, and general elections. For the first time candidates of key races were able to answer questions asked by the viewer, live and unrehearsed via cable television.

In other cases the impact of cable TV on elections was unknown, or recognized as negligible. A League in New Hampshire reported that the local cable system "hired a programmer during the campaign and borrowed equipment to originate a series of interviews with candidates for the state legislature. They were carried at distinctly un-prime time, excited no comment in the community. It was only the second effort at local programming by the company. Its effectiveness was probably nil."

However, other Leagues reported highly successful use of cable, including candidate phone-ins, talk shows, debates, forums, and parallel appearances, as well as the broadcasting of election returns and even documentaries on issues.

Offensive language over the air was reported to have been used by two candidates: State Senator Milo G. Knutson of Wisconsin and J. B. Stoner, a gubernatorial candidate in Georgia. Describing Knutson's campaign, a League member said: "His scare tactics and use of foul language were used to frighten some of the less knowledgeable voters into voting for the Senator. He was able to get a large number of the blue collar and older votes with this method of campaigning."

In Georgia, according to a chapter report from that state, Stoner "used very offensive language against blacks. The case was carried to the FCC and they ruled in favor of the candidate," who continued his campaign full force and with no modification of language. Benjamin Hooks, the black FCC commissioner who voted with the majority, explained to WSB, Atlanta, that he had done it because "Angela Davis may be running next time."

In summing up, a Connecticut League reported:

> Because of the redistricting controversy and the delay in court decisions, the election campaigns in Connecticut have been brief and feverish. However, this situation has proved conclusively that a short, more intensive campaign can be more effective than the dull repetitive campaigns of the past. Coverage has been excellent both of candidates and issues and nobody has got bored.

One League in a small Florida community reported little local interest by citizens or media in either state or national electioneering and then asked a difficult question: "No interest because no information—or no interest on the part of radio or TV because they think they won't have an audience?"

Still, the League chapters and the DuPont correspondents identified more than 200 local radio and TV stations which they rated worthy of commendation for the quality of their political coverage.

Among them was WRKL, a daytime radio station in New City, a small community in Rockland County, New York, which had won a DuPont Award for its unusually thorough political coverage in 1968. In 1972 WRKL increased both its budget and time allotted to political coverage, making it possibly the most politics-prone station in the nation. In 1968 the station had used a total of 500 political news stories and interviews; in 1972 the number exceeded 1,300. For the first time reporters were sent to the national conventions, and the station was one of the few in the country which gave its listeners a second chance to hear McGovern's acceptance speech, as well as Nixon's. It arranged nine hour-long debates by local politicians during the fall election campaign and gave thirty additional candidates time on its talk show "Hot Line." The station's presence at political meetings and other party affairs was constant throughout the year. WRKL reporters brought back substantial stories from no less than 220 of these events in the first eleven months of 1972.

WRKL had a Western counterpart in KSSS Radio, Colorado Springs, which scheduled 50 one-hour phone-in appearances by candidates for local and statewide office in addition to debates between candidates on several controversial issues included on the Colorado ballot.

Other radio stations also did conspicuously well in their political coverage: KFWB, Los Angeles, in a thirty-two-part series explained what the twenty-two propositions on the California ballot were all about. It offered reprints of the series and got more than 5,000 requests.

WIBC, Indianapolis, managed to catch Indiana politicians out more than once, the most important instance being a voting fraud at the state Democratic convention which other news media blinked at.

KTOK, Oklahoma City, in addition to thorough coverage of the primaries, conventions, and general election, did a series of politically related documentaries.

KPRC, Houston, sent two reporters and two special commentators (one to cover youth) to each of the national conventions and gave full coverage to important state political gatherings. According to the news director:

> We presented candidates in races that were not receiving much coverage from the newspapers. Specifically, we covered every legislative district. This is a coverage problem in a metropolitan area of nearly 2 million people . . . there was no way for a voter to get any non-partisan view of a candidate, except by listening to KPRC radio daily.

KTRH, Houston, completely banned paid political ads to the point of running CBS network political speeches but refusing to accept money for them. The radio station also did a good job on debates, giving time to minority-party candidates and undertaking its own polls.

KASU, radio station of the State University of Arkansas, researched, wrote, and produced a series of forty biographical sketches on all candidates for Jonesboro city offices, broadcasting each of them twice just before the general election.

A total of thirty-four public TV stations were singled out by the League and DuPont correspondents. Possibly the most impressive job again was done by KERA, Dallas, which may have been the only station, public or commercial, that managed during the primaries to get 200 candidates on the air at some length. Later coverage included detailed reporting on all the major races in Dallas County as well as adjacent Tarrant County, plus panel shows and simultaneous interviews of all candidates for the same office by a team of newsmen. KERA was also one of the few stations which attempted to profile candidates in some detail.

WBGU-TV, Bowling Green, Ohio, produced the only weekly

statewide public affairs program, piped to nine other Ohio stations. It also was one of the few stations which felt compelled to give equal time to the American Independent Party. Mel Martin, director of news and public affairs, commented:

> The media erred badly in ignoring John Schmitz, as he was certainly as valid a candidate as Wallace. His criticisms were justified, and his lack of exposure showed up election day . . . as he got about one tenth the votes Wallace did. Regardless of how one feels about what Schmitz had to say . . . (I found it repulsive) he should have been covered. Here at WBGU the AIP got as much coverage as the Republicans and Democrats.

WTTW, the Chicago public TV channel, without a regular news department, still presided over two 2½-hour polithons (repeated three times) for Illinois candidates, which represented the most extensive effort to inform the electorate in the Chicago area and was given credit by some for the defeat of Mayor Daley's protégé, state's attorney Edward V. Hanrahan. KPBS, San Diego, did an impressive job of covering the California campaigns in 20 hour-long, prime-time programs concentrated in the month of October.

KQED, the public TV outlet in San Francisco, claimed to have given its viewers the first straight explanation of the maneuvering on the South Carolina challenge some minutes before the vote was completed, and the "only full account of how and why the McGovern machinery messed up the abortion vote—and alienated many of McGovern's people." It also "experimented with a different form of candidate representation"—a debate in which candidates asked each other questions. KQED claimed to be the only San Francisco station to have contestants in major races appear face-to-face.

The station was also more fastidious than most in the matter of presidential spokesmen.

> In our judgment, the "surrogates" did not merit equal attention if the purpose of their trip was purely to speak for the President. In those cases where more was involved —such as Volpe coming to see BART [Bay Area Rapid Transit system], Morton coming to inspect a wildlife area, Stein speaking on wage price controls, we did cover, but we restricted coverage to the issue part of the trip.
>
> On some occasions we did probe the financing and true purpose of "surrogates" pretending to do government business and actually doing nothing but campaign work.

KQED looked on the relation of politics to broadcasting with a somewhat jaundiced eye. Jonathan Rice, its assistant general manager, wrote:

> It is asking too much to expect candidates to be candid and honest in dealing with the press, and it is unreasonable to expect campaign planners to substitute substance for the current successful practice of arranged, meaningless TV events on the campaign trail. As long as radio and TV, particularly local stations, are content to spend their money to make cheap political spots for the evening news, candidates will happily participate. And as long as most TV stations refuse to present—or are prevented from presenting—one candidate without the other, those candidates who fear public debate and probing will get off the hook.
>
> It is up to television to turn down the nonsense, concentrate on real events and issues and tell people what's going on whether or not a particular candidate likes it. The day the press bus is empty when a candidate rides to the beach to prove his love of nature, is the day maturity will have entered TV political reporting.

On November 7, what various observers had called the most over-reported, over-polled, over-complained-about campaign in history came to an end.

The Justice Department had never had so many complaints, thanks to the new campaign spending act. The FCC had never heard from so many irate constituents, thanks to the new sensitivity to "balance" and "fairness," nor had the Fair Campaign Practices Committee. For what *The New York Times* had called a "dreary" campaign, 1972 had broken a record number of records.

Early in the morning of November 7 NBC's "Today" show coyly reported that the returns from Dixville Notch, New Hampshire, were in. The mountain hamlet which, according to Frank McGee, had always voted for the loser in presidential elections had cast ten votes for Nixon, three for McGovern.

Later in the day Nixon, who had not been seen in forty-eight hours, emerged to vote, going to his San Clemente polling place in a big black limousine. Television viewers could see him voting, from the knees down, after he dropped and retrieved his ballot. They saw McGovern going to vote in South Dakota, and Shriver and Agnew in Maryland.

At 6:30 P.M. all three networks came on with their special election-night coverage in settings that looked respectively like a poker chip holder, a nuclear reactor, and the men's room in

Bruno's Pen and Pencil. At 8:30 NBC announced that it was absolutely sure Nixon was going to win. At 8:52 CBS concurred, and at 9:20 ABC—which had been holding back the news to accommodate Governor Reagan in California, who was nervous about its possible influence while the polls in his state were still open—finally conceded. By shortly after midnight both candidates had made their singularly laconic acknowledgments of victory and defeat.

At 2:00 A.M. the networks departed from their fancy sets and called it a very expensive day. They had spent $9 million since nightfall, projecting and confirming the election of a sure-shot winner.

Oddly, there was a remarkable amount of Monday morning quarterbacking.

The most caustic may have come from the winning camp. On November 11 Charles W. Colson, special counsel to President Nixon, addressed the New England Society of Newspaper Editors at Kennebunkport, Maine, a stone's throw from where Senator Muskie had declared his candidacy nearly a year earlier. Mr. Colson, in the course of an attack on CBS and *The Washington Post,* gave his own view of what had been happening in the United States for the past few months:

> Through all of the commentary on Tuesday night, repeatedly I listened to Brinkley, Chancellor, Sevareid, Cronkite, Reasoner and their friends tell us how remarkable it was that an "unpopular" President could be winning the biggest, most spectacular landslide in modern history: now there is a strange contradiction in that conclusion.
>
> Webster says that popular means "approved by the people"; forty-six million people, the highest total ever in American history, went to the polls to say that they approved of Richard Nixon's Presidency and want him to remain in Office for another four years.
>
> What the commentators were really saying was that because the American people have chosen as their President a man with whom those same commentators very fundamentally disagree, that it was an unpopular choice.
>
> Nonsense! What Richard Nixon stood for in this election is what the vast majority, sixty-one percent to be precise, the highest percentage for any Republican in history—also stood for.
>
> A second myth emerging is that President Nixon did not win the election; but George McGovern lost it. How often have you read in the last few weeks of the foibles and fail-

ures of George McGovern? He lost, so goes the mythology, because of the unfortunate Eagleton affair, the various staff errors in his campaign, the fact that he was outspent by huge Republican secret funds, that the Republican party subverted the whole political process, James Bond style, with a massive sabotage effort, unprecedented in American history, or that he never had an opportunity to explain his views.

To this I say humbug! First of all, in mid-July, right after the Democratic National Convention, *after* McGovern's stands on the issues were given massive exposure, but *before* the Eagleton affair and *before* George McGovern's flip flops on his $1,000 welfare schemes and spending and tax proposals, that is when the people first understood the difference between the two candidates on the issues, the Harris Poll found that President Nixon led George McGovern 55–35; the Gallup Poll, 56–37. With the undecided factored out, that is almost the identical margin by which the President was re-elected.

Secondly, I predict when all the final reports are made we will find that George McGovern spent more money in this campaign than did the President's Committee. It already appears that in the last three weeks of the campaign, McGovern outspent the Nixon campaign for media at least two to one.

Thirdly, as for the charge of subverting the whole political process, that is a fantasy, a work of fiction rivaling only *Gone With the Wind* in circulation and *Portnoy's Complaint* for indecency.

There one had it in précis, the entire campaign, in the official version.

Observations

As THE TEXT of the Survey demonstrates, it has been an exceptionally rough year for broadcasters. In view of the attacks upon them, justified or not, and past instances of corporate timidity, it is remarkable that any substantial treatment of controversial subjects got on the air. For those who stood firm, networks and local stations alike, the DuPont jurors have only admiration and praise.

However, there are many aspects of present-day broadcast journalism which trouble us as a body of citizens genuinely concerned with the quality of radio and TV news and public affairs.

When jurors assemble for the concentrated hours that are required to view the material that has been submitted to them, they are struck with the excellence of much of today's broadcast journalism. It is technically superb and pictorially beautiful, and many important subjects are brought to public light. However, what is packed into a few days' concentrated viewing looks different when measured against the sum total of broadcast hours. We feel there has been a decline in the number of courageous documentaries dealing with important subjects of controversy. The decline of the documentary in public television seems especially disturbing. Thanks to various pressures, the national public television documentary is almost extinct. Nor does there seem to be, according to announcements by the newly appointed heads of the Corporation for Public Broadcasting, any plan to resume such productions. We find this lapse regrettable.

The jurors react with profound skepticism to the Administration's positions, voiced repeatedly by Clay Whitehead and reflected in a presidential veto message, that (a) public television should be decentralized, with prime emphasis on local programming and local production and (b) public television should stay away from public affairs programming.

As for decentralization, much of the answer lies in elementary economics. The total programming funds available today, if distributed among the more than 212 local public stations, would finance only a minute amount of quality programming per station. Moreover, it is elementary common sense that most major cultural or public affairs productions should be cooperatively financed and produced through some type of centralized instrumentality. Of course, local stations and local programming should be encouraged and supported. The need obviously is for a reasonable blend of the centralized and the local.

As for public affairs programming, some of the jury believe that there have been occasional public broadcasting shows that were unbalanced, oversimplified, amateurish, and far short of the Caesar's-wife standards that tax-supported programming must achieve if it is to survive. Yet dozens of public broadcasting programs like "The Advocates," "Washington Week," and numerous discussion and interview shows have demonstrated that fairness can be attained. The BBC has also illustrated the potential. To kill all public affairs programming is shortsighted elimination of one of public broadcasting's chief functions.

One vital and unquestionable public affairs role for the local public station was well illustrated this year by WTTW in Chicago and KERA in Dallas. This was the function of providing full exposure, through debates and questioning, to state and local political candidates, including minor party nominees. This involves the kind of time allocations that commercial stations would or could never provide.

In the viewing year the jurors sensed a somewhat new mood in the documentaries they saw. There seemed to be fewer take-outs on major social ills, and more in-depth exploration of sensitive human beings caught in a tide of sweeping social change. Thus, a dramatic essay on the civil war in Ulster was seen largely through the eyes of Belfast children. Another essay explored attitudes toward death. Another, the thoughts and ruminations and expectations and lack of expectations of young workers in a Ford plant in California. Touching vignettes of the aging. A suburban family living and talking openly before the cameras. The meaning in human terms of the northward migration from the rural South. These were only a few examples of a trend that the jurors felt was particularly visible this year.

We are troubled by the fact that although revenues at the networks are once more increasing, there is no commensurate increase in the time allotted to regular news and public affairs programming, whether in network or local station schedules. We acknowledge that this is not solely management's fault. Both the public and the advertisers are implicated in the decline of important television programming of all sorts—the sponsors by consistently choosing the innocuous over the disturbing, the public by accepting what is offered without complaint. However, the suspicion remains that broadcasters have been far too ready to level down to the lowest common denominator of public taste and the corporate timidity of their sponsors.

Both the networks and the sponsors would make more plausible their protestations of unjust treatment by government agencies, dissident groups, and critics in general if their investment in the worthwhile were more conspicuous on television—regardless of the ratings.

Alternatives within over-the-air broadcasting, both commercial and public, seem limited, and time is running out. It therefore seems important to consider other measures of getting information to the American public directly and without interference. Over the long haul, the most promising seems to be cable TV. Therefore, the jurors would urge that everything possible be done to develop this new technology rapidly and in such a way that it is kept free of the undue influences which have hamstrung over-the-air TV and kept it from being of full use to the public.

We deplore the new sentence-counting techniques of broadcast critics who prefer syllable by syllable "balance" to truth and place conservative versus liberal bias above fact versus falsehood as the primary conflict in radio and TV journalism. We feel the journalist's job is not to satisfy the majority's notion of what is fair or unfair. His job is to dig out and describe the situation as it exists and to correct popular misconceptions—not abide by them. Whether the facts please conservative or liberal or neither should be of no concern to the journalist. "Advocacy" journalism for either side, in the opinion of the jurors, has to be bad journalism.

During the year there have been attacks on network newscasters for lack of balance and fairness. Some of those attacks have been political, not a new thing in 1972. In the main, the jurors believe, imbalance and unfairness on the major news broadcasts are rare. For integrity, striving for fairness, and general responsibility the jury must give high marks to these broadcasts and to the journalistic professionals who staff them. Theirs is a difficult assignment carried out with decency and honor. The year reconfirmed the importance of network news broadcasts in the complex business of informing the American public. In a sense, the early-evening news shows now set the daily agenda of America's concerns.

We continue to deplore the overcommercialization of radio

and TV, which involves not only the distracting and frivolous interruption of news and other informational programs, but the cluttering and disfigurement of the entire schedule.

We regret the continued second-class status given to important documentaries, which are placed in inconvenient and unpopular corners of the schedule, crowded into "black weeks," scheduled opposite each other, and otherwise variously ignored and manipulated to fulfill the requirements of commerce.

We are appalled at the infrequency with which excellent documentaries are returned to the air and superior local programs are broadcast beyond their own communities. Although the rerunning of entertainment programs, no matter how fatuous, is as inevitable as the return of Wednesday, the rerun public affairs show tends to be as infrequent as February 29.

For the past two years this jury has urged broadcasters to find some way to recapture excellent local documentaries and give them wider audience. It is, therefore, with considerable satisfaction that we greet the word from New York's public broadcasting station, WNET (Channel 13), that it has collected a number of these documentaries from around the country and will air them in a series called "Replay." Many of them are documentaries that have received awards and mention in the DuPont-Columbia Survey.

We question the continued trend to fragmentize and trivialize the news through gags, jokes, and other cosmetic and attention-getting devices. We also continue to find unsatisfactory the apparent rule-of-thumb that says that a given news item must not run more than a limited length of time.

We are encouraged by the growing number of stations which are giving the public access to the air, particularly those members of the public interested in correcting errors in news and public affairs programs which heretofore have too infrequently gone uncorrected.

Elie Abel
Richard T. Baker
Edward W. Barrett
Dorothy Height
John Houseman
Sig Mickelson
Michael Novak

The Alfred I. duPont–Columbia University Awards, 1971–1972

FRED FREED AND NBC NEWS, for **"The Blue Collar Trap"**

ROBERT MARKOWITZ AND CBS NEWS, for **". . . but what if the Dream comes true?"**

GROUP W, for **"The Search for Quality Education"**

JOHN DRIMMER AND WNJT, TRENTON, for **"Towers of Frustration"**

WTVJ, MIAMI, for **"A Seed of Hope"** and **"The Swift Justice of Europe"**

"THE 51ST STATE" AND WNET/13, for **"Youth Gangs in the South Bronx"**

RICHARD THURSTON WATKINS, "LIKE IT IS," AND WABC-TV, NEW YORK, for **"Attica: The Unanswered Questions"**

MIKE WALLACE, for outstanding reporting on CBS' **"60 Minutes"**

And for outstanding coverage of the 1972 political campaigns*

NATIONAL PUBLIC AFFAIRS CENTER FOR TELEVISION

KERA, DALLAS

* Dean Elie Abel disqualified himself from the judging in political coverage because of membership on the board of NPACT.

REPORTS AND COMMENTARIES

THE FOLLOWING ESSAYS are done each year by invitation of the editor. They are written by persons with a special competence and interest in fields relating to broadcast journalism which might otherwise not be covered by the Survey.

Blurred Image in the Electric Mirror

by Sig Mickelson

THE 1972 ELECTION should have given broadcast journalists their finest hour. It should have given them the classic opportunity to put to maximum use the editorial expertise, experience, and manpower and the sophisticated electronic paraphernalia they had been developing in the twenty-year period since television news first burst into the political arena in 1952.

Unfortunately it didn't. But it wasn't entirely broadcast journalism's fault. All the reportorial skills and electronic miracles available to television journalism couldn't do much to make sense out of a presidential campaign where the presidential candidates didn't seem to lay a hand on each other.

One can only sense a strange feeling of detachment watching coverage of the campaign. It all seemed so unreal. The president barely came out of the White House, and, when he did, it was for pomp and pageantry befitting a royal family. Media representatives were kept at a sufficient distance so as not to clutter up the royal environment or perhaps catch a slip of the tongue should one occur.

The challenger was accessible. No broadcast reporter faulted him on that score. But he was in the frustrating position of being on the offensive against a man who wouldn't come out of his corner to fight. As he flailed about swinging haymakers, he seemed to be hitting nothing but air. At least, there were no indications from television reporters that he had landed any solid blows.

There was another and perhaps more profound reason for broadcast journalism's transmission of a blurred picture. Ever since Vice-President Agnew's November 1969 speech in Des Moines, Iowa, castigating network news organizations and the Eastern Liberal Establishment in the Press, the Administration had been chipping away at network broadcast journalism's credibility. The campaign may not have intimidated the networks but it surely planted a few seeds of doubt among viewers, thus causing an erosion of the base of confidence from which television journalists had been operating. At the same time, the power of the incumbent to dominate the media, which stemmed, in part, from the impact of television, created a situation in which the president could campaign without appearing to campaign at all.

For those of us who had been intimately involved in television's first major venture into the political arena, the campaign of 1972 was a curiously unsatisfying experience. We had been confident through the decade of the fifties, and the Kennedy-Nixon campaign of 1960, that television was a new force on the political scene, a force which would bring candidates out into the open, encourage them to wage their campaigns in the living rooms of millions of voters, strip away pretension and gimmickry, and bring politics down to fundamentals.

It is obvious now that we were dreaming. Television news in 1972 had more reporters on the campaign trail than ever before. Their equipment was more efficiently packaged and delivered higher physical quality. Pickups could be made from any city of any size in the country. Editorial executives had conquered the logistical problems of moving bodies and equipment to the point where they could furnish coverage at nearly any city in the United States where a candidate or his surrogates could go. But what resulted was largely frustration. The focus seemed soft, and reality never seemed to come into sharp perspective.

It's difficult to generalize on the coverage of the campaign because there were really two campaigns. One was the skillful low-key effort to "re-elect the president." The other was Senator McGovern's haymaker assault on the occupant of the White House. The result was a series of paradoxes:

The campaign was said to be characterized by apathy, but there was a rash of complaints about unfair practices, many of them involving the media.

The Campaign Finance Act of 1971 was designed to control expenditures, but the campaign was the costliest in history.

The campaign to "re-elect the president" reached a new high level in packaging a candidate. But Senator McGovern wouldn't be packaged, or couldn't.

There was more emphasis than ever before on coverage in television-news broadcast and interview programs. But the president was never available to participate. As a matter of fact, he had virtually no contact with the press. One candidate was virtually always available, the other never.

The whistle stop was abandoned, but the jet stop replacing it is almost the same thing. The only real difference is that it covers a lot more geography.

It was predicted that there would be a shift away from short political advertisements to computerized direct mail. The direct mail was evident in unprecedented volume, but there didn't seem to be any diminution in the use of short commercials. In brief, there are virtually no generalizations that can be drawn in such a way as to be completely valid.

If there was any one aspect of the 1972 campaign that was in any way distinctive, it was the preoccupation with hard-news broadcasts. But even in the news programs, which were a major target of opportunity for both campaign organizations, there was a decided difference in technique brought about largely by the role of the two candidates. While Senator McGovern was scurrying around from crucial state to crucial state trying to reach three major media markets each day, the president was able to sit in the White House and make news as if it were a commodity coming off an assembly line. He could announce grain sales to the Soviet Union and China, sign an arms-limitation pact with the Soviet Union, inspect flood damage in Pennsylvania, flay Congress for profligate spending, veto nine appropriation bills with a plea for fiscal responsibility, and venture out of the White House in a well-organized pilgrimage to Independence Hall to sign a revenue-sharing bill.

The president was as carefully shielded from the political hustle-bustle as if he were flying through the campaign in a hermetically sealed space capsule. The environment was carefully controlled. The course was set by skillfully programmed computer technology. Minor course corrections were well within the preestablished parameters, and there was an air-lock hatch available for a few space walks such as the Philadelphia and Atlanta trips.

It is easy to understand the frustration of the reporters. When the chief executive did come out of the White House, reporters rode in buses without a line of sight on the presidential limousine. They followed proceedings furnished to them through a play-by-play report broadcast from a car nearer the president. There were no press conferences, no personal interviews—in fact, no contact.

So the reporters did what they had to do; they concentrated on the external aspects of the campaigning, and on the surrogates who were threshing around the country denouncing Senator McGovern and urging voters to "re-elect the president." But when the president traveled, about all they could do was estimate how many tons of paper were thrust into shredders on the tops of Atlanta's tallest buildings, to be blown into the streets by giant fans; they could count crowds, speculate on the Watergate affair, or report on bedlam and police whistles. There simply weren't any issues fully joined.

Senator McGovern, meanwhile, was bravely keeping his appointments and getting his coverage both nationally and locally. Television reporters faithfully recounted what he had to say. And from the point of view of the print media, he succeeded in getting just about an even break. Even in the face of the incumbent's enormous advantage in commanding the attention of the media, an ABC News study covering the campaign from pre-primary period to Election Day showed that there was virtually no difference in the quantity of attention given to the two major party candidates.

One of the reasons for the increased attention given by the candidates to straight news coverage was the new Campaign Finance Act, which presumably would restrict their paid advertising. Even more important, however, is the fact that sophisticated political consultants were aware of the large audiences available to news programs. They discovered that news on television, at least prior to the vice-president's November 1969 attack, had obtained a high degree of public confidence in contrast with the skepticism which seemed to be attached to the political commercial, particularly the short, hard-sell variety. Adverse reactions to the excesses in political commercials in the 1970 campaign contributed further to the attractiveness of news. Hard news gave the candidate exposure in the most favorable of circumstances. He could hitchhike on the prestige of the anchorman, who had a large personal following in his own right. And he could reach all shades of the political spectrum—supporters, uncommitted, and supporters of the opposition.

Two other old favorites of political campaign managers made a comeback in broadcast schedules of 1972: the half-hour television address and the use of radio for straight talks. The half-hour television address had been virtually abandoned in the middle 1950's. In its revival it had undergone some changes. No longer did the address originate in front of large crowds. Now it came from a quiet library or office setting. Film clips and graphic arts were used in greater quantity than ever before to spice up the performance, illustrate critical points, and create a change of pace. Telethons were used as usual, but there is no evidence of the "arena" type of programs which dominated the Nixon campaign in 1968.

The intensive use of radio by President Nixon in the closing weeks of the campaign (although he also used it to some extent in the 1968 campaign) was a startling throwback to pre-television days. The president delivered a wide variety of position papers in a number of fifteen-minute speeches delivered largely during daytime hours. He couldn't expect audiences nearly comparable to those he would have reached on television. But the price was cheap, and the aftereffects vastly outweighed the significance of the original appearances. Segments of the speeches were quoted extensively on television and radio, and in the newspapers. The performances themselves, however, were sufficiently unobtrusive for the president to be able to preserve his seclusion and maintain the splendid fiction that he was really not campaigning at all. He was only reporting on his stewardship to the electorate.

Some of the financial support previously given to television commercials was diverted to direct mail, sometimes accompanied by telephone solicitation or personal house calls to individuals selected by complex computer programming. Increased sophistication in the use of computerized mailing lists, coupled with the fact that the Campaign Finance Act did not regulate direct mail, made this device particularly attractive. Although it will take many months before returns are in hand, preliminary evidence suggests that such mailings are valuable for soliciting campaign funds but substantially less useful in creating support for ideas.

The most favorable aspect of television participation in the political process was evident at the local station level rather than at the network. There were more debates, more special campaign programs, more candidates interviewed, and a greater variety of campaign programming than ever before. A reasonably large proportion of station managements apparently realized the values accruing to the station from intensive campaign coverage as well as the importance of their own roles in the democratic process.

Public television gave another dimension to local coverage. Station WTTW in Chicago, for example, produced a series of lengthy "politithons" in which candidates for office, important and unimportant, from parties large and small, left and right, and the smallest splinters were given an opportunity to be heard.

The networks still had their hands tied by Section 315, the equal-time provision of the Federal Communications Act. In dealing with Section 315, the local stations had a marked advantage. Their requirements to furnish equal time are limited only to the candidates officially on the ballots in their states. The networks, to the contrary, have a responsibility for giving equal access to all candidates for national offices throughout the nation. This year, for example, there were eleven qualified presidential and vice-presidential candidates. The total is somewhat fewer than the seventeen or eighteen that normally run for office in a national election year but still is a burden too heavy to assume if the two major party candidates are going to be given any reasonable and useful amount of time.

The biggest disappointment, however, is that television is not measuring up to its early promise.

It failed in 1972 largely because the candidates would not use its facilities to educate the voters.

It failed to have much real influence over the course of the campaign. It is unlikely that a considerable amount of additional money or effort put into political commercials, speeches, telethons, interviews, or arena programs would have changed enough votes to justify increasing the volume. As a matter of fact, it is doubtful whether any votes were changed at all.

It failed to get the candidates into the same ring as it had for the "Great Debates" of 1960.

It included a significant volume of coverage of the campaign in its news programs, interview and discussion shows, documentaries, political commercials, and five-minute or half-hour speeches. But the initiative was in the hands of the candidates, not the broadcasters.

It failed to get voters to the polls. The percentage turnout was the lowest in the television era.

As of the beginning of 1973, the future looks bleak. Television news has acquired skills, experience, remarkable electronic machinery, and sophistication. But there seems to be no place or way to use them. The political managers seem to have learned more. They discovered the methods required to bend news reports to their own ends and to take the leadership themselves. They have the momentum. It now remains to be seen whether broadcasters can recover the initiative. It will be easier for them in 1976, when the advantages of the incumbent will no longer be a deterrent. If broadcasters then can find the formula for leading rather than following, they can live up to all those optimistic predictions and glorious dreams of twenty years ago. If they can't, broadcasting may continue to be more a tool of the campaign directors than an instrument for voter education and a stimulus to interest in both the political process and issues.

Notes on the Drama of Politics and the Drama of Journalism

by Michael Novak

IN 1972 I found myself a "double agent." From February until August I followed the national press as a correspondent on the elections for *Newsday*. From August 7 until November 7, I worked on the staff of Sargent Shriver, spending most of those days on the campaign plane. My thoughts are still not thoroughly sorted. Notes on these two dramas follow . . .

In February 1972 few journalists reported credibly on the forces that would simultaneously win the nomination for George McGovern and lose the election for him. Throughout the spring features on "the new populism" did not succeed in capturing the subtle, complex moods of various groups in the electorate. In midsummer some newsmen were afraid to "underestimate" George McGovern—some predicted magic youth votes, magic registration figures, and other unknown potions . . .

As November 7 came, anomalies and paradoxes of the political situation still went largely unexplored. Anthony Lewis of *The New York Times* was reduced to asking: "What is the question?" Seldom, it seems, has the literate, "enlightened" segment of the population been so poorly informed about its fellow citizens.

Why?

Consider: There are almost 62 million registered Democrats. George McGovern, the Democratic candidate, won less than 29 million votes. *At least* 25 million Democrats did not vote at all. *At least* 36 million Democrats refused to vote for McGovern. When one accounts for Republicans and Independents, *not more* than 25 million Democrats actually voted for McGovern. Such disaffection from the Democratic presidential candidate is staggering.

How can so many ordinary Democrats be so disaffected from

a candidate who was for months a hero of educated people? And yet prove in congressional and state elections the fundamental health of the Democratic party?

When I read columnists in *The New York Times, The Washington Post, Newsday,* and other papers that I encounter, and when I watch the television news, I seldom—almost never—encounter interpretations of politics that match discussions among people I grew up with, in neighborhoods I still visit. Blacks, Chicanos, and Indians make the same complaint. Lower-class Jews voice it, as well. Psychologist Robert Coles, sociologist Richard Sennett, and others make the same point, so I know it is not idiosyncratic: When news reporters speak of "middle America," they seem vastly to oversimplify it, to miss it, to distort it. Perhaps they assimilate all of it to the bit of it *they* grew up in . . . They are too confident they know it all . . . and they don't show signs that they actually do . . .

They fail, for example, to distinguish WASP, rural, small-town "middle America" from urban, ethnic (Catholic or Jewish working class) "middle America." They fail to distinguish the many kinds of WASPs. The Alabama dirt farmer and the Protestant handyman, still poor despite two centuries in western Massachusetts, live in different psychic worlds. In politically significant ways, Minnesota farmers are not like those in Nebraska . . .

On television, meanwhile, the ethnic sameness inhibits our total trust: Cronkite, Reasoner, Smith, Huntley, Brinkley, Chancellor, and on down deep into the ranks. Couldn't *someone* be daring (I say facetiously) and slip in an Armenian anchorman, a Pole with an unpronounceable name, or (protect me) a very Jewish Jew? Not just a token name or face, of course, but a sensitive intelligence—someone who could give us confidence that he *understands* the precise nuances of the neighborhoods the news sometimes leads him into?

Instead, this tone of being above it all . . .

How representative of the many diverse neighborhoods of America are the writers and broadcasters? There are two parts to this question.

1. From what neighborhoods do they actually spring? Where are their roots? What are their present connections? We could benefit by a sociological portrait of perhaps the twenty top television newsmen, the twenty most widely read columnists, the

twenty top national radio broadcasters, and the fifty top national political reporters of the press. Such a portrait might show us how deeply experienced in America's diversity our journalists are.

2. How well do the chief writers and broadcasters understand the various regions, neighborhoods, interest groups, and other political forces it is their business to report? In how many different sorts of neighborhoods could their work be greeted—not, perhaps, with agreement—but with at least a grudging nod: "Yes, that's our neighborhood"? It is remarkable, for example, that follow-up studies of the reporting of the Attica prison riot indicated that neither the families of the inmates nor the families of the guards felt that their own cultural situation was presented accurately. It is quite plausible that the journalists present had, by and large, little experience in, or nuanced comprehension of, *either* of those cultural worlds.

Much more than we realize, becoming a journalist means entering into a quite special form of culture. At parties and receptions and on occasions when one has free time to dispose of, one soon learns to seek out and to prefer the company of fellow or sister journalists. One has "more in common" with them. One shares a similar sense of excitement, a related set of skills, a cultivated ambience of anecdote and wit. Individual differs from individual in background, learning, taste, and personality. Nevertheless, an outsider discerns a spirit of fraternity, a world as intact as "the clerical world" or "the academic world."

It is not surprising that journalists, especially in the national press corps, identify more with one another than with the sociological groups to which they earlier belonged through regional, neighborhood, ethnic, educational, or class ties. Becoming a member of the national press corps is of enormous cultural and psychic significance in one's life. By comparison to it, all other forms of belonging may not only pale but seem inferior, subject to detached study.

Members of other cultural groups often experience the arrival of the national press as a foreign invasion—an invasion of people from a different culture entirely. "Ego civis Romanus sum," St. Paul once said, with the pride that induced deference. "Coming through, national press!"—contemporary imperialism of the spirit.

"I'm going to be real!" a little black lad in Pittsburgh squealed last April after Hubert Humphrey, in the glow of his own joyous smile *and* the television lights, had shaken the boy's hand in a Pittsburgh street at twilight. "I'm going to be real."

Television in particular—but also the other media—construct a most important form of daily reality. In a political campaign, what doesn't make television or the papers fails (for millions and millions) to exist. Nothing. Emptiness. Zero. Even my best-informed friends have only the vaguest knowledge of what Sargent Shriver said and did. As if it had never happened . . .

Even little children watch television on the average of four hours a day. What a great chunk of awareness the ingestion of television constitutes. The real world. The world out there. The more glowing world, more structured, more urgent, more important, more moral, more political, more effective world. Out there are events. Out there is news. ("I am never on the news, nor families like mine, nor people like us—we don't count" . . . so millions think.)

So there is a teasing, ambivalent glow on the face when we suddenly realize that television cameras are coming down *our* street. "We will be real."

It is quite possible, I think, that people are losing faith in government not because of government but because of television. Television creates an image of reality, then tries to show what's "behind" the reality ("analyzes" it), then reports on the skills politicians develop in "using" television.

So that one never knows *when* or *what* or *whom* to believe. Is a crowd's "spontaneous reception" a carefully contrived prop? Is a press conference a *result* of news or a contrivance for *manufacturing* news? Illusion and reality blend indistinguishably . . .

"He's much handsomer than he looks on television," the lady says, fulfilling a need to check a sense of living under illusion with the evidence of flesh. "I didn't know he was so tall!" Like a Greek god, the candidate is singled out by lights and cameras in every crowd: a halo, a penumbra of otherworldly reality. He walks in a sphere few others share.

Why should anyone have any confidence in him? Superior reality is but another form of unreality.

Television empties politics of credibility—not in the dimension of truth and falsehood, but in the dimension of reality and unreality.

From sharing the ways of the press to serving as a staff member for Sargent Shriver. From one part of the plane to the other —what a different set of responsibilities, preoccupations, perceptions.

Amazing, to have a dozen or more staff workers do days of research to get up an event (say) in Detroit, preparing background, press statement, and perhaps a speech; to inspect the site and then later to have advance men on the spot days before arrival; to compile thick "trip books" full of information on local persons, events, issues; to go through hours of staff debate about taking a position on the given issue—and then to see how much of this effort surfaced, or failed to surface in the national and the local media.

Politics is like staging a play.

News reports comment mostly on the technique.

The "insider" books—like Theodore White's—may have destroyed actual reporting. Hardly anyone reports what the candidate actually *says* or *does;* interest in technique leads reporters *behind* the scenes. It's like putting on a play with the audience watching the backstage changes.

[There seems to be a studied effort to avoid the material laboriously prepared by candidate and staff, although sometimes it is solid stuff. There seems to be high interest in casual exchanges, offhand remarks, bits of spontaneous drama. It's a little like going to college for the parties.]

The whole nation is bored by issues, but piety demands that campaigners should campaign on them. So candidates *look* for them—a little like fishing. A baited hook, wait to see if the media or the public bite. But by this time "issues" are less principled, more symbolic; personified, dramatized, not "rational." Another way in which politics and journalism are both forms of drama.

The politician's play really has to be sharpened to a most elementary point—"focused"—to catch one minute on the evening news. But how to get the press to focus on the point the politician is focusing on? How get both to do the same play?

Politics and news reporting run in contrary directions. In a sense, a politician does well to forget politics and to concentrate on how the media operate. The media have certain laws. They run in a direction of their own, willy-nilly. Wrong to think they *follow* the politician, *report* the politician. No, they have their own necessities: morning and afternoon deadlines, space, thematic shape, demands of competition, traditions of perception. No use fighting against these necessities. The media are one more intractable reality a politician needs to respect rather than to try to reform. Examples (some elementary):

1. For better staging, the politician does well to allow writers and producers to see his script just long enough in advance to plot *their* stories. The politician may be busy from sun-up until midnight—no matter, the space or time the media have to fill is finite, and they must select. From a media standpoint, 99 percent of campaigning cannot be reported.

2. Newsmen find many more of their stories killed or paragraphs chopped than an outsider might imagine. Even to get "in" the paper or "on" the news is a daily, competitive struggle. So the press is jumpy. There's "inside" drama on its side, too.

3. The tradition of American journalism demands "news." An "angle." Something "different." Something "fresh." The world isn't made that way—"There's nothing new under the sun," men believed for thousands of years—and good politics is seldom a matter of novelty. But journalism has a voracious appetite for novelty. So you must go against both nature and politics, if you want coverage. (No wonder people suspect politicians will "do anything" to get their picture in the papers—a most untrustworthy crew, like circus people. As a politician you *need* the coverage. So, sell a little more of your soul . . . Is it just as corrupting to sell yourself for news as for lucre?)

Commentators, I think, fail to see how *corrupting* the practices of journalism truly are: the cult of celebrity, the cult of "news," the manipulative skills of "riding the wire," supplying two new daily "leads," "grabbing headlines," manufacturing "events" and "statements." Journalists speak as if *money* were the great corrupter of our times; but the corruption of intelligence and imagination by the demand for "news" is deadly . . . One source of the widespread revulsion against the culture of the media: a dim perception of the phoniness involved in being a "newsmaker."

Now, the professed mission of the media is to "enlighten" the public. There may be hypocrisy in that. Like clergymen, journalists explain the odium sometimes directed against them by saying, "We present truths people don't like to face." But the anticlericalism of the Age of Broadcasting is directed at those who decide what is real, who transubstantiate a whole world of shadowy movements into the real world of "events in the news."

It takes faith to identify the news with reality—faith in another world than the world of flesh.

4. The media follow narrative lines. They tell stories—parables—morality plays. The narrative lines have long-range rhythms, middle-range and short-range rhythms. In 1968, as Paul Weaver has pointed out in *The Public Interest,* the story of Humphrey was (a) the story of the underdog and the obstacles besetting him; (b) the story of the underdog gathering courage to confront one obstacle after another; (c) the story of momentum and "rags-to-near-riches." A classic American story.

In 1972 this same story, with a new leading man, carried the media from February to July. Thrown in for good measure was the story of the good guy in the white hat cleaning up the town —and of the town (shades of Chicago's Al Capone and the ministers of Cicero) throwing him out. All America is torn between loving the good guy and wanting to do him in. (Not least the more "issue-oriented" and "causey" of our writing intellectuals: the rise and fall of George McGovern in *Harper's, New York, The Atlantic Monthly,* etc. Has ever a man been so *speedily* put down by friends?)

From early June onward the story was: "The Moralist has clay feet." The clay feet crumbling. And crumbling . . . People *hate* a preacher . . . Journalists respect power, toughness, technical finesse—respect these most. Contempt for mere virtue, and an ultimate hidden hatred for nice guys. Deep in the American character. Most highly esteemed: professional killers. Hard-to-fool professionals!

It is important for politicians to catch the narrative line the media are following—and plan either to surprise and disrupt it, or to flatter it by riding it.

Journalists don't like to be proven wrong by events. So they are always anticipating today a story line that will hold up along the road. Once established, a story line serves as a connecting link from day to day—gives the coherence necessary for intelligibility.

If the story line *isn't* the story the politician is trying to tell, he ought to know that quickly and do something about it. But the function of a story line is to guide perception and to supply a device for screening and selection: once implanted, a story line is self-fulfilling and difficult to alter.

Journalists are more often trapped by their own story lines

than by any of the other sources of "bias" frequently mentioned: running with the pack, leaning toward the political left, jaundiced professionalism, etc.

A story line not only serves as self-protection; it is a necessity inherent in journalistic form.

America is so huge and various that a national politician needs a staff of dozens, plus years of experience, before he knows the faces, names, facts, historic forces, and local ways of perceiving that enable him to act accurately in every situation. The ordinary journalist has no such support; only a few who tend to be older have an impressive body of experience.

The journalist, moreover, remains in a peculiar way "above" or "outside" the local groups he encounters. By contrast, the politician must find a way to be "one" with them: to merge his identity with theirs. A journalist can take refuge behind "objectivity," and never break out of a habit of detachment. A politician, whether instinctively or against his personal grain, must lay his own subjectivity on the line, must make himself vulnerable, must try to find some psychic connection, awaken some bond of loyalty. A politician must *go out* to people (even if his manner is patrician, aloof, cold) in a way a journalist need not.

It would be a step forward if newspapers, radio stations, and television networks gave us accurate thumbnail biographies of their reporters. All reporting is angular, perspectival, selective. It would be far more "objective," or at least honest, if we had in mind the finite, distinctive story along whose trajectory each reporter sees what he sees. We could more easily "place" his work, catch its implicit intelligibility. (Facts we gradually learn about a favorite reporter or columnist shed light on his work, help us to interpret.)

Persons are not machines, not instruments without an organic history. Words do not live in a nonhistorical, abstract vacuum. Words are personal utterances; they get a large part of their meaning from the person who authors them. (The same sentence said by Nixon and by McGovern will, as often as not, have a significantly different meaning; so would the same speech, given by both.)

All the more is this true of television news: the personal signature of the newsman is as marked as that of a dramatist acting in his own play. The *reporter* tells (in one to four minutes, usually) what "the" story is for the day—he decides, from his part of the world. *He* had to invent it, create it, out of the chaos of a long campaign day.

(The written word allows for greater distance between speaker and word. The abstractness of print diminishes the immediacy of the personal presence. One can more easily pretend that the words authored themselves, without the intrusion of the writer. No matter: the nature of reporting is that it requires a *witness.* However impersonal the prose, the witness is human, incarnate, at a place, at a time—not the omniscient observer of some Victorian novel, but a mop of hair and a sack of bones with eyes and memory: *him* or *her,* no other.)

With many, I long for an end to the trappings of objectivity; for a frank acceptance of finiteness; for a direct recognition of personhood and its marvelous implications; for an honesty about what journalism can do and can't do (and politics, too); and for an attempt by journalists to overcome—as it seems—the educated person's disdain for the "unenlightened." I hope increasing numbers attempt to identify with, sympathize with; learn from, rebuke, and be rebuked by fellows in undershirts in their kitchens, and the clerks and insurance agents and pipefitters and pattern cutters who live in worlds, suffer pains, dream dreams which it is, alas, the function of education to isolate us from.

Is anything in America so divisive as "enlightenment"? One would hope journalists would not imagine themselves missionaries of that pretentious religion. One would hope more of them will report at least as much *from* the people *to* the enlightened as is now pressed upon the people from above.

Radio News—Promise and Performance

by Steve Knoll

BROADCASTERS frequently point with pride to polls taken by The Roper Organization which have found television to be the primary news source of the American people since 1963. Less often cited are the Roper findings as they pertain to radio. Yet these too are of interest. While the number of people giving television as their "source of most news" grew from 51 percent in 1959 to 60 percent in the latest Roper survey (conducted in 1971), those choosing radio declined from 34 percent in 1959 to 23 percent in 1971. Moreover, in 1968, when the poll asked, "Which would you say gives you the clearest understanding of the candidates and issues in national elections—radio, television, newspapers, or magazines?" radio fared poorest: only 4 percent selected the sound medium, compared with 57 percent for television, 23 percent for newspapers, and 10 percent for magazines.

A counterpoint to the Roper results is provided by a 1971 survey conducted by Opinion Research Corporation, which found that radio is the main source of news in the morning for 52 percent of Americans who are eighteen and older, as against 20 percent each for television and newspapers. This survey was commissioned, as it happens, by CBS Radio.

While few will deny that, as a New York disk jockey quipped, "more people listen to radio today than when it was popular," the Roper results carry a sobering message to radio broadcasters concerned about their medium's stature as a journalistic force. It could be that the inadequacy of much radio news—superficial at its best, incoherent at its worst—has become apparent to the average listener. That listener's response is not necessarily to turn off his set; radio's entertainment and service features remain of value to him. Yet, if the mass audience grows reconciled to the fact that it cannot learn the meaning of the news from radio, that would surely represent an unhappy omen for the medium.

The very limited appetite for news on the part of most American radio stations has long been painfully apparent to the national radio networks, which have been forced in recent years to eliminate or curtail some of their best news broadcasts to conform with station desires. Affiliates of some networks engage in what is known as "wild-spotting": carrying the commercials from network newscasts without carrying the newscasts themselves.

Van Gordon Sauter, CBS News executive producer for radio, feels that "a basic problem of radio news is that too many owners are blatant sharks—they derive substantial financial returns from the licenses while operating their news and public affairs departments at sub-poverty levels." In Sauter's view, which is widely shared among concerned radio newsmen, many station owners fail to give their news departments "moral assistance and leadership." Instead the departments "are frequently turned over to program directors, ex-disk jockeys who consider news intrusive, expensive, and, no doubt, subversive. There has been a perceptible increase in the quality of local print journalism in this country. I don't think the same can be said for radio journalism."

The "substantial financial returns" radio station owners derive from their franchises are spelled out in figures issued by the Federal Communications Commission and the National Association of Broadcasters. Radio profits in 1970—the last year for which FCC data are available at this writing—amounted to $92.9 million before federal income tax on revenues of $1,136.9 million. In 1971, according to an NAB survey, the median AM station made a pre-tax profit of $11,500 on revenues of $168,900.

An earlier NAB survey for 1970 found that in markets with greater than 2.5 million population, large stations (those with at least $1 million in total revenue) recorded a typical $570,300 profit. Counting only black-ink stations in that category, the median profit was $944,600, reflecting a profit margin of 25.51 percent. In none of the nine market sizes charted by the NAB—ranging from the largest to the smallest—does the "typical" station show a loss. And 1970, it will be recalled, was a recession year.*

---

* The 1971 NAB survey was based on responses from 1,380 AM and AM-FM stations. Excluded were independent FM's and combination AM-FM operations that filed separate returns for the FM. The 1970 NAB survey was based on responses from 1,374 AM stations.

Despite the resources at the disposal of the station owners, most critics would agree that commercial radio in America, like commercial television, falls considerably short of its potential, and for a similar reason: the quest for the sponsor's dollar is presumed to conflict with the pursuit of excellence in programming, and the former is given priority. Yet there are important differences between the program structures of radio and television as they have evolved during the past two decades. To some, a study of these differences suggests that television has at least retained its potential for excellence (i.e., an occasional oasis of cultural or informational refreshment), while radio has virtually committed itself to a diet of unrelieved mediocrity.

Although some radio broadcasters continue to air full-length public affairs programs and documentaries outside of the weekend "ghetto" time slots, such public-spirited stations are few and far between. An analysis of the reasons for this scarcity would not only help us to understand why radio is the way it is, but might also bring into question the notion that the availability of a large number of stations necessarily leads to diversity in program content. There may be an omen for cable television here.

While radio, like over-the-air TV, operates on a limited frequency spectrum, the concept of a "scarce resource" is purely academic in markets like New York, which has more than fifty AM and FM outlets. Yet it is apparent that in radio the proliferation of stations has not significantly enlarged the range of program choices. With the exception of some FM stations, notably the listener-supported Pacifica group, the intellectual and cultural minorities who were not being served in the heyday of network radio are not being served today. The programming structure has changed to meet the video competition, but the objective has remained constant: to attract the largest possible audience, as reflected in the ratings. The only modification of the rules accepted in recent years is the same one television has adopted: an increasing emphasis on reaching listeners aged eighteen to forty-nine, the demographic group favored by advertisers. The result of this change, in radio as in television, is that the needs and tastes of the over-fifty listener are increasingly neglected.

Yet television, for all its faults, has retained a structure of block programming, something radio has largely abandoned in favor of continuous formats. The block concept allows different program types, such as Westerns, comedies, and documentaries, to be blended harmoniously on a single evening's schedule. Granted, TV stations more often opt for a Western or a comedy than a documentary, but not because the documentary is deemed "inconsistent" with the other two genres. Indeed, in television, mixing up different program forms for the sake of variety is a common and accepted way of putting together a night's schedule. Television may not always achieve its potential for diversity in the fullest sense, but the block-programming structure leaves room for occasional intrusions of excellence. The point is fundamental.

The flexibility enjoyed by the video programmer is virtually unknown to his radio counterpart. True diversity within the programming of a single station is anathema to the basic dogma of format radio. That dogma is almost universally accepted. In a book entitled *Managing Today's Radio Station,* Jay Hoffer, program director of KRAK, Sacramento, argues that listeners expect uniformity in their radio stations. If the listener does not know what to expect next, the station defeats "the entire repetition-saturation philosophy that has made for the powerful resurgence of the overall medium of radio." ABC Television president Walter A. Schwartz, who served previously as president of the ABC Radio network and vice president–general manager of WABC, New York, once advised programmers at a Billboard Radio Forum that "in this age of specialization, your station is only as good as it is true to its format . . . . Everything you do, everything you play, everything you say or don't say, must give your call letters without your having to voice them. What you do and the way that you do it must be expected by your audience at all times."

The proponents of format radio have developed a rhetoric of their own to confer on their creation attributes it does not in fact possess. For example, they assert that in place of "vertical diversity" (translated: diversity within a single station's programming) there is "horizontal diversity." The contention is that as the listener goes up and down the dial, the diversity of the formats from which he can choose will more than compensate for the sameness of a single station's programming.

The theory is unexceptionable. The practice is something else. For the spectrum of formats employed in American radio today is a distinctly limited one. The overwhelming majority of stations play records (and commercials) the overwhelming majority of the time. Most carry at least one five-minute newscast per hour, although the trend in many sectors of FM is toward shorter newscasts of reduced frequency. (Indeed FM, which was once offered as a quality alternative to AM, has become largely an extension of it, operating on smaller budgets and with wider use of automation; robot radio stations abound on FM.)

The gradations of difference between music formats is a subject of interest to musicologists; yet for the listener-layman the gamut consists of five or six basic categories, from rock (underground or overground) on the one extreme to classical music on the other. This range may have been further narrowed in August 1971 when the FCC expressed apprehensions over free-form underground radio in words calculated to send a chill up the spine of any broadcaster involved with the format.

The FCC declared that the "free-form rock format, like a free-form classical format or a free-form anything format, gives the announcer [sic] such control over the records to be played that it is inconsistent with the strict controls that the licensee must exercise to avoid questionable practices."

In an interview with *Broadcasting* magazine, Allen B. Shaw, Jr., ABC vice-president in charge of the seven FM stations owned by that company, stated: "I agree in full with the FCC's ruling that free-form stations are not desirable. We have always exercised control of our programming and are constantly tightening up. We are out of the free-form thing entirely."

ABC's decision to "tighten up" its FM programming covered far more scope than the esoteric matter of music playlists. In an effort to lure the youth audience, the personalities on ABC's FM stations had been permitted to express antiestablishment political views, including sharp criticism of the Nixon administration. The rigid dictates of format radio were eased for the experiment. On the Fourth of July in 1970, and again in 1971, the stations broadcast "Self-Evident Truths," a one-hour documentary that artfully juxtaposed the libertarian rhetoric of the Founding Fathers and the Nixon-Agnew brand of oratory with telling effect.

ABC's return to a more conventional FM rock format thus represented a setback for the cause of free speech on commercial radio. Ironically, several months after ABC (FM) had reverted to form, the FCC issued a "clarification" of its original ruling, insisting that it had "merely referred to the commission's frequently reiterated concept of licensee responsibility over programming."

In many communities across the land, the disk jockeys that dominate the radio band have been complemented by "talk jockeys," a newer breed whose job is to blend not records but telephone calls from frequently irate, sometimes inarticulate listeners. "Two-way radio," as it is sometimes called, offers the public qualified access to the air. Too often the public's response indicates that giving the listener "access" is no guarantee of greater illumination on the issues of the day.

Talk-back radio has been trumpeted as the broadcast equivalent of the letters-to-the-editor section of a newspaper, but the comparison is inexact. The letters are confined to a small portion of a newspaper's total space. Moreover, they are not set into type as received, but are carefully sifted and frequently condensed before publication. And despite such precautions, the letters section generally lags behind the editorials and columns in providing informed opinion and perceptive analysis. With some exceptions, the letters-to-the-editor feature is mainly useful as a barometer of public opinion.

On two-way radio, by contrast, the "letters section" frequently constitutes the entire format. The "letters" are generally broadcast as received, "unopened," so to speak. The result too often is heat at the expense of light, or simply boredom.

Since most telephone talk shows deal with current affairs, it would seem desirable that the hosts be journalistically trained. This is not always the case, however. When an ill-informed host engages in verbal battle with an uninformed caller, there is much sound and fury, signifying nothing.

Yet the goal of establishing a dialogue with the community on public affairs, if not always met, is nonetheless admirable. The unwieldy characteristics of the format can be controlled when calls are screened, the agenda is limited to a given subject, and a guest expert is present. When such controls are imposed, and the program's host himself is knowledgeable, talk radio can serve its intended purpose. Some of the best results have been achieved when the conversation format is fused with a news broadcast, placing the callers in touch with the station's newsmen as well as with personalities in the news. A talk format on FM—as on New York's WRVR—seems to attract a more sophisticated listenership, suggesting an avenue that FM broadcasters in other markets might profitably explore.

(In May differences of approach among the WRVR staff surfaced as Michael Keating, a veteran political reporter, was dismissed as anchorman of the station's evening newscast. While Keating brought to his microphone many voices of dissent not normally heard on the air, the wisdom of his highly subjective approach to news coverage can certainly be questioned. Writing in *Newsday,* Keating explained: "the news was assembled with a view that held that the President is basically interested in reelection, not the welfare of the country; that Congress most often serves the corporations, not the people; that the military-industrial complex is really running things; that the worst corruptors in our society are not the dope pushers, but the bagmen, fixers, grafters and thieves who stride the halls of corporations and legislatures with dignity and authority. The reporters were told to forget about objectivity.")

In an age when the format ideology is accepted as gospel by most radio operators, it's ironic that one of the most commercially successful stations in the country, New York's WOR (AM), provides an unusually variegated service stressing civilized conversation. A talk station with a difference, WOR abjures the use of telephones, provides a wide range of discussion programs complemented by 15-minute newscasts on the hour and—blasphemy!—an occasional dash of popular music. There's a lesson there somewhere.

The homogenized character of most radio news, combined with its local orientation, has not left much room for development of the sort of colorful national personality that dominated the medium's "golden age." A few remain, mostly survivors of the earlier era. Yet since radio commentary today is delivered mostly in short takes rather than the old 15-minute form, the programming base upon which a commentator could establish a personal following is lacking. Of the new breed, one of the most compelling voices is that of Group W's Rod MacLeish. MacLeish's forte ranges from sharp-tongued political punditry to a moving essay "on the birth of kittens and other miracles."

Two of the leading "old-timers" are Lowell Thomas and Paul Harvey. The octogenarian Thomas, a veteran of more than forty years in radio news, continues on the air for ten minutes nightly.

The tradition of the conservative political commentator is maintained on the networks principally through the daily 15-minute broadcasts of ABC's Harvey and Mutual's Fulton Lewis III. The Chicago-based Harvey "may well be the United States' best-known newsman," according to *The Christian Science Monitor*. Such a description might surprise residents of the citadels of the East, who may fail to recognize the sway he holds over the rest of the country. In addition to his ABC Radio newscasts, which are carried on approximately five hundred stations, Harvey also is seen on a syndicated television program, and his column appears in some three hundred newspapers.

Taking into account his frequent ventures on the lecture circuit, Harvey's total earnings are commensurate with his celebrity, and place him in the same league as the top TV newsmen.

The nature of his broadcasts is difficult to convey in print, since a unique vocal style takes precedence over substance. The programs are akin to an entertainer's monologue, with adroit pacing and frequent "punch lines" as Harvey moves from item to item. Needless to say, the informational quotient is low.

For better or worse, Paul Harvey remains an island of programming in a sea of formats, serving as the exception that proves the rule. Yet overall, the dominance of local formats on the American radio landscape has wrought profound changes in the service provided by the four radio networks. The departure of "Arthur Godfrey Time" from the CBS Radio airwaves in April after twenty-seven years underscored the fact that stations looked to their networks principally as providers of abbreviated news, sports, and feature packages. The Godfrey program was seen as a vestige of another era, a half-hour block of entertainment programming.

Network radio's exclusive devotion to news, sports, and special events was not an unmixed blessing, however. The reasons for this were perhaps best explained back in 1958 by Edward R. Murrow, in his famous address before the Radio-Television News Directors Association. Murrow related, "I recently asked a network official, 'Why this great rash of 5-minute news reports (including three commercials) on weekends?' He replied, 'Because that seems to be the only thing we can sell.' "

Since 5-minute newscasts (6 minutes on CBS) are now the staple product of network radio seven days a week, Murrow's words take on even greater pertinence today. He asserted:

> In this kind of complex and confusing world, you can't tell very much about the why of the news in broadcasts where only three minutes is available for news. The only man who could do that was Elmer Davis, and his kind aren't about any more. If radio news is to be regarded as a commodity, only acceptable when salable, then I don't care what you call it—I say it isn't news.

Network radio today is full of clicks, beeps, subliminal tones, and verbal cues designed to accommodate local and network commercials of varying lengths within the structure of the hourly newscasts. The news itself is almost incidental. Stations play fast and loose with the network feed; a 4-minute newscast on one ABC Information affiliate is a 15-minute newscast on another, while a third may not carry it at all.

The principal talent required of a news writer is the ability to compress—to whittle down a story to two or three sentences while preserving a semblance of intelligibility. An increasing requisite for a newscaster is the ability to talk fast—the "running for a train" syndrome. One network has been known to periodically test its air men to make sure they were not slowing down.

The preoccupation with "pace" and "flow" and projecting a false sense of immediacy in much of radio news limits attention to content. Paradoxically, as news in such realms as politics, economics, and technology has grown increasingly complex, the amount of time available for intelligent exposition of contemporary problems has shrunk.

The able news staffs of the radio networks struggle manfully to do the best possible job in the least possible time. In January 1972 "CBS Views the Press" returned in the form of two capsule broadcasts on weekends, most of which were produced and written by Dale Minor, formerly a correspondent and executive with Pacifica Radio in New York. "CBS Views the Press" offered incisive, if at times distressingly truncated, critiques of broadcast as well as print journalism.

The leading television newsmen also had daily "strips" on the radio networks, in some cases affording them greater opportunity to analyze and comment on the news than they were permitted on television. Among those heard regularly were CBS' Walter Cronkite; NBC's John Chancellor, David Brinkley, and Edwin Newman; and ABC's Harry Reasoner, Howard K. Smith, Edward P. Morgan, Frank Reynolds, and Louis Rukeyser. Also of note was the CBS "Spectrum" series, featuring nine rotating commentators reflecting the gamut of political opinion, with three broadcasts just under three minutes each aired daily. The effect of such programs was to stimulate without satisfying, to implant a provocative thought or fresh insight in the listener's mind without providing the rounded analysis that only more time would allow.

Fortunately a few longer broadcasts survived, notably NBC's "Second Sunday" and ABC's "Perspective." Although both were produced under budgetary limitations, they nevertheless recalled Murrow's appreciation of radio's potential as "that most satisfying and rewarding instrument" of broadcast journalism. Occasional "instant specials" also provided a glimpse of that potential. For example, a CBS special on May 15, the day

Governor George Wallace of Alabama was shot, capitalized on radio's immediacy, deftly combining the harrowing sounds of the shooting and its aftermath with a review of Wallace's career and an eloquent commentary by correspondent Reid Collins.

But aside from historic events such as the Wallace shooting, the political conventions, and the president's trips to Russia and China, network radio specials—"instant" or otherwise—lasting fifteen minutes or longer were few and far between. In November 1966 the annual United Nations vote on the seating of Red China was the subject of a 25-minute CBS Radio report. But in October 1971, when the UN finally voted to admit Red China and expel the Nationalist Chinese, the only special coverage broadcast by CBS Radio took the form of two brief bulletins.

One of the most valuable series aired by CBS in recent years is "Debriefing," whose format consists of a correspondent interviewing a colleague at length about his assigned beat. Again, a comparison with 1966 illustrates the decline of such news-in-depth programming. "Debriefing" was begun in June 1966; eight 25-minute editions were presented between June and December of that year. By contrast, only one special "Debriefing" was broadcast in 1971: a 9-minute interview with Walter Cronkite following his return from a Middle East assignment.

While the radio side of CBS News has significantly expanded its resources, the network has steadily yielded to affiliate pressures for shrunken news. After a last-ditch effort at saving it, the full-length documentary is dead at CBS. In January 1968 the radio network inaugurated a monthly 25-minute series, "News Journal," in the hope that regularity of presentation plus the opportunity for local sponsorship would make documentaries attractive to enough stations to keep them on the air. It didn't work—even some all-news stations found "News Journal" a burden—and the series terminated at the end of 1969, the victim of poor clearances. The only documentaries now broadcast by CBS are the mini sort.

The start of 1972 saw CBS Radio continuing to bow to affiliates (including the seven CBS-owned stations, who represent some 30 percent of the network's total audience) by chipping away some more at the schedule. "Washington Week," which had been a first-rate analysis of the week's capital developments by members of the CBS Washington bureau, was cut from twenty-five to nine minutes. "The World This Week" went from fifteen to nine minutes; "The American Week," a

25-minute series narrated by Mike Wallace, left the air. And still more damage was done: a fourth one-minute "cutaway" (sixty seconds of news "filler" during which stations can air a commercial) was added to the morning "World News Roundup." And "The World Tonight," the network's 15-minute evening wrap-up, was re-formatted so that stations could cut out after the first nine minutes for local news and commercials. Many affiliates, including all-news WCBS, New York, and WTOP, Washington, D.C., eagerly seized this option. (WCBS and WTOP taped portions of the deleted segment—including Eric Sevareid's analysis—for later broadcast. Nevertheless, their action reflected a widely held view that the listener would not sit still for fifteen solid minutes of national and international news at the dinner hour.)

Indeed, most radio men are convinced that devoting more than two or three minutes to coverage of a single story is suicidal. Correspondent reports on network radio typically run to less than a minute. The doctrine of the limited attention span is one of the fundamental precepts of format radio. Yet there is no empirical evidence to support this view of the listener's habits. The burden of research, in fact, is to the contrary. For example, a 1966 study by R. H. Bruskin Associates commissioned by CBS Radio found that a majority of listeners—59 percent—preferred newscasts lasting ten minutes or longer. These findings did not deter CBS from cutting back most of its hourly newscasts to six minutes (with two minutes of commercials) in 1971.

The affiliate pressures that beset CBS are even stronger at the other networks. At NBC Radio they led to cancellation of "News of the World," the network's only daily 15-minute newscast, at the end of 1969. "The World and Washington," NBC's 15-minute Sunday evening news review, suffered a similar fate in April 1971. The latter series consisted of two segments: an analysis by NBC's State Department correspondent (initially Elie Abel, then his successor, Richard Valeriani) and a report by Ray Scherer, NBC's man in London. At the time of the series' demise, Scherer wrote to NBC News in New York to protest. He was told that if you put a program on the network that no one can hear, the effort involved is wasted.

"The World and Washington" represented the sort of program for which radio is uniquely suited: an attempt to place the events of the week in a clearer focus through astute analysis. Costs were minimal: "The World and Washington's" tab came to only $350 a week. Yet it's axiomatic that a network exists to serve its stations. When offered programs like "The World and Washington," the stations simply did not want to be served.

The clearance problems facing the radio networks, even on their New York flagship stations, were illustrated when President Nixon delivered a radio-only address to the nation from the Western White House on July 4, 1972. WABC and WNBC did not carry the speech (selected excerpts were used, of course, during later newscasts). All-news WCBS (AM) did air the address but omitted the follow-up analysis provided by Bernard Kalb in San Clemente in conversation with Reid Collins in New York. (Ironically WCBS [FM], a rock station, carried both the speech and the follow-up analysis.)

There were a few rays of light in an otherwise bleak picture. Special-events coverage represents a large share of network radio costs, yet sponsors for such coverage generally have been hard to come by, in part because of the clearance uncertainties. Thus it was a pleasant surprise when, in the summer of 1971, the Insurance Company of North America agreed to bankroll virtually all of NBC Radio's special programming, plus some regular features, through the end of 1972. The unprecedented buy, estimated at $2.5 million, included news bulletins. It became the responsibility of NBC News to decide when appending a commercial to a bulletin constituted bad taste. The bulletin announcing the death of Soviet premier Nikita Khrushchev was sponsored by INA; those on the attempted assassination of Governor Wallace were not.

There were some major exceptions to the INA purchase. "Second Sunday," the sole surviving documentary series on network radio, was not included. Neither was a half-hour special in March on "Busing and the Nixon Plan." NBC Radio officials denied that the controversial nature of the subject was related to the lack of INA sponsorship. They explained that because of the poor clearances accorded half-hour news specials, it would amount to "wasting" INA commercials by placing them on such programs. Most of the INA specials did not exceed ten minutes. INA also sponsored the "instant analysis" following presidential speeches.

NBC's "Monitor," a program whose birth in the mid-fifties was marked by exciting and innovative uses of radio journalism, has declined over the years to the point where its principal function is to serve as a merchandising vehicle for its advertisers. Defined by its creator, Sylvester (Pat) Weaver, as a "kaleidoscopic phantasmagoria," "Monitor's" early history was distinguished by a flexibility unknown in present-day radio. Money was no obstacle to news coverage. Neither was time. Hourly newscasts ranged from three to fifteen minutes—whatever the news required. Remote units and broadcast lines went wherever news was happening. The venturesome spirit underlying such endeavors is sadly lacking today.

The most radical change in radio networking in recent years occurred in 1968, when ABC switched from a single-network setup to one feeding four newscasts each hour to four different sets of affiliates. In effect ABC was transformed into an all-newscast network. When the move to the "quadnets" was made, the company launched an expansion program which it says cost $3 million to upgrade the New York headquarters as well as radio bureaus in Washington, Chicago, and Los Angeles.

While ABC Radio's resources are impressive, they cannot be fully utilized within the confines of a service laying primary stress on repetitive newscasts. Prior to 1968 the network had been unusually prolific in the area of special-events coverage; since then, it has lagged behind CBS and NBC because of the restrictions imposed by its new format. ABC generally does not broadcast "instant analysis" following presidential speeches, offering instead a few sentences of recapitulation and then signing off. This is done not to appease Spiro Agnew, but rather to minimize disruptions of the four-network service.

ABC is prohibited by FCC rules from selling its four networks in combination. Thus any special coverage fed simultaneously to all four cannot be made available for sponsorship. This precludes such arrangements as the NBC-INA deal, and means that the heavy costs of special convention, election, and space coverage cannot be recovered through sponsorship.

Commercially, the four ABC networks—which include the first national news service designed exclusively for FM—have performed well, lining up long lists of affiliates and moving ABC Radio, long plagued by deficits, toward black ink. However, this success has been achieved in part by permitting affiliates of some networks to carry only one minute of news with a commercial. ABC's pitch to stations stresses the "limited inventory" on each of its four services. The less a network has to offer, it appears, the more the stations like it.

When ABC devised its multi-network setup, consideration was reportedly given to establishing a news service for black-oriented stations. Ultimately this was not done because of the projected difficulty in obtaining a full network lineup for a black news service. However, in 1972 the Mutual Broadcasting

System, which for years had been unsuccessfully contesting the ABC operation before the FCC, decided to become a multi-network itself by adding news services for black and Spanish-language stations. At the same time, an independent group with primarily black management announced formation of the National Black Network.

The sudden competition for serving the black audience was a welcome, if overdue, development. Mutual entered the fray with the decided advantage of network lines already at its disposal. Stephen J. McCormick, Mutual's vice-president for news, said all he had to do was hire fifteen black newsmen, six editors, some supervisors, and some salesmen. In May Mutual's black network was on the air, while the rival NBN was forced to postpone its debut past the conventions.

In addition to the four major networks and their proliferating sub-networks, stations across the country were served by UPI Audio. Unlike its competitors, UPI Audio sold its service directly to subscribing stations rather than to advertisers. A station could maintain an "independent" image by using taped reports from UPI correspondents within the framework of local newscasts. (Some stations, primarily in smaller markets, made use of hourly newscasts which were also supplied by UPI.)

There were those in the industry who looked upon the UPI Audio approach as the wave of the future for all networks. According to this view, the networks would ultimately be reduced to providing national and international news inserts for use in locally produced programs, while perhaps continuing to feed complete newscasts to those stations that still wanted them. Observers pointed to Group W, which in the fifties had bolted the networks, choosing instead to build up its own worldwide news organization, feeding insert material to its stations. Three of the Group W outlets are all-news. It was partly the competition from Group W that forced CBS Radio to reverse a long-standing policy and add such inserts—the "overset" from regular newscasts—to its network service. To some at CBS News, this represented a lowering of standards, since the network had no control over the setting in which its correspondents were heard.

In the battle between programs and formats, formats carried the day. In many respects journalism was the loser. Like a steamroller crushing everything in its path, a "repetition-saturation" radio format dominates the entire broadcast schedule. Anything that does not conform with the format is tossed aside; full-length documentaries or news specials are *verboten.* "Consistency" of a station's sound at all hours is the paramount consideration.

Of course, few radio men will admit that their news coverage lacks depth. And so another rhetorical abomination on a par with "horizontal diversity" is concocted: "cumulative depth."

What is "cumulative depth"? It's the concept of "mini-documentaries," also popular in television. Instead of a self-contained hour or half-hour documentary, the program is splintered into fragments scattered over the broadcast day. The individual segments are often not much longer than a commercial spot. Yet taken as a single entity—even though they are not scheduled as such—the sprinkling of inserts is said to add "cumulative depth" to news coverage.

"Cumulative depth" is an inventive euphemism for what Sander Vanocur has termed "snippet journalism." A documentary presented in snippet form is not a true documentary. The average listener will be able to catch only one or two of the fragments. Impact is lost, and without impact, a documentary lacks one of its principal assets. Imagine if such high-impact television documentaries as "The Selling of the Pentagon" and "Hunger in America" were presented in the form of 5-minute segments televised over a week-long period at various times in the schedule, and you have some idea of what has happened to the radio documentary.

Programming in fringe periods, of course, can be a totally different story. In the presentation of public affairs and documentaries, many stations "get religion"—appropriately enough —on Sundays. Either early in the Sabbath morning or late into the night, the minimal percentages of nonentertainment programming promised to the FCC are chalked up. In this way the vast majority of listeners will never know that the station's basic format has been disrupted.

The radio documentary remains alive, but barely kicking, at Group W, since the chain's efforts often wind up in the Siberian time zones where the only audience is at the transmitter. In mid-1972 the Group W stations were offered "Breakdown," a series of thirteen half-hours narrated by Rod MacLeish probing the failures of technological systems ranging from transportation and health care to public schools and power. In New York all-news WINS relegated "Breakdown" to Sunday nights at 11:00. In Boston WBZ carried the series at 5:30 A.M. on Sundays; WIND, Chicago, opted for 2:00 A.M. on Mondays. The rest of the group chose less obscure time slots, but it was clear that the status of the documentary was lower at Group W radio than in the company's TV sector, where productions of the Urban America unit are carried in prime time by all the Westinghouse stations.

In a notice of inquiry aimed at defining what constitutes "substantial service" for a television station, the FCC has suggested a range of 3 to 5 percent, *including 3 percent in prime time,* as a representative figure for public affairs programming. If such a stipulation were applied to radio's prime time, the requirement would be viewed by the format-ridden operations as not merely onerous but devastating.

If the doctrine of the limited attention span were the only shibboleth afflicting radio news today, there would still be room for some astute reporting in the few minutes in which major stories are covered. Yet there are other inhibiting dogmas as well. High up on the list is a devotion to "sound," the compulsion to interrupt a newscaster's voice at regular intervals to air the tape-recorded noise of an event or the voice of a newsmaker. These are called "actualities," and they are not always inappropriate. Yet the reliance of radio journalism on "sound" is akin to television's dependence on "picture."

At one time, when television was showing the formalities attending the arrival of a foreign dignitary at the White House, radio was analyzing the reasons for the visit and its policy implications. Today radio is more likely to be carrying the audio portion of the welcoming ceremony.

Television's reliance on sight values constitutes an open invitation to radio to fill in the gaps. After all, the essence of news is ideas, and ideas rarely translate easily to a visual presentation. Yet by attempting to function as second-best television, radio negates its potential as a medium of ideas.

While a TV newsman is constrained to tailor his narrative to fit the available film or videotape, a radio newsman is often forced to build his report around the available actualities. "Sound" for the sake of sound, regardless of its technical quality or informational value, can be as oppressive a tyrant on radio as "picture" on television. The better radio news shops try to avoid the promiscuous use of actualities. In many cases a concise summary of a speech—with a few well-chosen words of analysis—is far more illuminating than a replay of two or three sentences in the speaker's own words for the sake of "sound."

A Group W news executive once observed of radio journalists, "We cover the news conferences. By God how we cover them . . . . We don't miss any because they're easy, accessible and if our reporter doesn't know enough to ask an intelligent question we can still record 'sound' . . . that all-important 'sound'! This simply isn't enough."

Many all-news stations tend to underplay the fact that they are radio, strange as that may seem. This is because they conceive of themselves as public utilities. As one all-news executive put it, "You turn on the faucet, you get water. You turn on the gas, you get heat. You turn us on, you get news." In this context, the decision of WCBS, New York, during the past year to change its on-air identification from WCBS Newsradio 88 to WCBS News 88 may take on special significance. As a Group W official once remarked of the all-news format, "Radio is incidental. We have become an information source."

A comparison of all-news radio with the telephone company's time and weather services would be unfair, since the scope of the all-news service is broader. Yet basic similarities exist. In attempting to provide news headlines and weather, traffic, and sports information at any time of the day to anybody who might be tuning in for a few minutes, the all-news outlets must also try to hold on to the long-term listener. Each station strikes its own compromise between these two conflicting imperatives. Some employ musical sound effects or a background news ticker as show-biz gimmicks. On most all-news stations, the newscasters also read the commercials, and the separation point between news and ad copy is not always clear.

If Ed Murrow was right that news packaged as a commodity isn't really news, then the seemingly contradictory phenomenon of the no-news all-news station becomes understandable.

Despite advances in technology, the standards of radio journalism have declined during the past two decades. As Murrow observed, "In order to progress, it need only go backward." What was once a 15-minute commentary with no middle commercial is now a 3-minute commentary sandwiched around a blurb.

Today the title of "program director" is almost a misnomer. As one industry official has defined the position, "A program director is a fellow who's confronted with a bunch of commercials on one side and a bunch of music records on the other. His idea of his job is to put the two together without any dead air."

If public television is designed to serve as an alternative to "private" television, the need for a similar alternative to commercial radio may be even more pressing. The fact is that such alternatives do exist: the Pacifica group, the better college FM stations around the country, and, since April 1971, NPR, the National Public Radio network.

"We are trying to define the literacy of broadcast journalism a little more," explains William H. Siemering, NPR director of programming. The primary vehicle for this endeavor is "All Things Considered," a daily 90-minute program of news, analysis, and features carried by virtually all of the network's 140 stations, most of which are educational FM's. "All Things Considered" draws heavily on the resources of member stations, with consequently greater emphasis on middle America than can be found on commercial network news. The program is also served by NPR's own Washington staff, plus daily feeds from the British Broadcasting Corporation, correspondents for *The Christian Science Monitor,* Reuters, Agence France-Presse, the Associated Press, and other news services. Commentary on broadcasting itself falls within the network's scope through the services of Judy Bachrach, TV critic of the *Baltimore Sun,* and Edith Efron, author of *The News Twisters.*

NPR's public affairs programming makes the efforts of the commercial networks seem puny by comparison. Representative of the range of the public radio network's special coverage are the twelve hours in March 1972 devoted to the hearings of the Senate Subcommittee on Communications concerning the surgeon general's report on the effects of TV violence; more than fifteen hours in March covering Fairness Doctrine debate before the FCC; ten hours of coverage in June from the United Nations Conference on the Human Environment in Stockholm, and many more hours of UN debates, Congressional hearings, and National Press Club luncheons.

NPR also covered the hearings of the Democrats' Platform Committee in June, but due to the budgetary cutbacks in public broadcasting, was able to provide only a morning-after "highlights package" during the week of the convention itself. A similar pattern was followed for coverage of the Republican convention in August. (NPR is financed by the Corporation for Public Broadcasting.)

The Pacifica Radio network, which also compiled a distinguished public affairs record throughout the year, offered extensive live convention coverage, while the commercial networks presented selective coverage.

The function of backgrounding the news was admirably served by "Insight," a daily half-hour on WQXR, New York, featuring Clifton Daniel, associate editor of *The New York Times,* in conversation with *Times* staffers at home and overseas. There was no reason why the commercial networks, with their superior resources, could not offer a similar series. Yet to do so would require a major reorientation of their thinking, and more particularly that of their affiliates.

It appears that the stature of radio journalism has been harmed by the trend toward abbreviated news. No one can deny that radio performs an important function as a headline service, companion to the lonely and surrogate phonograph. In time of emergency, ranging from tornado to power blackout, radio's alert performance has received deserved acclaim. Yet it is not enough to be allowed glimpses of the medium's potential when disaster strikes.

The dimension of depth can be returned to radio news only if the program form is resurrected. This would not entail revolutionary change; a modest infusion of diversity into the current schedules is all that is needed.

Sports and Television: The Perfect Marriage

by Dick Schaap

THE MARRIAGE between sports and television is a marriage made in heaven. Heaven, as everyone in both businesses knows, is in Manhattan, on the east side of Sixth Avenue, somewhere between the high-40's and the mid-50's.

Sports and television were made for each other, in the sense that each fulfills the other's deepest needs. Sports offers television honest drama, plots with unpredictable twists. Television, in turn, offers sports exposure, which is nice, and money, which is essential.

There is considerable evidence that each partner has served the other well. The American Football League, for instance, might have died quickly and quietly if the National Broadcasting Company had not elected to risk time and money on the project. The decision benefited both sides; the AFL lived, prospered, and merged with the NFL, and NBC wound up with its share of a huge Sunday afternoon audience plus a shot, every other year, at the Super Bowl, a biennial bonanza. The American Basketball Association could never have mounted a serious threat to the established National Basketball Association without the potential of TV revenue. The same holds true for the World Hockey Association in its war with the National Hockey League.

Television, of course, has bestowed all these gifts upon sports out of the goodness of its heart—and for the goodness of its pocketbook. The top sports attractions—the Super Bowl, the Masters golf tournament on CBS, the World Series on NBC, the U.S. Open golf championship and Monday Night Football on ABC—don't have to search for sponsors; they have to turn them away. These events command high ratings, the lifeblood of television, and a good percentage of the sports audience presumably stays tuned for whatever follows the athletic event.

The drawing power of sports was most remarkably demonstrated during the 1972 Olympics, when ABC's prime-time coverage earned incredible ratings, at times more than 60 percent of the viewing audience in some major cities.

Obviously, the marriage between sports and television is idyllic—on the surface. But both businesses know about fallen idylls, and, beneath the surface, the TV-sports relationship has flaws, flaws worth considering.

Ironically, it was the 1972 Olympic coverage, one of the historic highpoints of sports programming, that pointed up one potentially critical flaw. Stated simply, it is that television tends to look upon sports events as shows, not as events.

In the midst of ABC's imaginative, even brilliant Olympic camerawork—bringing swimmers and runners, rowers and divers vividly to life—a jarring news event popped up: the Arab attack upon the Israeli athletes. Suddenly sports coverage dissolved into news coverage, and the difference between the two was obvious. The fact that the ABC team of sports reporters adjusted to the new situation with varying degrees of skill is beside the point.

As the horror story unfolded—the taking of the hostages, the tense wait in the Olympic Village, the abortive rescue attempt at the airport—ABC offered extensive live coverage, telling exactly what was happening at each precise moment, as far as its staff could determine.

This was exactly the opposite of what ABC had done during its coverage of the Olympic competition. Every night, by the time the Olympic coverage came on the air in the United States, the day's events in Munich had long been finished. But the ABC reports coldly and calculatedly feigned suspense, pretended that the outcome of each event was still unknown. Would Mark Spitz win his fifth gold medal? Would he win his sixth? His seventh? Anyone who'd been listening to the radio—or, for that matter, watching early-evening news reports on ABC stations—knew the answers to those questions well before the nightly Olympic telecast went on. But the ABC anchorman perched in Munich had to play dumb, had to draw false drama from each event. NBC did exactly the same dishonest thing with its coverage of the Winter Olympics in Japan.

This may be considered terrific showmanship in some circles, but, by any decent standard, it is absolutely terrible journalism. Unless the television networks are ready to concede that sports reporters are not journalists, and that the events they cover are not news, then the system is an unforgivable sham.

The ultimate beauty of the Olympic coverage was the camera-work, and the camerawork, honest in itself, wouldn't have suffered at all from integrity at the microphones. Why couldn't the Olympic anchorman come on at the top of the show, review the major results of the day, then say, "OK, now we'll show you how it all happened, now we'll show you the highlights."

True, a viewer who didn't know how the Russian-American basketball game, for instance, was going to turn out would have been robbed of some of the drama by being told the outcome in advance. But is it worth sacrificing honesty for drama? And isn't drama without honesty simply melodrama?

Under normal conditions sports events on television are live events, the outcome unknown, the drama real, no contrivance necessary. But this is no excuse, in those rare instances when sports events are presented on videotape or film, for pretending that the situation is normal, the event live. If television, in its sports coverage, cannot adjust to the abnormal situation, then maybe the time has come to put all sports events into studios, save field production costs, keep the results a secret, and present the events on the air as merely an athletic version of "The Newlywed Game."

The taped Olympic coverage—the creation of false immediacy—may be a rare incident, but the illness it points up is not rare. There is a great deal of less dramatic evidence that television considers sports purely entertainment, not news. (Back to the marriage analogy: TV Weds Sports = Millionaire Weds Chorus Girl, for surface appearance, not substance.) Take the Masters golf tournament, for example. CBS has presented the tournament for years without ever mentioning how much money the winner of the Masters receives. CBS doesn't mention money because the people who run the Masters forbid it.

Yet money is a terribly important factor in golf; pro golfers, in fact, are ranked each year by the amount of prize money they've earned. Golf is the only sport in which the main measure of a man is his income. But CBS, in covering the Masters, ignores dollars and sense for fear of offending the Masters organizers. The fear is real. Representatives of ABC are invariably on hand at the Masters, enjoying the tournament and waiting for CBS to do something, anything, to arouse the displeasure of the people who run it. ABC would then happily step into the CBS slot, and ABC, too, despite its pride in its reportorial treatment of sports, would almost certainly agree never to mention cold cash.

In its coverage of almost every major sport, television too often becomes a patsy for what it covers. ABC, CBS, and NBC all provide network coverage of professional football—and all three fear putting on any halftime or between-games reportage that might offend the football establishment. Instead the networks pick up stadium shows that are so saccharinely patriotic and corny they would drive both Thomas Jefferson and Lawrence Welk out of the stadium. NBC, the major outlet for baseball, tries hard to avoid antagonizing the baseball establishment; it shies away from coverage of the controversial or the unflattering.

Up to a point, the public is willing to put up with this marriage of convenience between sports and television, a marriage in which each gives up a little of itself to pacify the other.

But the public used to be willing to tolerate newspapers whose sports reporters were coddled and bribed by the sports they covered. Baseball teams paid the living expenses for newspapermen on the road; boxing promoters openly bought writers for favorable exposure. The newspaper approach to sports was rah-rah and gee-whiz, with a little evangelism thrown in. Eventually this system died, destroyed by its own dishonesty. Newspaper readers became more sophisticated; they demanded independent judgment and decent journalism.

Television viewers are becoming more sophisticated, too, and even though right now they are still mesmerized by the fact that they see for nothing the games they once had to pay to view, this feeling can wear off, especially if the trend toward overexposure of the major sports continues. Television sports follows the same pattern as television entertainment. If one show about doctors succeeds, then put on ten shows about doctors; if bigotry is in, flood the air with bigotry; if one Super Bowl is great, ten Super Bowls would be sensational. Football is the sport in the worst danger of overexposure—you can view games on Saturday, Sunday, and Monday, watch replays on Tuesday and Wednesday, then check the highlights on Thursday and Friday—but baseball, basketball, tennis, golf, and hockey could all fall victim to the same syndrome. In time the audience is going to weary of games, and then the sports departments of television networks are going to have to provide something different. They would be wise to start now.

If the marriage between sports and television is going to flourish, then—I suspect—two ingredients are essential: more aggressive and knowledgeable reportage and more genuine humor.

Television's strength, in all areas, is its *impact,* its ability to strike an emotional chord, not its *depth,* not its ability to probe far below the surface. Still, this is no excuse not to attempt to ferret out some truths. As an example, the most important story in sports in 1973 is the future of the reserve clause, that traditional device that ties players in most professional sports to one team—as long as that team wants them. The story of the reserve clause is a complicated one, but it is not one that cannot be treated by television.

In fact, television could probably give the complicated story some life—by showing how a player is tied to one area and restricted to a certain style of living, even though the opportunities for him may be far greater elsewhere. The story would not have to be a series of talking heads, each explaining his own viewpoint, for and against the reserve clause; it could incorporate action footage from a variety of sports; it could give a glimpse of the meetings of players' unions; it could show the different types of opportunities available in different areas. It could be done, excitingly, if television wants to risk antagonizing the sports establishment.

It is remarkable how little humor has crept into television's coverage of sports—which helps explain the success of Don Meredith on the Monday Night Football games. Sports traditionally has been so fertile a field for humor—Ring Lardner, for prime example—that it should be irresistible to television. Occasionally—as in a memorable CBS golf broadcast when a relatively obscure pro named Rocky Thompson reviewed one of his own rather disastrous swings—humor does pop up in television's sports coverage, and when it does, when it is honest, spontaneous, and funny, it is brilliant.

Sports has almost as many funny characters as politics has, and these characters and their doings lend themselves perfectly to television.

The New York Mets, for example, have a pitcher named Tug McGraw. I once wrote a story in which I said McGraw was insane. The next time I saw him, he said, "Thank you."

Twice I brought McGraw on television to play himself. The first time, right after the baseball players' strike, he came on and sang "The Star-Spangled Banner"; he said that after nine days on strike, he had to review the words. The second time, he came on and gave a clinic about how you learn to write autographs on the curved surface of a baseball. He said that the only trouble is, once you learn, whenever you want to write home to your folks you have to wrap a piece of stationery around a baseball.

I think somebody who talks like that is a healthy influence on any marriage.

TV Drama in the U.S.A.: The Great Drought of 1971–1972

by John Houseman

The affinity between television news and drama has often been pointed out. John Houseman, writer and distinguished man of the theater in all its forms, comments in the following essay on the fate of television drama and how it might bear on the future of television news.

IN SEPTEMBER 1959, in its cover story, "Great Stars, Great Stories," *TV Guide* printed a forecast of the new season's television drama:

> Not since the days of "Studio One" and "Philco Playhouse" has the air been so filled with dramatic excitement . . . . There are two new half-hour drama series at CBS and the promise of another exciting year from "Playhouse 90," "Hallmark's Hall of Fame," DuPont's "Show of the Month" and the various Rexall and Revlon specials . . . . Four stories by Ernest Hemingway will be dramatized by CBS; "NBC Startime" and a new Sunday drama series will include star-studded teleplays and David Susskind will release his much-talked-about "The Moon and Sixpence" starring Sir Laurence Olivier.

> And don't forget the "G.E. Theatre," "Alfred Hitchcock Presents," "The Loretta Young Show," "Shirley Temple's Story-book," "The Desilu Playhouse," "Alcoa Theatre" alternating with "Goodyear Theatre" and "Armstrong Circle Theatre" alternating with the "U.S. Steel Hour."

In a rundown of coming attractions are promised, among others, Geraldine Page, Jason Robards, Larry Blyden, John Forsythe, Ralph Bellamy, Arthur Kennedy, Art Carney, Rosalind Russell, Jerry Lewis, Ingrid Bergman, Alec Guinness, Frank Sinatra, Mickey Rooney, James Stewart, George Gobel, Claudette Colbert, Robert Preston, June Allyson, Dick Powell, Julie

Harris, Maurice Evans, Thomas Mitchell, Tony Randall, and David Wayne. Writers include Archibald MacLeish, Maxwell Anderson, Henrik Ibsen, William Shakespeare, Sinclair Lewis, Rod Serling, Graham Greene, Cervantes, Ernest Hemingway, Philip Barry, Sidney Howard, Pat Frank, and Thornton Wilder.

Schedules of the three major networks during that winter show that between three and four hours were devoted each night to TV drama—a total of close to thirty hours a week of prime time. A glance at the *New York Times* Sunday television pages during the recent 1971–1972 season reveals that there were weeks, last winter, when, outside of the Public Broadcasting stations, there was literally nothing on the air that would qualify, by standards I shall presently attempt to define, as television drama.

These are statistical facts of the entertainment business. They reveal a drastic change in American viewing habits and public taste, and though, as usual, it is unclear whether such mutations follow public sentiment or are, in fact, imposed on the public, for economic and other reasons, by those who control the instruments of communication, it is evident that for the moment at least, American TV drama is very close to death.

It is not my intention, in this brief survey, to shed nostalgic tears over the dear, departed days of Television Drama, but, rather, to note its decline and to question what effect this may be having on the cultural and social attitudes of this country's more than two hundred million inhabitants.

Television drama, as produced by the major networks in the fifties, was the aristocrat of the airwaves, an important element in TV advertising and a substantial source of revenue for networks and agencies alike. Though its audiences never quite equaled, in sheer numbers, those of the top quiz and comedy shows, they were large, loyal, and involved. The productions were costly, prestigious, and occasionally controversial. They ranged from standard, established material to original works of which not a few had direct relevance to the world for whose entertainment they were created. Inevitably they were uneven in texture and quality, but they had variety and individuality and they were consistently high in the kind of emotional and imaginative energy that frequently distinguishes a new medium: this in marked contrast to the prefabricated slickness that characterizes almost all the big-time series and films produced today for television.

For its creators TV drama was an exciting and demanding

adventure. It was surprisingly free from interference and offered unusual opportunities to the young to express themselves. It gave actors a chance to play a variety of parts; many new writers (freer on the whole than their better-paid colleagues in motion pictures) did their first serious work there before going on to success in other media; directors, in particular, found themselves facing exciting creative challenges in which precedent and routine experience were of little help. On one show alone ("Playhouse 90") there were five staff directors, all in their twenties and all at the beginning of their careers, each of whom rank today among the top film directors of the world. Around them, on each major network, were gathered expert and competitive production crews, all rigorously trained and all high in morale and the professional courage and imagination required to turn out a full-length "live" TV drama every few days.

Today, like the shows and the audience they created, those producing units have disappeared—scattered and destroyed through lack of use. On those rare occasions when a network, with great fanfare, announces an isolated dramatic "special," the chances are better than even that it will be produced abroad —in Great Britain, Canada, or continental Europe. For the decline and death of TV drama, it must be noted, is a purely American phenomenon. In England (where, incidentally, radio drama continues to flourish) it remains a highly prized and creative activity, performed by Britain's leading actors, written, produced, and directed with energy and pride and a considerable expenditure of money. This money is apparently well spent, for the appeal of British TV drama extends far beyond the confines of the United Kingdom. "The Forsyte Saga" has been a smash all over Europe—including the Soviet Union. And its success in the United States has helped, over the past year, to bring about an astonishing situation.

Of the TV drama presently available to the American public, more than half comes over the limited facilities of the Public Broadcasting Service, formerly known as National Educational Television. And of PBS' dramatic programming for 1971–1972, more than half was imported from England, the product of the British Broadcasting Corporation. If these importations have filled the vacuum left by the collapse of our native product the reasons are obvious: quality and price. Even on our educational stations it costs a minimum of approximately $150,000 to produce a full-length dramatic show. The rental cost of the British import runs, I believe, to less than one tenth of that figure. At that price shrewd, "public spirited" sponsors are not hard to find. This has resulted in the following absurdity: that in this, the richest and most elaborately cultured nation in the world, during one of the most critical, challenging, and formative periods in its history, the only dramatic programs regularly available to its citizens, week after week, were concerned with:

1. The marital affairs of an English monarch of the early sixteenth century.
2. The personal and political crises in the life of his daughter, Queen Elizabeth of England.
3. The court intrigues surrounding the rise and fall of a British general and his wife two and a half centuries ago.
4. The emotional and financial vicissitudes of an English middle-class family of the late-Victorian and Edwardian era.

Add to these a number of English, French, and Russian classics, performed in English accents from an entirely British point of view. The fact that these shows were well written, excellently directed, and beautifully played does not diminish the absurdity of the situation or lessen the cultural dangers of this new colonialism.

It may be objected that this is a distorted and biased picture and that the American public is, in fact, receiving its dramatic nourishment in other forms. First of these are the countless "series" in which we are invited, each week, to follow complications in the lives of cops, ranchers, lawyers, doctors, fathers, housewives, bigots, private eyes, foreign agents, and the like. The truth is that for all their violent action and hysterical emotion these shows, with few exceptions, do not qualify as drama: they are cramped, melodramatic, formalized, and mechanical, with low credibility and little identification. For all their semblance of realism and relevance, they give their audience little to feel or think about. (That holds true also, with very few exceptions, of the 60- or 90-minute films turned out by the networks for the television market.)

Second, it could be argued that there *is* drama on the home screen—thousands of hours of it, all day and all night, in the form of old films, most of them of better quality than TV drama at its best. There is no question that a million-dollar movie has been more lavishly produced, more expensively cast, and more smoothly edited than most television shows—thrown together under pressure in a few days for a mere fraction of the average feature film's original cost. Still, it is no substitute for TV drama. There is a basic difference between a show made for exhibition in a theater six to twelve months hence and one designed for immediate viewing on the intimate home screen. This was particularly true of "live" television in the fifties: for all its handicaps and imperfections it had a relevance and a directness of communication that is only rarely to be found in a movie—especially if the movie, however good, was made anywhere from five to forty-five years ago.

Finally, it could be maintained with some truth that much of the dramatic, human material whose absence I am lamenting does, in fact, find its way into the best of our current "documentaries." Of our own DuPont Award winners over the past two years, I can think of half a dozen which, through the conflicts they illustrated and the empathy they aroused, fully qualified as dramatic shows. But those are few and far between and do not, to any appreciable degree, fill the vacuum of which I am complaining. (There, too, we seem to be going through a period of attrition. As the prime air-time devoted to documentaries diminishes and they become increasingly absorbed into the generally arid pattern of news shows, the opportunities for developing the human relationships and the personal elements in the social situation that is being "documented" become correspondingly less.)

What, exactly, is the nature of my beef? Why do I continue to grieve over a form of show-business which, by the test of the marketplace and the rules of supply and demand, is apparently obsolete? Without indulging in cultural platitudes may I reply that I firmly believe in the value of having a nation live out its personal and collective hopes and anxieties in dramatically reflected projections, and that I feel that the almost total absence of such vicarious experiences on the country's dominant medium of communication is a regrettable and, possibly, a serious thing.

A colleague of mine to whom I described my uneasiness over this deficiency in the American diet sent me the following note of agreement:

> On cultural matters—what happens to young people when there are no dramatic models for them to imitate
> —Not from the Bible
> —Not from literature (who reads books these days?)
> —Not from extended family or neighborhood relationships
> —Not from theater (inaccessible to most)
> —From TV?

Just the image of stimulus response, minute to minute.

It is this mechanical, shallow, contrived pattern of stimulus-response—both violent and comic—that dominates the airwaves today and provides almost none of that identification, recognition, and release that is derived from a vicarious dramatic experience, no matter how simplistic or limited. To this absence may be attributed, I suggest, much of the apparent callousness and indifference with which American TV audiences are accused of viewing the most harrowing and distressing scenes of disaster and suffering—so long as they take place outside the range of their own immediate perception.

I suggest further—though I would have difficulty in proving it—that this dearth of dramatic experience is having its effect on other branches of the medium, notably on its handling of the news. With a few brilliant exceptions (such as certain interviews, some of the war coverage, and the recent reporting of the Olympics, with its combination of technical expertise and well-documented human values) the flat, weary delivery and visual repetitiveness that characterize the formats of most of the nation's leading news shows reveal a dearth of creative imagination among their producers that may have its roots in a lack of experience and an absence of competitive contact with that most demanding and adventurous of television genres, the Drama. Conversely, in its recent demands for more entertaining and colorful personalities on its news shows, may not the American public be expressing its hunger for an empathy of which it is deprived in its current TV diet?

Have I overstated the case? In my regret over the demise of dramatic television am I exaggerating its consequences? Straws in the wind blowing past me as I write indicate that I am not alone in my uneasiness and that the pendulum is getting ready to swing the other way. Shocked and disturbed by the phenomenal success of the imported BBC shows, the commercial networks and educational television both are showing signs of considering a resurrection of American TV drama in the seasons to come. May I express the fervent hope that in their anxiety to restore the balance, they will not merely attempt to repeat their former achievements or imitate their successful transatlantic competitors, but will take time and thought to conceive and develop forms of drama, classic and contemporary, that are original and indigenous. In selecting the personnel who are to create this new drama, one trusts they will not overlook some of those who have shown energy and imagination during the lean years:

1. The documentary makers who, through this disturbed period of our history, have continued to extract dramatic and significant human values from our social and economic crises.

2. The eager and dedicated men and women (producers, directors, actors, and designers) who, over the past decade, have moved out of the ruins of centralized, commercial Broadway into the new and fruitful field of popular, regional, and community-supported theater.

Add to these the writers (not only the established names but also the young), the playwrights, novelists, and journalists who have found little or no employment under the medium's present hierarchic hiring habits, but who, if helped and encouraged, will find in television drama, as their predecessors did twenty-five years ago, an exciting and satisfying form of creative expression. Between them, and in collaboration with all those other fresh talents that never fail to appear wherever vital dramatic activity is in progress, they may help to infuse energy and emotion into the enervated body of American television.

APPENDICES

Appendix I

Remarks of Clay T. Whitehead, Director,
Office of Telecommunications Policy,
Executive Office of the President, at the
International Radio and Television Society
Newsmaker Luncheon, Waldorf-Astoria
Hotel, New York City, October 6, 1971

THIS IS a major speech—I read the advance billing and felt I had to say that. I was also billed as one of the youngest and most controversial figures in government and communications. Before I've even opened my mouth, Nick Johnson hates me.

Before I read that advance billing, we had planned one of my usual speeches. You know—a state of the universe message. But after a year of stating and restating the problems, I guess I can't get away with that any more. So this won't be that kind of speech, but I've gotten attached to the format, so I'd like to spend a little time on the state of broadcasting. I don't claim to have the expertise that any of you have in broadcasting; but in the first year of OTP's life, we've been exposed to many of the relationships between government, broadcasting, and the public. Today, I want to focus on those relationships.

I'll probably sound a bit naive to you when I say that some of these relationships don't make sense and should be changed. But why can't they be changed?—especially when they are the cause of many of our problems. The Communications Act isn't sacrosanct. It's a 37-year-old law that was intended to police radio interference—and it has frozen our thinking about broadcasting ever since. But something more than that is needed in a day when the *electronic* mass media are becoming *the* mass media.

There are a number of directions to choose from, and I'm here to propose one—one that redefines the relationships in the Communications Act's triangle of government, private industry, and the public.

But before I tell you what my proposals are, let me first tell you why I think a change is needed and why you should want one too.

Look at the current state of the broadcasting business. You sell audiences to advertisers. There's nothing immoral about that, but your audience thinks your business is providing them with programs. And the FCC regulates you in much the same way the public sees you. It requires no blinding flash of originality on my part to see that this creates a very basic conflict.

CBS's Programming Vice-President says: "I've got to answer to a corporation that is in this to make money, and at the same time face up to a public responsibility . . . ." His counterparts at the other networks have the same problem. They all have to program what people *will* watch—what gets the lowest cost-per-thousand. Sometimes that's what the people *want* to watch, but more often than not it's the least offensive program.

But you don't care what I think about your programs—and you shouldn't have to care what any government official thinks about your programs.

But what does the public think? The signs aren't good.

Look at the new season: Twenty-two new prime-time network law and order shows and situation comedies fill in between movies and sports. It's the same old fare. *Life*'s Harris poll is being interpreted to show that there is wide public dissatisfaction with the entertainment you offer.

Kids and teen-agers are developing an immunity to your commercials. Do you doubt that advertisers are questioning the effectiveness of TV as a sales medium?

How long will you be able to deliver our children to food and toy manufacturers? Parents are calling the Pied Piper to task—there were 80,000 letters to the FCC concerning the ACT petition alone.

Consider the anomaly of blacks as your most faithful viewers and your most active license challengers.

I suppose it looks like I'm just another critic taking cheap shots at TV. But there's another side to the broadcasting business. In my part of Washington, it's no insult to call someone a successful businessman. You have created a successful business out of the air—people *do* watch television. Sure your success is measured in billions of dollars, but it's also measured in public service and all those sets in use.

But your success is taking its toll. It's giving you viewership, but not viewer satisfaction—public visibility but not public support.

You've always had criticism from your audience but it never *really* mattered—you never had to *satisfy* them; you only had to *deliver* them. Then the Reverend Everett Parker read the Communications Act. You all know the outcome of the *WLBT–United Church of Christ* case. Once the public discovered its opportunity to participate in the Commission's processes, it became inevitable that the rusty tools of program content control —license renewal and the Fairness Doctrine—would be taken from the FCC's hands and used by the public and the courts to make *you* perform to *their* idea of the public interest.

Surprise! Nick Johnson is right. The '34 Act is simply being used and enforced. But where is that taking us?

Look at where we're going on license renewals. In city after city, in an atmosphere of bewilderment and apprehension, the broadcaster is being pitted against the people he's supposed to serve. The proxy for the public becomes the patsy who is held responsible for the Vietnam War, pollution, and the turmoil of changing life styles. As the East Coast renewals come up again, you're snickering about ascertainment—sure it was designed for Salina, Kansas, and not New York City—but I'll wager you'll all wrap yourself in interview sheets when your applications are filed in March. But that won't make you less vulnerable at renewal time because you can have no assurance that your efforts over the years will count for anything if a competing application is filed. "Substantial performance" becomes "superior performance" at the drop of a semantic hat and means that the government has finally adopted program percentage minimums. That's the current price of renewal protection.

So while we all talk about localism, we establish national program standards. You go through the motions of discovering local needs, knowing that the real game is to satisfy the national standards set by government bureaucrats. But it's not a game. Right now your programs are being monitored and taped and the results will be judged under the FCC's 1960 Program Statement. Can you be safe in *all* fourteen program categories?

The Fairness Doctrine and other access mechanisms are also

getting out of hand. It is a quagmire of government program control and once we get into it we can only sink deeper. If you can't see where it's leading, just read the *Red Lion* and *BEM* cases. The courts are on the way to making the broadcaster a *government* agent. They are taking away the licensees' First Amendment rights and they are giving the public an *abridgeable* right of access. In effect, the First Amendment is whatever the FCC decides it is.

However nice they sound in the abstract, the Fairness Doctrine and the new judicially contrived access rights are simply *more* government control masquerading as an expansion of the public's right of free expression. Only the literary imagination can reflect such developments adequately—Kafka sits on the Court of Appeals and Orwell works in the FCC's Office of Opinions and Review. Has anyone pointed out that the fiftieth anniversary of the Communications Act is 1984? "Big Brother" himself could not have conceived a more disarming "newspeak" name for a system of government program control than the Fairness Doctrine.

I'm not seriously suggesting that the FCC or the courts want to be "Big Brother" or that 1984 is here, or that we can't choose a different path from the one we now seem to be on. You are at a crossroads—now you're probably clutching your "Chicago Teddy Bears" and wondering when Whitehead is going to get to the point. The point is: We need a fundamental revision of the framework of relationships in which you, the government, and the public interact. The underpinnings of broadcast regulation are being changed—the old *status quo* is gone and none of us can restore it. We *can* continue the chaos and see where we end up. But there has to be a better way.

I have three proposals. They are closely related and I want you to evaluate them as a package that could result in a major revision of the Communications Act. The proposals are: *One,* eliminate the Fairness Doctrine and replace it with a statutory right of access; *two,* change the license renewal process to get the government out of programming; and *three,* recognize commercial radio as a medium that is completely different from TV and begin to *de*-regulate it.

I propose that the Fairness Doctrine be abandoned. It should be replaced by an act of Congress that meets both the claim of individuals to use of the nation's most important mass media and the claim of the public at large to adequate coverage of public issues. These are two distinct claims and they cannot both be served by the same mechanism.

Access: As to the first of them—the individual's right to speak: TV time set aside for sale should be available on a first-come, first-served basis at nondiscriminatory rates—but there must be no rate regulation. The individual would have a right to speak on any matter, whether it's to sell razor blades or urge an end to the war. The licensee should not be held responsible for the content of ads, beyond the need to guard against illegal material. Deceptive product ads should be controlled at the source by the Federal Trade Commission. This private right of access should be enforced—as most private rights are enforced—through the courts and not through the FCC.

License Renewals: As to the second claim—the opportunity of the public to be informed on public issues: This is the type of "public interest" traditionally protected by regulatory agencies, but it should be done in a manner which recognizes it as an overall right, which cannot sensibly be enforced on a case-by-case basis. It can best be protected, I suggest, not in countless proceedings involving individual complaints, but in the course of the renewal process. The licensee would be obligated to make the totality of programming that is under his control (including public service announcements) responsive to the interests and concerns of the community. The criterion for renewal would be whether the broadcaster has, over the term of his license, made a *good faith* effort to ascertain local needs and interests and to meet them in his programming. There would be no place for government-conceived program categories, percentages, and formats, or *any* value judgment on specific program content.

There should be a longer TV license period with the license revocable for cause and the FCC would invite or entertain competing applications *only* when a license is not renewed or is revoked.

I believe these revisions in the access and renewal processes will add stability to your industry and avoid the bitter adversary struggle between you and your community groups. They recognize the new concerns of access and fairness in a way that minimizes government content control.

I'm not saying that this will eliminate controversies. But it will defuse and change the *nature* of the controversies.

Radio De-regulation: We can go further with radio. Yesterday I sent a letter to Dean Burch proposing that OTP and the FCC jointly develop an experiment to *de*-regulate commercial radio operations.

We proposed that one or more large cities be selected as deregulatory test markets in which radio assignments and transfers would be *pro forma*. Renewals would not be reviewed for programming and commercial practices. And the Fairness Doctrine would be suspended. The experiment should be only a first step. For most purposes, we should ultimately treat radio as we now treat magazines.

These are my proposals. The proposals are just that—I have no legislation tucked in my back pocket that we are about to introduce. But, I will work for legislation if there is support for these proposals. In short, my message on all these proposals is that we've tried government program control and bureaucratic standards of fairness and found that they don't work. In fact, they can't work. Let's give you and the public a chance to exercise more freedom in a more sensible framework and see what that can do.

There is one further aspect of freedom I would like to discuss. Some people suggest that this Administration is trying to use the great power of government licensing and regulation to intimidate the press. Some even claim to see a malicious conspiracy designed to achieve that end. They must ascribe to us a great deal of maliciousness, indeed—and a great deal of stupidity—in the attempt to reconcile their theory to the facts. It is not this Administration that is pushing legal and regulatory controls on television, in order to gain an active role in determining content. It is not this Administration that is urging an extension of the Fairness Doctrine into the details of television news—or into the print media.

There is a world of difference between the *professional* responsibility of a free press and the *legal* responsibility of a regulated press. This is the same difference between the theme of my proposals today and the current drift of broadcasting regulation. Which will you be—private business or government agent? —a responsible free press or a regulated press? You cannot have it both ways—neither can government nor your critics.

Appendix II

Remarks of Clay T. Whitehead, Director,
Office of Telecommunications Policy,
Executive Office of the President, at the
Forty-seventh Annual Convention,
National Association of Educational
Broadcasters, Miami, Florida,
October 20, 1971

IT WOULD BE refreshing for you, I'm sure, to hear a convention
speaker dwell on all the good things that public broadcasting
has accomplished—after all the accomplishments are real. But
government policy making doesn't usually concern itself with
good news; it deals with problems, and policy is my topic today.

Public broadcasting occupies a very special role in my Office
and in the Executive Branch generally. It is one of the few
elements in our communications system that has had a policy
blueprint. The policy for public broadcasting—even its very
name—was the result of deliberate study, public discussion, and
legislation in the form of the 1962 ETV Facilities Act and the
1967 Public Broadcasting Act. Much of the policy has been
developed and administered by the Executive Branch.

The process of developing policy is a continuing one. After
four years of experience with the system created by the Act,
you and OTP are asking whether the policies that guide public
broadcasting work—where they have taken us and where they
are taking us. The process has taken much longer than we all
wanted it to take. But now I'd like to talk to you about the

factors that have shaped our thinking about public broadcasting and how we view the policy questions.

I honestly don't know what group I'm addressing. I don't know if it's really the Forty-seventh Annual Convention of NAEB or the first annual meeting of PBS affiliates. What's your status? To us there is evidence that you are becoming affiliates of a centralized, national network.

For example, CPB calls PBS our fourth national TV network —and the largest one at that, with over 210 affiliates. Don Quayle's National Public Radio may be the only real national radio network we have—I half expect Arthur Godfrey—or maybe David Susskind—to be hired to do a "morning magazine" show for NPR. I see NAEB's ETS Program Service transferred to PBS and NPR. Because of CPB's method of funding program production, it's less than candid to say the production system is a decentralized group of seven or eight regional centers. Who has real control over your program schedules?

On a national basis, PBS says that some 40 percent of its programming is devoted to public affairs. You're centralizing your public affairs programs in the National Public Affairs Center in Washington, because someone thinks autonomy in regional centers leads to wasteful overlap and duplication. Instead of aiming for "overprogramming" so local stations can select among the programs produced and presented in an atmosphere of diversity, the system chooses central control for "efficient" long-range planning and so-called "coordination" of news and public affairs—coordinated by people with essentially similar outlooks. How different will your networked news programs be from the programs that Fred Friendly and Sander Vanocur wanted to do at CBS and NBC? Even the commercial networks don't rely on one sponsor for their news and public affairs, but the Ford Foundation is able to buy over $8 million worth of this kind of programming on your stations.

In other kinds of programming, is it you or PBS who has been taking the networks' approach and measuring your success in rating points and audience? You check the Harris poll and ARB survey and point to increases in viewership. Once you're in the rating game, you want to win. You become a supplement to the commercial networks and do *their* things a bit better in order to attract the audience that wants more quality in program content.

The temptation to make your mark this way has proven irresistible. The press is good. You've deserved the limelight much sooner, but it's coming now with truly outstanding efforts in the up-coming "Electric Company" and "Sesame Street" and "Forsyte Saga" and the BBC's other fine dramatic and cultural shows. You do this job brilliantly. You *can* pick up where the commercial networks leave off. You can do their children's shows, their drama, their serious music, their in-depth informational programs—you can even be their "farm system" and bring up young, minority-group talent to work in the "majors" in New York and Los Angeles.

You *can* program for the Cambridge audience that WGBH used to go after—for the upper middle class whites who contribute to your stations when you offer Julia Child's cookbook and Kenneth Clark's "Civilisation." It also has the advantage of keeping you out of the renewal and access conflicts now faced by commercial broadcasters. With a few notable exceptions, maybe the community activists don't think you're meaningful enough in your own communities to warrant involving you in these disputes.

As the fourth national network, things are looking pretty rosy for you. Between 1968 and 1970, national broadcast hours went up 43 percent. This year alone PBS is sending an average of two hours a night down the interconnection lines. But local productions of instructional and "public" programs continue a decreasing trend—down 13 percent from 1968 to 1970. The financial picture at the local stations looks bleak, even though CPB can now raise the range of its general support grants to between $20,000 and $52,000 per TV station. But it's still not enough. The average TV station's yearly operating costs are over $650,000 and the stations are suffering—Delaware may be without a state-wide system, local programs are out on WHYY in Philadelphia, things look bad elsewhere—even at the production centers.

Money alone—great bales of it—would solve a lot of the problems. CPB would be able to fund programs on America's civilization and programs on the Adams family instead of the Churchill and Forsyte families. The production centers could be more independent and the other local stations could devote more energy to programming, ascertainment and community service instead of auctions, fund-raising gimmicks, and underwriting grants. More money could even lessen the internal squabbling that seems to occupy so much of your attention.

But money alone won't solve the basic problems that relate to the structure of public broadcasting—a structure that was to be built on a bedrock of localism. I've read Arthur Singer's speech last June at Boyne Highlands and I've read the Carnegie

Commission Report and the legislative history of the '67 Act. Singer wins—the reality of 1971 doesn't match the dream of 1967.

Do you remember that the Carnegie group put its principal stress on a strong, financially independent group of stations as the foundation of a system that was to be the clearest expression of American diversity and excellence; that the emphasis was on pluralism and local format control instead of a fixed-schedule, real-time network, and that this view was reflected in the House, Senate, and Conference reports on the '67 Act; that CPB was supposed to *increase* options and program choices for the stations; and that the Carnegie Commission wanted general operating funds to come from HEW because of the concern that the corporation not grow too big or become too central. As Dr. Killian put it, if stations had to look to the corporation for all their requirements, it would lead "naturally, inevitably, to unwise, unwarranted and unnecessary centralization of educational broadcasting." The concept of dispersing responsibility was essential to the policy chosen in 1967 for public broadcasting Senator Pastore said on the floor of the Senate that, "since the fundamental purpose of the bill is to strengthen local noncommercial stations, the powers of the Corporation itself must not impinge on the autonomy of local stations."

The centralization that *was* planned for the system—in the form of CPB—was intended to *serve the stations*—to help them extend the range of *their* services to *their* communities. The idea was to break the NET monopoly of program production combined with networking and to build an effective counterforce to give appropriate weight to local and regional views.

In 1967, the public broadcasting professionals let the Carnegie dreamers have their say—let them run on about localism and "bedrocks" and the rest of it—let them sell the Congress on pluralism and local diversity—and when they've gone back to the boardrooms and classrooms and union halls and rehearsal halls, the professionals will stay in the control room and call the shots. The professionals viewed the Carnegie concept of localism as being as naive and unattainable as the Carnegie excise tax financing plan. They said that no broadcasting system can succeed unless it appeals to a mass audience in one way or another; that networking in the mold of the commercial networks is the only way to get that audience; that a mass audience brings a massive reputation and massive impact; that it's cheaper, more effective, more easily promoted, simpler to manage, and less demanding on local leadership than the system adopted by the Congress; *and they are right*. But is *that* kind of public broadcast system worth it? Is it what *you* want? What your community needs? What's best for the country?

You've been asking yourself these questions. For you, the past few months have been a time for self-analysis and hard questions—from Singer's Boyne speech, to the Aspen meetings; the Jack Gould–Fred Friendly debate on the pages of the Sunday *New York Times;* the discussion that's been going on between my Office and CPB; and the emotional debate within public television over the FBI sequence on "Dream Machine." Your public debate has focused on the fundamental issues and you're to be admired and respected for it.

You are grappling with the policy imposed on a going enterprise in 1967. That policy was not only intended to change the structure of ETV, it was also supposed to avoid the structure of commercial TV and to steer clear of a government-run broadcast system. There are trade-offs in this policy. For example, if you imitate the commercial structure, all we have is a network paid for by the government and it just invites political scrutiny of the content of that network's programs. We're asking a lot of you when we expect that you implement the policy chosen for public broadcasting. But some of you haven't succumbed to despair yet. Some of you don't want to be a fourth network. Some of you are trying to make the policy work.

For example, PBS will be trying to use its interconnection for program distribution as well as networking; it's trying to broaden the base of small station representation on its Board; CPB is trying to devote more funds to general operating grants; as long as there is a centralized network, Hartford Gunn is trying to make it work in a responsible manner despite the brickbats and knives that come his way; some local stations are really trying to do the job that *must* be done at the community level. I recognize this. I appreciate the problems you face.

CPB seems to have decided to make permanent financing the principal goal and to aim for programming with a national impact on the public and the Congress to achieve it. But look at the box that puts you in. The local station is asked—and sometimes willingly accedes—to sacrifice its autonomy to facilitate funding for the national system.

When this happens, it also jeopardizes your ability to serve the educational and instructional needs of your communities. All the glamor is packed into your nighttime schedules and the tendency is to get more public attention by focusing on the news, public affairs, and cultural programs that are aimed for the general audience. But there must be more balance in your service to your communities. In quantitative terms, your schedules are already split equally between instructional and general programming. But in qualitative terms, are you devoting enough of your resources to the learning needs of your in-school and in-home audiences?

Do any of you honestly know whether public broadcasting— structured as it is today and moving in the direction it seems to be headed—can ever fulfill the promise envisioned for it or conform to the policy set for it? If it can't, then permanent financing will always be somewhere off in the distant future.

The legislative goals for public broadcasting—which I hope are our common goals—are:

1. to keep it from becoming a government-run system;
2. to preserve the autonomy of the local stations; and
3. to achieve these objectives while assuring a diversity of program sources for the stations to draw on in addition to their own programs.

When you centralize actual responsibility at a single point, it makes you visible politically and those who are prone to see ghosts can raise the specter of government pressure. When you, as local stations, are compelled by the system's formal structure, its method of program distribution, the mere lack of a programming alternative, or simple inertia to delegate formulation of your program schedules to a central authority, how can you realistically achieve the objective of local autonomy. All we are left with is the central organization and its national programs and *that* was never intended to be an end in itself. When the struggle is simply between the Washington center and the New York center, it doesn't much matter who wins. It probably isn't even worth the effort.

You've been told at this convention all that you should *do* —that you should *be*—as cablecasters, minority-group employers, public telecommunications centers and the lot. But is *enough* expected of you when you are branch offices of a national, public telecommunications system? It would be a shame for you to go into the new world of electronic education centers offering a dazzling array of services without engaging in the most exciting experiment of all—to see if you as *broadcasters* can meet your wide responsibilities to your communities in instructional and public programming. It's never been tried and yet, as a policy, it's America's unique contribution to broadcasting—it's our concept of mass communications federalism.

Your task then is one of striking the most appropriate balance in determining the local station's role in the public broadcast system—a balance between advancing the quality of electronic instruction and the quality of programs for the general public and, ultimately, the balance between the system's center and its parts. You have to *care* about these balances and you have to *work* for them. We in government want to help, but the initiative must come from you.

Appendix III

Message from President Nixon to the House of Representatives, June 30, 1972

I FIND it necessary to return without my approval H.R. 13918, which is intended to provide increased financing for the Corporation for Public Broadcasting and to modify the Public Broadcasting Act of 1967 by making various changes in the structure of the noncommercial, educational broadcasting system.

Public broadcasting can and does make important contributions to our Nation's life by presenting educational and cultural programs of diversity and excellence. Programs such as "Sesame Street" and "The Electric Company" already have begun to repay the far-sighted decision the Nation made in the 1950's when channels were reserved for educational purposes. Public broadcasting deserves to be continued, and to be strengthened.

The legislation before me, however, offers a poor approach to public broadcast financing. It ignores some serious questions which must be resolved before any long-range public broadcasting financing can be soundly devised, and before the statutory framework for public broadcasting is changed.

There are many fundamental disagreements concerning the directions which public broadcasting has taken and should pursue in the future. Perhaps the most important one is the serious and widespread concern—expressed in Congress and within public broadcasting itself—that an organization, originally intended only to serve the local stations, is becoming instead the center of power and the focal point of control for the entire public broadcasting system.

The Public Broadcasting Act of 1967 made localism a primary means of achieving the goals of the educational broadcasting system. Localism places the principal public interest responsibility on the individual educational radio and television stations, licensed to serve the needs and interest of their own communities. By not placing adequate emphasis on localism, H.R. 13918 threatens to erode substantially public broadcasting's impressive potential for promoting innovative and diverse cultural and educational programming.

The public and legislative debate regarding passage of H. R. 13918 has convinced me that the problems posed by Government financing of a public broadcast system are much greater than originally thought. They cannot be resolved until the structure of public broadcasting has been more firmly established, and we have a more extensive record of experience on which to evaluate its role in our national life.

This Administration has demonstrated its dedication to the principle of public broadcasting by increasing appropriations to the Corporation sevenfold in the past three years, from $5 million in FY 69 to $35 million in FY 72. On top of this, I have requested an additional 30 percent increase for next year to $45 million. The funding proposed in H.R. 13918, which almost doubles next year's appropriation, and more than doubles the following year's appropriation over FY 1972, is unwarranted in light of the serious questions yet unanswered by our brief experience with public broadcasting.

I urge the continuation of carefully measured annual funding for the Corporation, under the existing statutory framework, subject to regular budgetary oversight and review. Specifically, I ask the Congress to follow my budget recommendation by enacting a one-year extension of the Corporation's authorization and providing it $45 million. Since interim funds for the Corporation are included in a continuing resolution currently before the Congress, there should be no interruption of the Corporation's activities.

Appendix IV

Remarks of Clay T. Whitehead, Director, Office of Telecommunications Policy, Executive Office of the President, at the Sigma Delta Chi Luncheon, Indianapolis Chapter, December 18, 1972

On December 18, 1972, Clay T. Whitehead, director of the office of Telecommunications Policy, delivered the following speech at a luncheon meeting of the Indianapolis chapter of Sigma Delta Chi.

With its references to "imbalance," "bias," "ideological plugola," and "elitist gossip" and its exhortation to network affiliates to "exercise the responsibility of private enterprise" in screening network programs—particularly news and public affairs—the speech confirmed for the already jittery news departments their worst apprehensions of Administration intent.

IN THIS calm during the holidays, we in Washington are thinking ahead to 1973—among other things, planning our testimony before Congressional committees. For my part, I am particularly concerned about testimony on broadcast license renewal legislation. Broadcasters are making a determined push for some reasonable measure of license renewal security. Right now they are living over a trap door the FCC can spring at the drop of a competing application or other renewal challenge. That is a tough position to be in, and, considering all the fuss about so-called "intimidation," you would think that there wouldn't be much opposition to giving broadcasters a little more insulation from government's hand on that trap door.

But there *is* opposition. Some tough questions will be asked —even by those who are sympathetic to broadcasters. Questions about minority groups' needs and interests. Questions about violence. Questions about children's programming; about reruns; about commercials; about objectivity in news and public affairs programming—in short, all questions about broadcasters' performance in fulfilling their public trust. These are questions the public is asking. Congress is asking the questions, too: Senator Pastore on violence; Senator Moss on drug ads; Representative Staggers on news misrepresentations. Despite this barrage of questioning, the Congress is being urged to grant longer license terms and renewal protection to broadcasters. Before voting it up, down, or around, the Congress will have to judge the broadcasters' record of performance.

And where do we see that performance? It leaps out at you every time you turn on a TV set, and it's definitely not all that it could be. How many times do you see the rich variety, diversity, and creativity of America represented on the TV screen? Where is the evidence of broadcasters doing their best to serve their audiences, rather than serving those audiences up to sell to advertisers? And, most disturbing of all, how do broadcasters demonstrate that they are living up to the obligation—as the FCC puts it—to "assume and discharge responsibility for planning, selecting, and supervising all matter broadcast by the stations, whether such matter is produced by them or provided by networks or others"?

It's been easy for broadcasters to give lip service to the uniquely American principle of placing broadcasting power and responsibility at the local level. But it has also been easy—too easy—for broadcasters to turn around and sell their responsibility along with their audiences to a network at the going rate for affiliate compensation.

The ease of passing the buck to make a buck is reflected in the steady increase in the amount of network programs carried by affiliates between 1960 and 1970. It took the FCC's prime-time rule to reverse this trend, but even so, the average affiliate still devotes over 61 percent of its schedule to network programs. This wouldn't be so bad if the stations really exercised some responsibility for the programs and commercials that come down the network pipe. But all that many affiliates do is flip the switch in the control room to "network," throw the "switch" in the mailroom to forward viewer complaints to the network, sit back, and enjoy the fruits of a very profitable business.

Please don't misunderstand me when I stress the need for more local responsibility. I'm not talking about locally-produced programs, important though they are. I'm talking now about licensee responsibility for *all* programming, including the programs that come from the network.

This kind of local responsibility is the keystone of our private enterprise broadcast system operating under the First Amendment protections. But excessive concentration of control over broadcasting is as bad when exercised from New York as when exercised from Washington. When affiliates consistently pass the buck to the networks, they're frustrating the fundamental purposes of the First Amendment's free press provision.

The press isn't guaranteed protection because it's guaranteed to be balanced and objective—to the contrary, the Constitution recognizes that balance and objectivity exist only in the eye of the beholder. The press *is* protected because a free flow of information, and giving each "beholder" the opportunity to inform himself, is central to our system of government. In essence, it's the right to learn instead of the right to be taught. The broadcast press has an obligation to serve this free flow of information goal by giving the audience the chance to pick and choose among a wide range of diverse and competing views on public issues.

This may all seem rather philosophical. Cynics may argue that all television, even the news, is entertainment programming. But in this age when television is the most relied upon and, surprisingly, the most credible of our media, we must accept this harsh truth: the First Amendment is meaningless if it does not apply fully to broadcasting. For too long we have been interpreting the First Amendment to fit the 1934 Communications Act. As many of you know, a little over a year ago I suggested ways to correct this inversion of values. One way is to eliminate the FCC's Fairness Doctrine as a means of enforcing the broadcasters' fairness obligation to provide reasonable opportunity for discussion of contrasting views on public issues.

Virtually everyone agrees that the Fairness Doctrine enforcement is a mess. Detailed and frequent court decisions and FCC supervision of broadcasters' journalistic judgment are unsatisfactory means of achieving the First Amendment goal for a free press. The FCC has shown signs of making improvements in what has become a chaotic scheme of Fairness Doctrine enforcement. These improvements are needed. But the basic Fairness Doctrine approach, for all its problems, was, is and for the time being will remain a necessity, albeit an unfortunate necessity. So, while our long-range goal should be a broadcast media structure just as free of government intrusion, just as competitive, just as diverse as the print media, there are three harsh realities that make it impossible to do away with the Fairness Doctrine in the short run.

First, there is a scarcity of broadcasting outlets. *Second,* there is a substantial concentration of economic and social power in the networks and their affiliated TV stations. *Third,* there is a tendency for broadcasters and the networks to be self-indulgent and myopic in viewing the First Amendment as protecting only their rights as speakers. They forget that its primary purpose is to assure a free flow and wide range of information to the public. So we have license renewal requirements and the Fairness Doctrine as added requirements—to make sure that the networks and stations don't ignore the needs of those 200 million people sitting out there dependent on TV.

But this doesn't mean that we can forget about the broader mandates of the First Amendment, as it applies to broadcasting. We ought to begin where we can to change the Communications Act to fit the First Amendment. That has always been and continues to be the aim and intent of this Administration. We've got to make a start and we've got to do it now.

This brings me to an important first step the Administration is taking to increase freedom and responsibility in broadcasting.

OTP has submitted a license renewal bill for clearance through the Executive Branch, so the bill can be introduced in the Congress early next year. Our bill doesn't simply add a couple of years to the license term and guarantee profits as long as broadcasters follow the FCC's rules to the letter. Following rules isn't an *exercise* of responsibility; it's an *abdication* of responsibility. The Administration bill requires broadcasters to exercise their responsibility without the convenient crutch of FCC program categories or percentages.

The way we've done this is to establish two criteria the station must meet before the FCC will grant renewal. First, the broadcaster must demonstrate he has been substantially attuned to the needs and interests of the communities he serves. He must also make a good faith effort to respond to those needs and interests in all his programs, irrespective of whether those programs are created by the station, purchased from program suppliers, or obtained from a network. The idea is to have the broadcaster's performance evaluated from the perspective of the people in his community and not the bureaucrat in Washington.

Second, the broadcaster must show that he has afforded reasonable, realistic, and practical opportunities for the presentation and discussion of conflicting views on controversial issues.

I should add that these requirements have teeth. If a station can't demonstrate meaningful service to all elements of his community, the license should be taken away by the FCC. The standard should be applied with particular force to the large TV stations in our major cities, including the fifteen stations owned by the TV networks and the stations that are owned by other large broadcast groups. These broadcasters, especially, have the resources to devote to community development, community service, and programs that reflect a commitment to excellence.

The community accountability standard will have special meaning for all network affiliates. They should be held accountable to their local audiences for the 61 percent of their schedules that are network programs, as well as for the programs they purchase or create for local origination.

For four years, broadcasters have been telling this Administration that, if they had more freedom and stability, they would use it to carry out their responsibilities. We have to believe this, for if broadcasters were simply masking their greed and actually seeking a so-called "license to steal," the country would have to give up on the idea of private enterprise broadcasting. Some are urging just that; but this Administration remains unshaken in its support of the principles of freedom and responsibility in a private-enterprise broadcasting system.

But we are equally unshaken in our belief that broadcasters must do more to exercise the responsibility of private enterprise that is the prerequisite of freedom. Since broadcasters' success in meeting their responsibility will be measured at license renewal time, they must demonstrate it across the board. They can no longer accept network standards of taste, violence, and decency in programming. If the programs or commercials glorify the use of drugs; if the programs are violent or sadistic; if the commercials are false or misleading, or simply intrusive and obnoxious; the stations must jump on the networks rather than wince as the Congress and the FCC are forced to do so.

There is no area where management responsibility is more important than news. The station owners and managers cannot abdicate responsibility for news judgments. When a reporter or disk jockey slips in or passes over information in order to line his pocket, that's plugola, and management would take quick corrective action. But men also stress or suppress information in accordance with their beliefs. Will station licensees or network executives also take action against this ideological plugola?

Just as a newspaper publisher has responsibility for the wire service copy that appears in his newspaper—so television station owners and managers must have full responsibility for what goes out over the public's airwaves—no matter what the origin of the program. There should be no place in broadcasting for the "rip and read" ethic of journalism.

Just as publishers and editors have professional responsibility for the news they print, station licensees have final responsibility for news balance—whether the information comes from their own newsroom or from a distant network. The old refrain that, quote, "We had nothing to do with that report, and could do nothing about it" is an evasion of responsibility and unacceptable as a defense.

Broadcasters and networks took decisive action to insulate their news departments from the sales departments when charges were made that news coverage was biased by commercial considerations. But insulating station and network news departments from management oversight and supervision has *never* been responsible and *never* will be. The First Amendment's guarantee of a free press was not supposed to create a privileged class of men called journalists, who are immune from criticism by government or restraint by publishers and editors. To the contrary, the working journalist, if he follows a professional code of ethics, gives up the right to present his personal point of view when he is on the job. He takes on a higher responsibility to the institution of a free press, and he cannot be insulated from the management of that institution.

The truly professional journalist recognizes his responsibility to the institution of a free press. He realizes that he has no monopoly on the truth; that a pet view of reality can't be insinuated into the news. Who else but management, however, can assure that the audience is being served by journalists dedicated to the highest professional standards? Who else but management can or should correct so-called professionals who confuse sensationalism with sense and who dispense elitist gossip in the guise of news analysis?

Where there are only a few sources of national news on television, as we now have, editorial responsibility must be exercised more effectively by local broadcasters and by network management. If they do not provide the checks and balances in the system, who will?

Station managers and network officials who fail to act to

correct imbalance or consistent bias from the networks—or who acquiesce by silence—can only be considered willing participants, to be held fully accountable by the broadcaster's community at license renewal time.

Over a year ago, I concluded a speech to an audience of broadcasters and network officials by stating that:

> There is a world of difference between the *professional* responsibility of a free press and the *legal* responsibility of a regulated press. . . . Which will you be—private business or government agent?—a responsible free press or a regulated press? You cannot have it both ways—neither can government nor your critics.

I think that my remarks today leave no doubt that this Administration comes out on the side of a responsible free press.

Some Information About the
Alfred I. duPont–Columbia University
Awards for 1972–1973

EACH YEAR the awards are based upon research done in conjunction with the annual DuPont–Columbia Survey of Broadcast Journalism. There is no set number of awards or permanent categories for the awards, which will vary according to evidences of outstanding performance in news and public affairs during the year. Local and network radio, local and network television, as well as syndicated material, will be surveyed.

Although categories for the awards will not be set in advance, concerned parties are encouraged to suggest to the jurors examples of broadcast journalism which they feel are particularly worthy of attention. They are also invited to suggest subjects for research.

Suggestions for those wishing to participate:

1. Any concerned person, group, organization, or broadcast station may bring to the DuPont jury's attention material dealing with performance in broadcast news and public affairs.

2. If such information concerns a specific program, it should include the following particulars: (a) the time, the date, and the station carrying the program, (b) the subject of the program, (c) the reason the program is being singled out. If possible, there should be notification enough in advance of air time to permit jurors to view or hear the program at the time of the original broadcast. In any event, supporting material such as tapes, films, or scripts should be retained as documentation. *However, supporting material should not be submitted unless expressly asked for by the Director.*

3. If information submitted concerns long-term performance of an individual, a station, or other institution,

names or call letters should be given, as well as a full statement of the reasons for the submission.

4. The Director will also welcome suggestions of subjects for investigation or research to be dealt with in the Survey.

5. Nominations may be made throughout the year for programs aired between July 1, 1972, and June 30, 1973. Nominations must be postmarked no later than midnight, July 2, 1973.

6. All materials submitted will become the property of Columbia University.

7. All inquiries and correspondence should be addressed to:

> Director
> The Alfred I. duPont–Columbia University
>   Survey and Awards
> Graduate School of Journalism
> Columbia University
> New York, N.Y. 10027

Acknowledgments

DURING THE PAST YEAR the jurors and the Survey have received generous assistance from a great number of organizations and individuals. Although it is not possible to list all those who have helped in some way, we would particularly like to express our gratitude to the following: the news directors and newsmen from the networks and individual stations who answered questionnaires, furnished tapes and films, and did the real work with which this volume and these awards are concerned. Each year their contributions to the Survey, direct and indirect, increase.

We would also like to thank the awards and public information departments of the commercial and public television networks; the faculty of the Columbia School of Journalism, particularly Professor W. Phillips Davison; also the national office of the League of Women Voters and the hundreds of local League chapters who participated in this year's political survey; Ida Sloan Snyder and Valerie Russell of the National Board of the YWCA and the many members of the YWCA who helped in a special Survey project; the A. C. Nielsen Company, especially Bill Behanna, and the staffs of the Federal Communications Commission; the National Association of Broadcasters; the National Cable Television Association; the White House; and the Office of Telecommunications Policy.

The research and reportorial assistant for this year's Survey was Steven Petrou. Peggy Brawley supervised the checking and editing of the final manuscript. Michael Meadvin took care of the arrangements for award submissions; Rosemary Guevara and Teresa Grippo contributed secretarial assistance. Jane Vittengl, DuPont program assistant, prepared the manuscript.

Louis Cowan, director of special projects for the Columbia University Graduate School of Journalism, made invaluable contributions to both the Survey and the broader activities of the program upon which it is based.

Again, special mention should be made of the continuing coverage of broadcast journalism by *Variety, Advertising Age,*

Broadcasting magazine, *TV Digest, The New York Times, The Wall Street Journal,* and *TV/Radio Age,* which furnished the editor, Marvin Barrett, and the jurors with an invaluable record of the subject throughout the year.

Facilities for the screening of awards were provided by the commercial networks, WNET/13, and the Television Center of Brooklyn College.

As a reading of the text will indicate, much of the most interesting material came from the correspondents now located in sixty-five of the major broadcast markets across the country. Their faithful attention to the news activities of their local stations and the resulting comments and recommendations are of great importance to the continuing success of the Survey and Awards.

Index

Abel, Elie, 188
"Action Line" (WDIO), 88
Action for Children's Television, 84, 214
advertising (*see also* sponsors):
    cigarette, 8, 81–82, 91
    political, 101–102, 134–135, 137–138, 145–146, 165–167
    public attitude toward, 7, 76–77
    regulation of, 78–80, 82–84, 86–87, 91
"Advocates, The" (PBS), 156
Agnew, Spiro, 39–40, 48–49, 117, 133, 136, 140, 163, 166, 190
Agronsky, Martin, 119
Ailes, Roger, 98, 101
"Alias Smith and Jones" (ABC), 11
"All Things Considered" (NPR), 195
Altmeyer, Paul, 16
"America" (NBC), 9
American Broadcasting Company (ABC), 10–11, 14, 24, 40, 61, 85, 121, 129, 131, 133, 197–200
    ABC News, 7, 57–58, 166
    ABC Information, 186
    ABC Radio, 181, 184, 186, 190
"American Week, The" (CBS Radio), 187–188
Anderson, Jack, 45, 118, 126
Angelico, Richard, 31
"Anna and the King of Siam" (CBS), 146
antitrust suits vs. networks, 61–62
"Arthur Godfrey Time" (CBS Radio), 185
"Attica: The Unanswered Questions" (WABC), 159
Avco Broadcasting, 86–87

Bachrach, Judy, 195
"Banks and the Poor" (PBS), 12, 23, 31
Banzhaf, John, III, 91
"Bearcats!" (CBS), 10–11
"Behind the Lines" (PBS), 12, 27
Billboard Radio Forum, 181
"Bill Moyers' Journal" (PBS), 12
"Blue Collar Trap, The" (NBC), 22–23, 156, 159
Bohm, M. R., 89
"Breakdown" (Group W Radio), 192
Brinkley, David, 109, 121, 125, 153, 170, 186
British Broadcasting Corporation (BBC), 9, 156, 195, 205, 208
Broadcasting, 111, 182
Brown, Clarence J., 71
Brown, Willie, 121, 123
Buchanan, Patrick, 61–62
Bumble Bee Tuna, 87–88
Burch, Dean, 54, 58, 82, 85–86, 93, 217
"Busing and the Nixon Plan" (NBC Radio), 189
"Busing, Some Voices from the South" (Group W), 16–17
Business Executives Move for Peace in Vietnam (BEM), 84, 216
"Business of Blood" (NBC), 31
". . . but what if the Dream comes true?" (CBS), 20–22, 156, 159

cable TV, 29, 93–96, 147–148, 157
campaign, presidential:
    direct mail in, 138, 165
    postconvention, 1, 5, 132–142, 152, 154, 163–168

campaign, presidential (cont.):
preconvention, 97–98, 106–116
Campaign Finances (Penniman), 99
campaign spending, 98–101, 107–112, 136, 138, 145, 152, 164, 166–167
campaigns, local, 114–116, 142–152, 167–168
"Candidates '72" (University of North Carolina ETV), 115
Carnegie Commission report on ETV, 68, 221–222
"Carolina Candidates '72" (WFMY), 146
Carr, Martin, 8–9, 22
"Chance for a Lifetime, A" (Group W), 18
Chancellor, John, 12, 14, 52, 63, 121, 124, 128, 131, 153, 170, 186
"Chicano" (CBS), 10–11
"Children of Poverty" (WNBC), 23
Chisholm, Shirley, 49, 107–108, 113–114
"Christmas at the White House," 63
"Chronolog" (NBC), 9, 14–15, 31
"City Desk" (WYES), 28
Clark, Dick, 143
Clark, Michele, 121
"Class . . . and the Class Room" (Group W), 18
Collins, LeRoy, 92
Collins, Reid, 189
Colson, Charles W., 153–154
Columbia Broadcasting System (CBS), 3, 8–11, 14–15, 40–41, 48, 50, 61, 64, 84, 95, 102, 109, 118, 120–125, 129, 131, 153, 159, 197, 214, 220
  CBS Broadcast Group, 56
  CBS News, 9, 39, 46–47, 88, 90, 93, 138, 179
  CBS Radio, 178, 185–188, 190–191
"CBS Evening News, The," 34, 110, 140
"CBS Morning News, The," 36, 49
"CBS Reports," 9, 20
"CBS Thursday Night Movie," 10–11
"CBS Views the Press," 186

Comegys, Walter B., 62
"Come to Florida . . . Before It's Gone" (WJCT), 74
Committee to Re-Elect the President, 136–137
Communications Act of 1934, 53–54, 100, 113, 167, 213–216
communications subcommittees, in Congress, 54, 195
"Company Town" (CBS), 15
Congress, 15–16, 30, 51–53, 63, 69, 71, 73–74, 88, 98, 100, 165, 195, 222, 226
Connally, John, 60, 134, 139
conventions, presidential
  of 1968, 117, 128, 129
  of 1972, 5, 118–131
Cooper, Dan, 31
Corporation for Public Broadcasting (CPB), 53–54, 68–69, 71–75, 105, 155, 195, 220–223, 226–227
counter-advertising, 81–84, 120
Cox Communications, Inc., 94–95
Crawford, Clare, 25
"Crisis in the Courts" (KGBS), 30
Cronkite, Walter, 14, 49, 121, 124–125, 129, 153, 170, 186, 187
Crutchfield, Charles, 64
Curtis, Thomas, 75

Daniel, Clifton, 195
Dann, Mike, 126
Davis, Peter, 8–9
Davis, Sid, 132
Day, James, 70
"Day in the Presidency, A," 63
"Dean Martin" (NBC), 11
debates, political, 106–108, 112, 139–140, 148, 151, 167
"Debriefing" (CBS Radio), 187
Democratic National Committee, 123, 126, 137
Democrats for Nixon, 136–137
documentaries, 8–10, 12, 13, 19–25, 27, 70–71, 74, 103, 105, 155–156, 158, 180, 189, 192, 207, 209
Dole, Robert, 40, 141
"Dragnet," 13
drama on TV, 203–209
Drew, Elizabeth, 61
Drimmer, John, 25, 159
Drinan, Rev. Robert, 122, 124–125

Eagleton, Thomas, 45, 122, 126–127, 135, 137, 140, 154
"Economy vs. the Environment, The" (KCFW), 35
Educational Television Facilities Act of 1962, 219
Efron, Edith, 46–47, 61, 195
"Election Game, The" (WJCT), 115–116
"Electric Company" (PBS), 221, 226
"Elizabeth the Queen" (PBS), 206
"Enemy of the People, An" (CBS), 15
equal time (*see also* Fairness Doctrine), 43, 56, 64–65, 79, 100–101, 105, 112–113, 167–168
ETS Program Service, 220
"Eyewitness News" (WABC), 24

"Face the Nation" (CBS), 112–113, 126, 140–141
Fair Campaign Practices Committee, 137, 152
Fairness Doctrine, 53–58, 64, 77–78, 83, 91, 100, 105, 147, 195, 215–216, 218
Federal Bureau of Investigation, 41, 50, 69, 223
Federal Communications Commission, 40, 43, 52–59, 62, 64, 76–78, 80, 82–83, 86, 88, 93–96, 100–101, 103, 112–113, 133–134, 137, 145, 148, 152, 179, 182, 190, 192–193, 195, 214–217
Federal Election Campaign Act of 1972, 98–99, 112, 136, 138, 152, 164, 166–167
Federal Trade Commission, 73, 76–83, 91, 127
"Feedback" (WJCT), 31
"Fifty-First State, The" (WNET), 28, 159
First Amendment, 40, 46, 50–51, 56, 80, 120, 216
"First Churchills, The" (PBS), 206, 221
"First Tuesday" (NBC), 9
Fisher, Andrew, 18
"Flip Wilson" (NBC), 11
"Florida Forum" (WCKT), 107–108

Ford Foundation, 28, 69, 94, 103, 220
format radio, 181–182, 184–185, 191–192, 194
"Forsyte Saga, The" (PBS), 205, 206, 221
Fouser, Don, 12
Frank, Reuven, 49, 120, 131
Frankel, Max, 120
Freed, Fred, 22–23, 159
"Free Time" (WNET), 29
"French Chef, The" (PBS), 221
Friendly, Fred, 93, 220

Gardner, Allen D., 99
Gardner, John, 99, 101–102
Garfield, Susan, 18
Garth, David, 108
Gartner, Michael, 99
General Foods, 89–90
"Glen Campbell Goodtime Hour" (CBS), 97
Godfrey, Arthur, 185, 220
Goldberg, Arthur, 98
Goodman, Julian, 120
Gould, Jack, 3
Graham, Rev. Billy, 60–61
Gray, L. Patrick, 41, 43
"Great American Dream Machine, The" (PBS), 12, 25, 69, 72, 223
Gregory, Dick, 119
Group W, 16–18, 119, 132, 159, 184, 191–194
Guggenheim, Charles, 102, 111–112, 134
Gunn, Hartford N., Jr., 70, 72–73, 129, 223
GWETA (Washington, D.C.), 74

Haldeman, H. R., 40
Harris, Henry W., 94
Harris Poll, 44, 154, 214, 220
Hart, John, 49
Hartke, Vance, 107, 108
"Harvest of Shame" (CBS), 23
Harvey, Paul, 184–185
Helms, Jesse, 41, 44
Herman, George, 126
"Heroes and Heroin" (ABC), 24
Hooks, Benjamin, 148–149
"Hot Line" (WRKL), 149
Hubbard, Ray, 119

Hubert, Dick, 18
Humphrey, Hubert, 46, 49, 107–113, 123, 136–138, 172, 175
"Hunger in America" (CBS), 8, 23, 31, 192
Huntley, Chet, 170

Illinois Broadcasters Association, 55
International Radio and Television Society, 53, 213
International Telephone and Telegraph Corporation, 45, 118
interviews, political (*see also* debates), 63, 110, 115–116, 122–123, 133, 148, 165, 167
"In the News" (CBS), 86
"Involvement" (KGBS), 30
Iowa Educational Broadcast Network, 27, 144
Ireland, Charles, 3
Israel, Larry, 48
"Issues and Answers" (ABC), 112–113, 139–140

Jackson, Henry, 49, 107–108, 110–111
Jacobs, Paul, 69
Johnson, Lyndon B., 44–45, 63, 135
Johnson, Nicholas, 55, 86, 93, 101, 213, 215
Jones, Clarence B., 94
Justice, Dept. of, 16, 61–62, 118, 152

KABC (Los Angeles), 29, 119
Kalb, Bernard, 189
Kaplow, Herb, 10
Karayn, Jim, 129–130
Kass, Benny, 92
Kastenmeier, Robert, 95
KASU (Jonesboro, Ark.), 150
KCFW (Kalispell, Mont.), 34–35
KCPX (Salt Lake City), 30–31, 37
KDKA (Pittsburgh), 59–60, 105
Keating, Michael, 183
KERA (Dallas–Fort Worth), 19, 70, 114–115, 150, 156, 159
KETV (Omaha), 36
KFWB (Los Angeles), 30, 150
KGBS (Los Angeles), 30

KGO (San Francisco), 36
Kilpatrick, James J., 119
Kissinger, Henry, 45, 64, 138
Klein, Herbert, 60, 81, 84
Kleindienst, Richard, 48
KMPC (Los Angeles), 119
KOLO (Reno), 103
KOVR (Sacramento), 13, 25
KPBS (San Diego), 151
KPIX (San Francisco), 37
KPLR (St. Louis), 25, 143–144
KPRC (Houston), 150
KQED (San Francisco), 25, 29, 74, 105, 151–152
KRAK (Sacramento), 181
KRNT (Des Moines), 144
KRON (San Francisco), 20, 36
KSL (Salt Lake City), 30, 100
KSSS (Colorado Springs), 149
KTEN (Oklahoma City), 115
KTLA (Los Angeles), 30
KTOK (Oklahoma City), 37, 150
KTRH (Houston), 150
KTTV (Los Angeles), 30
Kuralt, Charles, 20–21
Kushner, Valerie, 123
KVAL (Eugene, Ore.), 38
KVOS (Bellingham, Wash.), 57
KWTV (Oklahoma City), 18–19, 37, 88
KYTV (Springfield, Mo.), 31

Laird, Melvin, 48, 136
Lange, Jim, 88
Lardner, Ring, 201
"Leaving Home Blues" (NBC), 8, 22, 156
Lehrer, Jim, 12, 70
Leiser, Ernest, 10
Lemon, Robert, 103
Lewis, Anthony, 131, 169
Lewis, Fulton, III, 184
licenses of broadcasters, 2, 53, 79
   renewal challenges, 58–60, 120, 214–215, 217
"Like It Is" (WABC), 25–26, 159
Lindsay, John, 49, 107–110
Lisagor, Peter, 119
Loomis, Henry W., 75
"Longstreet" (ABC), 11
Lower, Elmer, 57–58
"Loyal Opposition, The" (CBS), 64

McAllister, William, 33
McCarthy, Eugene, 49, 107–108
McClellan, John, 95
McCloskey, Paul, 107
McCormick, Stephen J., 191
Macdonald, Torbert, 54, 69, 73–74, 95
McGee, Frank, 152
McGovern, George, 34, 49, 102, 107–113, 116, 119, 121, 123–127, 132–141, 149, 152–154, 164–169, 175–176
McGregor, Clark, 141–142
Mackin, Cassie, 121–122, 124
MacLeish, Rod, 17, 184, 192
MacNeil, Robert, 69, 130
Macy, John, 71, 75
Magnuson, Warren, 91
Managing Today's Radio Station (Hoffer), 181
"Marcus Welby" (ABC), 131
Markle Foundation, 94
Markowitz, Robert, 20, 159
Martin, Mel, 151
"M*A*S*H" (CBS), 146
Mason, Kenneth, 87
Matney, Bill, 10
"Meet the Press" (NBC), 43, 112, 126
Meredith, Don, 201
Metzenbaum, Howard, 98
"Migrant" (NBC), 8, 31
Miller, Jack, 143
Mills, Wilbur, 49, 107–108, 111
Minor, Dale, 186
Mississippi Authority for Educational TV, 74–75, 105
Mitchell, John, 136–137, 141
"Mod Squad" (ABC), 131
Monday, 40–41
"Monday Night Football" (ABC), 197, 201
"Monitor" (NBC Radio), 189–190
Montana Television Network, 35
Morgan, Edward P., 186
Moss, Frank, 53–54, 91
Moyers, Bill, 12, 45–46, 72, 73, 130
Murphy, George, 98
Murphy, John, 86
Murrow, Edward R., 185–186, 194
Muskie, Edmund, 34, 49, 97–98, 106–108, 110–111, 134, 136, 153

Mutual Broadcasting System, 184, 190–191

"Nader Report, The" (PBS), 12
National Advertising Review Board, 80, 91–92
National Association of Broadcasters, 6–7, 60, 80–81, 84, 87, 101, 120, 179
National Association of Educational Broadcasters, 67, 219–220
National Black Network, 191
National Black Political Convention, 94 .
National Broadcasting Company (NBC), 8–9, 11, 14–15, 22, 31, 40–41, 61, 85, 118, 120–125, 129–131, 197–198, 200, 220
  NBC News, 10, 49, 120, 159, 188
  NBC Radio, 186–190
"NBC Nightly News," 40, 52, 109
National Educational Television, 70–71, 74, 205, 222
"NET Journal" (PBS), 12
National Opinion Research Center, 6
National Public Affairs Center for Television, 14, 69, 72, 74, 109, 129, 142, 159, 220
National Public Radio, 67–68, 195, 220
Newman, Edwin, 186
"News Journal" (CBS Radio), 187
"News of the World" (NBC Radio), 188
"Newsroom" (KERA), 19
"Newsroom" (KQED), 29, 74
"Newsroom" (WETA), 28
News Twisters, The (Efron), 46, 61, 195
Ney, Edward, 102
"Nichols" (NBC), 11
Nielsen, A. C., surveys, 6, 9–11, 134
Nixon, Richard, 34–35, 46, 49, 62–65, 182, 189
  1968 campaign, 135–136, 167
  1972 campaign, 98, 100, 107, 120, 127–128, 130, 133–141, 149, 152–154, 163–168, 176

Nixon, Richard (cont.)
  opposition to, 40, 44, 70
  and public TV, 73–75, 226–227
  trip to China, 5, 9, 13–14, 63–
    64, 135, 187
  trip to Russia, 5, 45, 63, 135, 187
Noble, Gil, 25–26
Northshield, Robert, 23
"Not to *My* Kids, You Don't!"
  (CBS), 16
November Group, 135–137

Office of Telecommunications Man-
  agement, 53
Office of Telecommunications Pol-
  icy, 52–54, 95, 213, 217, 219
Olympics, 5, 145, 198–199, 208
O'Neill, Thomas P., 100
Opinion Research Corporation,
  178
O'Toole, John, 101
"Ottinger Rule," 111
"Owen Marshall" (ABC), 11

Pace, Frank, 75
Pacifica Radio, 119, 180, 186, 194–
  195
Pappas, Ike, 109–110
Parker, Rev. Everett C., 56, 215
"Pasquinizo Story, The" (KCFW),
  35
Pastore, John, 95, 222
Peers report, 44
"People Talk, The" (KFWB), 30
Perkins, Jack, 124
"Perspective" (ABC), 186
Pettit, Tom, 127
"Picasso Is 90" (CBS), 10–11
Pitofsky, Robert, 82
"Playhouse 90" (CBS), 203, 205
"Politics and Humor of Woody
  Allen, The" (PBS), 70
"Politics and Public Broadcasting"
  (NPR), 67
Post-Newsweek stations, 48, 119
Powell, Lewis F., Jr., 41–42
Powledge, Fred, 75
President Nixon and the Press
  (Keogh), 48
press conferences, 63, 65, 139, 165,
  172
"press release" videotapes, 33, 106,
  112, 132–133

primaries, presidential, 1, 98, 106–
  116
prime time TV:
  network percentage of, 7, 62
  politicians' access to, 62–64,
    101–103, 133–134
  public access to, 6, 56
"Projection '72" (NBC), 34
public access to media, 29–31, 55,
  79, 120, 158, 182–183, 217
  to cable TV, 29, 94
public affairs programs, 2, 6–7, 9–
  11, 13, 55–56, 67–75, 79–80,
  84, 94, 103, 156, 180, 192,
  195, 220
Public Broadcasting Act of 1967,
  68–69, 219, 226
Public Broadcasting Service (PBS),
  12, 14, 51, 68–72, 75, 105,
  129, 204–205, 220–221, 223
Public Interest, The (Weaver), 175
public opinion of media, 5, 27,
  37–38, 41, 43–44, 46–47, 51–
  52
public television, 12, 53–54, 67–75,
  93, 155–156, 219–226, 227–
  228
"Public Television . . . A Question of Survival" (Powledge),
  75
Putnam, George, 30, 64

Quaal, Ward, 101
"Quarterly Report" (NBC), 10–12
Quayle, Don, 220

radio:
  news programs on, 12–13, 178–
    196
  public access to, 29–31, 139,
    182–183, 217–218
  public opinion of, 6, 178
ratings, 9–11, 130–131, 197
Reasoner, Harry, 7, 10, 14, 121,
  153, 170, 186
recall, audience, 7, 86–87
Red Lion case, 216
"Replay" (WNET), 158
reporters, TV, 1, 52, 121–123, 125,
  130–131, 147, 170–177
Republican National Committee,
  40, 60, 72, 103, 141

Reynolds, Frank, 139–140, 186
Rice, Jonathan, 152
Rivera, Geraldo, 24–25
Robertson, J. L., 41
Rogers, Robert, 14
Roper Survey, 178
Rowan, Carl, 119
Rukeyser, Louis, 186

Safer, Morley, 48
Salant, Richard, 39, 46–47, 90, 93, 131
Sarnoff, David, 3
Sauter, Van Gordon, 179
Save Our Schools Committee, 16
"Scan Goes to Jail" (KQED), 25
Scherer, Ray, 188
Schneider, John, 56
"School Busing: The Trial of Two Cities" (KWTV), 18
Schorr, Daniel, 50–51
Schoumacher, David, 10
Schwartz, Tony, 134–135
Scott, Ron, 36
"Search for Quality Education, The" (Group W), 16, 159
"Second Sunday" (NBC), 186, 189
"Seed of Hope, A" (WTVJ), 24, 159
"Self-Evident Truths" (ABC Radio), 182
"Selling of the Pentagon, The" (CBS), 8, 23, 31, 40, 42, 64, 192
Selling of the President, The (McGinniss), 136
"Sesame Street" (PBS), 221, 226
Sevareid, Eric, 7, 121, 153, 188
"Seven Summits, The" (NBC), 63
Seymour, Dan, 77, 92–93
Shachtman, Tom, 23
Shakespeare, Frank, 75
Shannon, William V., 125–126
Share the Savings (WMAQ-TV), 88–89
Shaw, Allen B., Jr., 182
Short Course in Cable, A (United Church of Christ), 94
Shriver, Sargent, 127, 133, 140, 169
Shultz, George, 136, 139
Sidey, Hugh, 119
Siemering, William H., 195
Silverstein, Morton, 12

Simon, Norton, 98
Singer, Arthur, 221, 222, 223
"Sixty Minutes" (CBS), 9–11, 15, 43, 48, 159
"Six Wives of Henry VIII, The," 90, 206
Sloan Commission on Cable Communications, 95–96
"Slow Justice of Florida, The" (WTVJ), 24
Smith, Howard K., 121, 170, 186
"Soap Box" (KPLR), 143
Sorensen, Theodore, 79–81, 92
"Spectrum" (CBS), 186
sponsors and programming, 3, 5, 10, 87–89, 93, 118, 123, 156–157, 189
Staggers, Harley O., 40
Stanton, Dr. Frank, 95–96, 102–103, 113, 120
Steinfeld, Dr. Jesse, 86
Sterling Manhattan cable TV, 94
Stern, Andrew, 7
Stewart, John, 120
"Suffer the Little Children" (NBC), 23, 156
Super Bowl, 197, 200
"Survival Kit for Consumers" (WCCO), 88
Susskind, David, 220
"Swift Justice of Europe, The" (WTVJ), 24, 159

"Take Des Moines . . . Please" (Iowa Educational Broadcasting Network), 27
TelePrompTer, 29, 94–95
telethons, 15, 116, 133, 151, 166–168
Television Bureau of Advertising, 79, 81, 92
Television/Radio Age, 92
Thiele, Edward M., 76–77
"Thirty Minutes With . . ." (PBS), 61
"This Child Is Rated X" (NBC), 8
Thomas, Lowell, 184
Ticket-Splitter, The (DeVries and Tarrance), 103–104
Tiernan, Robert O., 100
"Today" (NBC), 40, 43, 113, 152
Top Value TV, 121

"Towers of Frustration" (WNJT), 27, 159
Townley, Richard, 18–19
Trafficante, Santo, Jr., 34
Treyz, Oliver, 133–134
"Truth in Advertising" survey, 90–91
TV Cable Company (Fort Walton Beach, Fla.), 147–148
TV Guide, 46, 120, 203
"TV's Failed Promise" (Vanocur), 50

United Church of Christ, 55–56, 94
UPI Audio, 191
U.S. Open Golf Championship, 197
University of North Carolina Educational TV, 115
Utley, Garrick, 124

Valeriani, Richard, 188
Vanocur, Sander, 39, 50, 69, 130, 192, 220
Viacom, 61
"Vietnam Hindsight" (NBC), 15

WABC (New York), 24, 84, 159, 181, 189
WABF (Baton Rouge, La.), 34
Wallace, George, 5, 49, 107–108, 110, 122, 136, 151, 187, 189
Wallace, Mike, 15–16, 129, 159, 188
Walters, Barbara, 40
Ward, Scott, 7
"Washington Week" (CBS Radio), 187
"Washington Week" (PBS), 156
Watergate affair, 129, 137, 140
Watkins, Richard Thurston, 25, 159
WBAL (Baltimore), 103
WBAP (Fort Worth–Dallas), 13, 57
WBBM (Chicago), 38, 115
WBGU (Bowling Green, Ohio), 150–151
WBT (Charlotte, N.C.), 64
WBZ (Boston), 115, 192
WCBS (New York), 31, 48, 84, 188, 189, 194
WCCB (Charlotte, N.C.), 57
WCCO (Minneapolis), 88

WCKT (Miami), 51, 56–57, 107–109, 119
WCMB (Harrisburg, Pa.), 34
WDIO (Duluth), 32, 88, 103, 105
Weaver, Paul, 175
Weaver, Sylvester (Pat), 189
Weaver, Warren, Jr., 138
Westfeldt, Wallace, 40–41
Westen, Tracy, 55
Westerman, Sylvia, 140
WETA (Washington, D.C.), 28
WFMY (Greensboro, N.C.), 57, 106, 115, 146
WFTV (Orlando, Fla.), 37
WGBH (Boston), 221
WGN Continental Broadcasting Company, 101, 103
WHIS (Charleston, W. Va.), 33
Whitehead, Clay T. (Tom), 52–56, 58, 60, 67–69, 71, 73–75, 81, 93, 155, 213–226, 228–234
"Who Has Lived and Not Seen Death" (WNBC), 23, 156
WHP (Harrisburg, Pa.), 34
WHYY (PBS, Philadelphia), 221
WIBC (Indianapolis), 150
Wicklein, John, 48
WIIC (Pittsburgh), 25
Wiley, Richard, 54
"Willowbrook—The Last Great Disgrace" (WABC), 24, 32
WIND (Chicago), 192
WINS (New York), 192
"Wintersoldier" (WNET), 71
Wiseman, Frederick, 12
WISH (Indianapolis), 59
WISN (Milwaukee), 36
Witherspoon, John, 68, 75
WITN (Washington, D.C.), 59
WJCT (Jacksonville), 31, 74–75, 115–116
WJZ (Baltimore), 25, 32–33, 105
WLBT–United Church of Christ case, 215
WLS (Chicago), 31
WLW (Dayton), 25
WMAQ (Chicago), 88–89, 103
WMAR (Baltimore), 81
WMVS (Milwaukee), 110
WNBC (New York), 23, 83–84, 189
WNET (New York), 15, 28–29, 70–72, 74, 159
WNJT (Trenton), 27, 159

WNYC (New York), 14
WOR (New York), 184
Wordham, Bill, 140
"World and Washington, The" (NBC Radio), 188–189
"World News Roundup" (CBS Radio), 188
World Series, 197
"World's Largest Television Studio, The" (Top Value TV), 121
"World This Week, The" (CBS Radio), 187
"World Tonight, The" (CBS Radio), 188
WPIX (New York), 27
WQWK (State College, Pa.), 88
WQXR (New York), 195
WRAL (Raleigh, N.C.), 41
WRC (Washington, D.C.), 25
WRKL (New City, N.Y.), 149
WRVR (New York), 15, 183
WRTV (Indianapolis), 144
WSAZ (Huntington, W. Va.), 133

WSB (Atlanta), 148
WSBA (York, Pa.), 51–52
WSOC (Charlotte, N.C.), 19, 59
WTLV (Jacksonville), 59
WTMJ (Milwaukee), 34
WTOP (Washington, D.C.), 84, 119, 136, 188
WTTW (Chicago), 151, 156, 167
WTVJ (Miami), 24, 108–109, 159
WTVT (Tampa, Fla.), 34
WVEC (Norfolk, Va.), 19
WVUE (New Orleans), 25, 31
WWDC (Washington, D.C.), 51, 88
WYES (New Orleans), 28
Wysocki, Richard, 109–110

Yankelovich, Daniel, 76–77
Yorty, Sam, 49, 107–108, 113–114, 119
Yost, Charles, 91–92
"Youth Gangs in the South Bronx" (WNET), 159